RENAISSANCE DIPLOMACY

'A first oration: Aeneas Sylvius Piccolomini, ambassador of the Council of Basle, presents himself at the court of Scotland.'

RENAISSANCE DIPLOMACY

by

GARRETT MATTINGLY

NEW YORK / RUSSELL & RUSSELL

To

BERNARD DeVOTO

*to whom for a long time I have always brought my hardest
problems. And never in vain.*

FIRST PUBLISHED IN 1955 BY HOUGHTON MIFFLIN COMPANY

REISSUED, 1970, BY RUSSELL & RUSSELL

A DIVISION OF ATHENEUM PUBLISHERS, INC.

BY ARRANGEMENT WITH HOUGHTON MIFFLIN COMPANY

L. C. CATALOG CARD NO: 70-102520

PRINTED IN THE UNITED STATES OF AMERICA

CONTENTS

70719

CONTENTS

PART FOUR

EARLY MODERN DIPLOMACY

FOREWORD

SOMEWHAT more than thirty years ago the studies out of which this book has grown were begun at Harvard University under the guidance of Roger Bigelow Merriman. I then intended a history of Anglo-Spanish diplomatic relations in the sixteenth century. An alert reader may be able to detect, in the frequency with which illustrations from the Spanish embassy in England occur in some of the following chapters, a trace of that original plan, but there is really very little of it left.

Work on it was interrupted by other interests, by personal distractions and by those intrusions of current events which have disarranged most people's lives in the recent past. Each time I took up the manuscript again I found that its interest for me had changed, that I was asking different questions and being obliged to range always further afield for answers. Spreading out so far, of course, has increased the danger of error in fact and in interpretation. I can only plead that I could not understand specific diplomatic negotiations without more knowledge of their background than I found ready to hand. In particular, I needed to know more of the growth of diplomatic institutions, of the uses they were designed for and the assumptions people made about them and of the spirit which gave them life.

So I was finally led to write, not the narrative of a particular embassy, but a general account of the development of Western diplomacy in its formative period. It seemed worth doing for two reasons. In the first place, although all civilizations of which we have any record have had some set of diplomatic institutions, ours took a turn some time after 1400 which differentiated it from all other sets in history. This new development seemed to me a characteristic symptom of the new power relations of the nascent modern world, and therefore possibly instructive about the period of history from which we are emerging, and about how people adapt their institutions in an age of change. In the second place, little proved to have been written, even for specialists, about the development of European diplomatic institutions before 1648, and of that little only a small fraction in English.[1]

[1] See general note on bibliography, p. 299.

FOREWORD

Historians have argued so much about the Renaissance in recent years, and have so stretched and contracted and pulled about its meaning, that the word has fallen into a kind of disrepute. For some time I hesitated to use it in the title of this book, and called the manuscript, to myself, 'The beginnings of modern diplomacy'. But on reflection, 'modern' seemed as tricky a word as 'Renaissance'. Would not a reader be justified in expecting a book called 'The beginnings of modern diplomacy' to be about the San Francisco Conference or the founding of the League of Nations rather than about things that happened in the fifteenth and sixteenth centuries? It seemed better, then, to use the only name we have for that period of Western history which begins with Petrarch and ends with Descartes or, in terms more appropriate for this study, begins with the emergence in northern and central Italy of the first purely secular states and ends with the failure of the last effort to re-impose a medieval unity on Europe.

The diplomacy of this period assumed its characteristic form between 1420 and 1530 in a time which we all call the Renaissance, however we may differ about the limits of the term. Resident embassies, the distinguishing feature, were an Italian invention. They were fully developed in Italy by the 1450s and spread thence, like other Renaissance innovations, to the rest of Europe around 1500. And like other Renaissance innovations, they continued to develop along the lines laid down throughout the period which ended in 1914, so that their first stage may also properly be called the beginning of modern diplomacy. The new Italian institution of permanent diplomacy was drawn into the service of the rising nation-states, and served, like the standing army of which it was the counterpart, at once to nourish their growth and to foster their idolatry. It still serves them and must go on doing so as long as nation-states survive.

They may not survive for ever. Technological progress, which made possible the nation-state system of the West, with its bitter rivalries and colonial empires, now promises to end it. We are experiencing another major change of phase, more rapid and violent than the Renaissance. We are again called on for creative adaptations, for inventiveness in political institutions and particularly in the machinery of international relations. It would be presumptuous to hope that this study could be of much use in so grave

FOREWORD

a task. But it may be some help to understand the beginning of the story before we come to its end.

Archival research for this book has been made possible by the generosity, at different dates, of Harvard University, of the John Simon Guggenheim Memorial Foundation, and of the Columbia University Council for Research in the Social Sciences. During many years the patience and helpfulness of scores of librarians and archivists have laid upon me debts of gratitude which can receive here only the most general acknowledgment, but my especial thanks are due to Don Miguel Bordonau Mas, Inspector-General of the Spanish Archives, for the marked kindness and distinguished courtesy with which he assisted my last researches in Spain. Parts of several chapters of this book were discussed by the Columbia University Seminar in the Renaissance with, I hope, consequent improvement. I am grateful to Professor Felix Gilbert and Doctor Hans Baron for valuable suggestions, to Professor P. O. Kristeller for the constant benefit of his wide knowledge of Italian humanism, and to Professors Leo Gershoy and Edward C. Mack for their encouragement, and their criticism of the manuscript. My indebtedness to my friend Bernard DeVoto for help over many years with every phase of this study is greater than he realizes or than any dedicatory phrase could suggest. In its penultimate form, this book passed under the wise and kindly eye of Professor J. E. Neale, I hope to its advantage. In the research and in the writing, from first to last, my wife has had so large a share that this is really as much her book as mine.

Rome,
March 15th, 1954

13

PART ONE

MEDIEVAL DIPLOMACY, FIFTEENTH CENTURY

CHAPTER 1

THE LEGAL FRAMEWORK

B Y the first quarter of the fifteenth century the diplomatic institutions of the Latin West were already highly developed. Like the society they served, they were dynamic, not static. They had been changing with that society throughout the centuries since Western civilization had risen from the wreckage of the barbarian invasions. Like most Western institutions, they showed traces of ancient Germanic customs and of Byzantine and Islamic influence, but were mainly an adaptation to a new environment and new ends of the classical Mediterranean tradition as it had been preserved by the clergy of the Roman Catholic Church.

By 1300 the fusion of all these influences had long been completed, and the secular powers of Christendom had already learned all they could from the papacy about the machinery of diplomacy, as about other kinds of governmental machinery. After another century of development, Western secular diplomatic institutions were perhaps as highly elaborated as any previous set in history, although still plastic enough to be adapted to new uses. In fact, a good many early fifteenth-century rules, procedures and types of documents survived the disintegration of medieval Europe almost unchanged and may still be recognized in contemporary diplomatic practice, surprisingly little altered by the passage of five hundred years. During the transition from medieval to modern times, in diplomacy as in some other fields, formal institutions changed less than might have been expected. It was the objects of policy and the vision of society which changed.

Today coherent sense can be made out of medieval diplomatic institutions only by reference to the values they reflected. Looked at from a point of view which takes a jarring congeries of hostile sovereignties to be the natural order of the world, medieval 'international law' seems formless, and medieval diplomacy, in theory and practice, absurd. As formless and absurd it has generally been described, even by writers who ought to have known better. One finds even the wisest speaking with approval here of a paragraph of theory or there of a stroke of practice, as they recognize a similarity to the theory and practice of their own time, in the tone of adults praising the cleverness of precocious children. But the world of 1400 was not childlike. It merely retained different basic assumptions from those of the age which is now ending. Its institutions took different shapes from ours and its self-explanations used different words because, although swept forward in the grip of change, its articulate élite still clung to a different, an older style of thinking.

From the point of view of diplomacy the chief difference was that the West, in 1400, still thought of itself as one society. Christendom was torn by the gravest internal conflicts, by religious schism, doctrinal dispute, and the endemic warfare of class against class, people against people, faction against faction, king against king. But Latin Christendom still knew itself to be one.

This sense of unity compels recognition on even the most cursory study, yet it eludes precise and satisfactory statement. Modern attempts to define it are likely to seem pedantic and remote from actuality, like modern attempts at gothic architecture — at once alien to our daily world and unconvincing to specialists. This is the less surprising since throughout the period when Latin Christendom was a living reality, saints and philosophers, poets and propagandists were constantly seeking to capture in universal terms the essential quality of its unity, without ever winning the unqualified agreement of even a majority of their contemporaries.

The easiest thing to say about the unity of Christendom is that it was complex and protean, sensitive to change and adaptable to circumstances, so that it took on different aspects for different observers. It would never have been stated in quite the same terms or with quite the same emphasis in Italy as beyond the Alps, by a friar as by a parish priest, by a merchant as by a knight. Guelph and Ghibellines, canonists and civilians, realists and nominalists argued about it endlessly. It changed subtly in form and meaning for every generation between the Council of Clermont and the Council of Trent. To describe it as if it depended upon the functioning of some system of political or legal administration, or as if it ever attained, or even ever, as a whole, consciously sought to attain, to a given ideal as stated by St. Thomas or Dante or Nicholas of Cusa is to go surely wrong about it. But not so far wrong as it would be to deny that a belief in the actual unity of

18

Christendom, however variously felt and expressed, was a fundamental condition of all medieval political thought and activity.

We shall understand medieval diplomatic conventions better, therefore, if we begin, not with the various magistrates, popes and emperors and kings, feudal lords and city states, among whom in complicated patterns allegiance was apportioned, but with the collective unity, the people. They had no common name for themselves except Christians. In their more tolerant moods they regarded the Jews among them as guests and strangers to be preserved until the Second Coming. They were willing, at times, to admit to their society the Greek Orthodox schismatics along their eastern frontier. Their theorists granted that even infidels, as the possessors of rational souls, could claim some place in the general community of mankind. But in general, the Latin West inclined to lump Jews, heretics, schismatics and pagans together as outsiders and natural enemies, while preserving, even in the bitterest internal quarrels, a sense of solidarity in one Catholic faith, a solidarity more intimate and complex in its ties than anyone quite knew how to express.

Besides thinking of themselves as Christians, the people of Latin Christendom also thought of themselves, more or less consciously, as Romans. No one had yet come to tell them that Rome had fallen a thousand years ago and given Europe over to the Goths; or that they were the Goths to whom it had been given over. It did not occur to their poets or to their legislators that Hector, Alexander and Julius Caesar were any more alien to their heritage than Arthur, Charlemagne and Godfrey of Bouillon, or than Joshua, David and Judas Maccabeus. Especially around the Mediterranean, where classical reminiscence was strongest, lawyers and Ghibelline intellectuals liked to speak of the people of Christendom as the Roman people, the *populus romanus*. But Germany also, even those parts of Germany where no Roman legion had ever tarried, knew its king as Roman emperor, and continued to elect him, on the plea that to allow the throne of Caesar and the temporal lordship of the world to pass by inheritance, like a farm, was unbecoming its peculiar dignity. Equally in France and Britain and Spain, where the kings acknowledged no imperial suzerain, men felt the tug of the imperial past, and traced their national histories to ancient Rome. Even in Ireland, and among

19

Norwegian fiords, and on the Polish plain, literate Celts and Norse and Slavs whose ancestors had never seen the eagles thought of themselves as belonging somehow to the world, not merely of papal, but also of imperial Rome.

This sense of a common bond, political as well as religious, never found adequate expression in political institutions. The actual social structure of power, the difficulties of travel and communication, the confused pattern of local and regional differences prevented any such expression. The authority of the Holy Roman Empire, like the magical *peau de chagrin*, shrank every time an emperor invoked it, until finally it could hardly be stretched to cover more than the narrow hereditary domain of some German princeling. But the collapse of the empire and the schism of the papacy underlined a sense of unity which had never really depended on any fountain-head of authority, and the society for which pope and emperor alike were more important as symbols than as rulers found a name more definite than Christendom.

As the age of the great councils approached, one heard more frequently and with a wider reference of the Christian Commonwealth, the *res publica Christiana*. At Constance and at Basel the name was a battle cry to rally the enlightened against the divisive despotisms of Church and State. Its combination of Roman pride and Christian faith was more than a mere aspiration; it was almost a reality. In the documents of chanceries and the reasoning of lawyers, as well as in the exhortations of preachers and the dreams of scholars like Nicholas of Cusa, it stood for the common interests of the community of Latin Christendom, interests which all men agreed were real and vital, however difficult it proved to give them practical political expression. As the watchword of those common interests the term *res publica Christiana* survived the failure of the councils, the Lutheran revolt, and the beginning of the Habsburg-Valois wars. The breaking-up of Christendom in the sixteenth century finally drained the Latin syllables of most of their meaning. But their nostalgic echo continued to haunt men's consciences long after any actual Commonwealth of Christendom had ceased to be a possibility.[1]

If the *res publica Christiana* found no other political expression, it had achieved, by the last century or so of the Middle Ages, something like a common body of law. Or perhaps 'achieved' is not the right word. The common body of law was not so much achieved as always assumed and increasingly realized,[2] the area of its most nearly complete realization being in the realm we now call 'international' law. This included, of course, 'the international law of diplomacy', that is, the rules regulating the recognition and status of diplomatic principals, the behaviour and immunities of diplomatic agents, and the negotiations, validity and observance of diplomatic agreements.

Like most medieval law, this diplomatic part of it escaped anything like systematic codification and derived its force not from formal acts, not from statutes or edicts or treaties, but from generally accepted principles and old-established customs. Since the West was not thinking in terms of mutually discrete, sovereign national states, but was trying to develop legal rules for a great society, the doctrine about the status and intercourse of princes, the position of ambassadors and the sanctity of treaties must usually be disengaged from a miscellaneous mass of commentaries and *consilia* on other matters. Like the sense of unity of which it was an expression, the 'international law' of the Middle Ages was stated with varying emphasis by different writers, and defies any precise definition which could have commanded universal acceptance at any period. Yet there is an unmistakable core of agreement. Coherently enough, and without serious contradiction, the available literature describes the framework within which medieval diplomatic institutions were elaborated and the climate of opinion in which their evolution towards modern forms began.

One can distinguish three converging currents of tradition: ecclesiastical, feudal and imperial, or, if one prefers, Christian, German and Roman, embodied in canon law, customary law and civil law.

The international character of canon law is immediately striking. It was co-extensive with the Roman obedience, and therefore with the *res publica Christiana*. It was administered by its own hierarchy of courts throughout Christendom. These courts claimed and on the whole successfully asserted, besides exclusive jurisdiction over the intellectual élite of the West, the clergy, concurrent jurisdiction over the laity as well in all matters involving the laws of God. Jurisdictional disputes between secular and ecclesiastical courts were frequent and bitter, but no Christian judge cared to contradict the divinely revealed mandates on which the laws of the Church claimed to be based. In fact, therefore, a good many legal relationships were governed, throughout the Roman obedience, by the doctrines and principles laid down by the Church lawyers. Thus, for medieval Europe canon law supplied, in large part, the need for a code of private international law.

In addition, since the eleventh century, the canonists had been preoccupied with many of the problems which we think of as belonging to public international law, with the definition of sovereignty, with the sanctity of treaties, with the preservation of peace, with the rights of neutrals and noncombatants, and with the mitigation of the rigours of war. From the beginning of the investiture controversy it had been to the advantage of the papacy to strengthen the independence of the kings against the universal claims of the emperor, and in the maxim that 'each is master of his own house' its lawyers found the basic principle of sovereignty which later led kings in France and England and Castile to assert that they were emperors in their own domains.

On the premise that the violation of an oath was a breach of the moral law, punishable by excommunication, the canonists had erected a whole theory of the sanctity of treaties, and of the use of spiritual arms to enforce them. Because of its concern with peace among Christians, the Church elaborated laws of war meant to mitigate the consequences of internal strife in Christendom, to distinguish between just and unjust wars, and to justify intervention against unjust breakers of the peace.[3] Finally, because of the European-wide nature of its interests, intensified in the thirteenth century by its bitter struggles with the emperors, the papacy had been the first Western power to make a systematic use of diplomacy. Consequently thirteenth-century canonists had begun to develop a set of rules about the status, conduct and privileges of papal diplomatic agents. These rules, though they were too specialized to admit of simple appropriation for secular diplomacy, were general enough to make their adaptation to secular use by the canon-law trained chancellors of Western princes practicably inevitable.

Naturally, the enforcement of the Church's code of public international law met grave, and before long insuperable, difficulties. When the reformed papacy was at the height of its moral prestige, when enthusiastic monks and friars gave it an all-persuasive army of loyal and effective propagandists, even the toughest-minded monarchs flinched before the thunderbolts of Rome. Innocent III could actually appear what his successors long pretended to be, the suzerain of all earthly kings and arbiter of Christendom. But that was a brief moment. Within a century of Innocent's death, the kings of Europe had learned that they could snub and defy popes with impunity whenever they could not seduce or coerce them. Nevertheless, the authority of the canon law survived. Neither the Avignonese captivity, nor the great schism, nor the subsequent ridiculous and horrifying spectacle of three popes, all cursing, vilifying and excommunicating each other, succeeded in quenching the feeling of the West that all Christians, laymen as well as clergy, ought to try to live together under the laws of God.

Meanwhile the lay society of Western Europe was working out rules for living together within the framework of its customary laws. Among the burghers, the lines of trade spread the good customs of one town to another, and tended to create something like the beginnings of a common law for the merchants and seamen of the West.[4] Even more markedly, the code of knightly behaviour spread and generalized itself, and modified in doing so the law laid down by the Church. Henry V and Philip the Good, John II of Castile and James I of Scotland, and all the lords and captains remembered by Froissart and Monstrelet followed, in principle at least, a common code of chivalry which regulated the formal intercourse of feudal overlords and their barons in peace, and especially in war. Although influenced by the teachings of the Church,[5] the chivalric doctrines of the just quarrel, the formal defiance, the good war, the treatment of heralds and prisoners and noncombatants, the summoning of towns and the observation of truces and treaties contained much matter not to be found in the canonists, and drew their real authority from their general acceptance by the military caste.

If the validity of the third element, Roman civil law, had depended on the enforcing power of the emperor, as modern writers are sometimes inclined to posit, civil law by the middle of the fifteenth century should have been the weakest of the three. The power of the emperors to enforce anything outside their hereditary estates and their ability to intervene efficiently in

European affairs had never been less than in the anarchy of the early fifteenth century and the long, inglorious reign of Frederick III. In fact, however, the civil law as interpreted by its teachers in the universities was everywhere increasing in influence. In what we may call the international law of the fifteenth century, Roman law was the most important element, the warp on which the legal garment of the great society was being constantly woven. In part, this was because Roman law appealed to the rulers of the West, not only by the handles it offered to absolute power but also as a generalized and rational system, adapted to the needs of a civil society, to secular authority, and to pecuniary interests. In part, it was because of the familiarity of the maxims which had served the canonists since the twelfth century and the lawyers of the feudal kings since the thirteenth. And in part, because, to Western sentiments of unity, civil law, backed by the traditions of imperial Rome, seemed even to the most zealous defenders of local customs the only possible and general code for governing the relations of the whole complex community which thought of itself as the Christian protraction of the Roman empire.[6]

Had the civil law remained a dead and rigid inheritance from the codifiers of sixth-century Byzantium it could never have fulfilled a vital function in the fifteenth-century world. But it was in no such danger. The most influential fourteenth-century jurists were eager to keep it living and flexible. Bartolus of Sassoferato,[7] who gave his name to the leading school, no more thought of the law he taught at Perugia as something fixed since the age of Justinian than he thought of the terse, serviceable Latin in which he wrote and lectured as a language fixed in the age of Augustus. Though he tried to connect his precepts with the great tradition of the Roman past, he shared and encouraged the interest of his practical-minded students in the actual law of their contemporary world. His followers, the Bartolists, continued throughout the fifteenth century his effort to assimilate into the civil law the teachings of the Church and the customs of the Italian cities and of the transalpine peoples, so as to provide a single rational body of doctrine for the legal relations of the Western world. This grandiose conception of the civil law scarcely survived the sixteenth century. But the Bartolists were so far successful that throughout the period of change officials employed in foreign affairs were expected to be trained in civil and canon law. Indeed, down into the last decades of the seventeenth century, men usually spoke of the civil law as if it were what we now call international law.[8]

The civilians could not have gained so much had there been any fundamental disagreement between them and the canonists, or between either and the feudalists. But, in fact, all three groups of lawyers were working with materials into which feudal customs, Christian morals, and Roman juristic thinking had been inextricably and almost imperceptibly interwoven. This convergence reflected the sentiments of a society which, through the intercourse of princes and knights, merchants and pilgrims, and by the long labours of the Church, was being moulded into increasing unity in spite of its political diversity. It was in this harmony of sentiments that the 'international law' of the Middle Ages found its most effective sanction. For men, on the whole, were agreed that there must be a common body of law valid for all the Commonwealth of Christendom. And they were agreed, too, that finally everyone, even the kings, even the emperor, even the popes ought to be subject to this law.[9]

CHAPTER II

DIPLOMATIC PRINCIPALS AND DIPLOMATIC AGENTS

THE same sense of unity which led men to think of themselves as living in one society under the rule of a common law made it difficult for them to formulate a precise theory of diplomatic principals. The political realities of the later Middle Ages made it more difficult still. Our modern notion of an international society composed of a heterogeneous collection of fictitious entities called states, all supposed to be equal, sovereign and completely independent, would have shocked both the idealism and the common sense of the fifteenth century. Such a society would have seemed to philosophers a repulsive anarchy, a contradiction to their basic assumption of a hierarchically ordered universe — almost a blasphemy. And the concept would have been equally uncomfortable to practical statesmen. When, in fact, large parts of the political map of Europe presented an intricate puzzle of partial and overlapping sovereignties, who was to say which of them were to be granted and which denied the right of negotiating with others?

Kings made treaties with their own vassals and with the vassals of their neighbours. They received embassies from their own subjects and from the subjects of other princes, and sometimes sent agents who were in fact ambassadors in return. Subject cities negotiated with one another without reference to their respective sovereigns. Such behaviour might arouse specific objection, but never on general grounds. The right of embassy was not spoken of in theory or regarded in practice as diplomatic representation, a symbolic attribute of sovereignty. It was a method of formal, privileged communication among the members of a hierarchically ordered society, and its exercise could be admitted or denied according to the relations of the parties concerned and the nature of the business in hand. The precise definition of a body of diplomatic principals had to wait for a revolution in men's thinking about the nature of the state.

The evolution of a general theory of diplomatic principals,

however, can be traced in the literature about diplomatic agents. In the thirteenth century, Gulielmus Durandus, long a leading canon law authority on the subject, could write, 'A *legatus* [through the Renaissance about the commonest term for a diplomatic agent] is anybody sent by another.' Durandus thus deliberately subsumed the highest ranking diplomats in Christendom, the papal legates *a latere* about whom he was writing, under a definition which included not only the representatives of princes, provinces and cities, but those of subordinate vassals and officials, and apparently, under appropriate circumstances, those of any corporation or individual.[1] Practice bore him out. In the thirteenth and fourteenth centuries, not only the princes and free cities of the empire, and the greater feudal nobles, but even merchant towns, even universities and craft guilds, sent formal quasi-diplomatic agents on occasion, apparently without anyone's questioning their right to do so, or finding it odd to refer to them as ambassadors (*legati*), while the legists continued to discuss diplomatic agents under the same rubrics which dealt with all agents legally empowered to act for others.

Nevertheless, even as Gulielmus Durandus wrote, the actual European powers, the diplomatic principals of the future, were taking shape. Edward I and Philippe IV, Alfonso X of Castile and Jaime II of Aragon played the diplomatic game on a different scale and with different counters from petty feudal lords and bishops. And it was beginning to be recognized that while Florence and Venice, Genoa and even Lubeck might play in such a game, genuinely subject towns, even if they were London or Paris, could not. Strong monarchs after 1300 did not receive ambassadors from their subjects on equal terms, or, except under the strongest compulsion, ambassadors from their rebels at all, and kings began to regard the reception of ambassadors from their own subjects by other rulers as a suspicious, if not a hostile, act.

Theory reacted to practice with less than its usual slowness. In Italy some city states once subject to the emperor or to the pope had, by the fourteenth century, clearly become sovereign and independent. A city of this class, said Bartolus, some seventy years after Durandus, was a prince in respect to itself, and, letting his eye wander further over Europe, he noted that rulers of the provinces of the empire who acknowledged no superior were equally

27

'princes' in their respective kingdoms. That is, such princes were, to use a cliché which Bartolus avoids, 'emperors in their own domains'.[2]

The foundation stone of the modern theory of sovereignty was thus laid and, in the first course of the new structure, the beginnings of a new theory of diplomatic principals. Ambassadors, Bartolus said, are to be presumed genuine if they are sent by just and valid governments. He does not quite say who these just and valid authorities are, or go so far as to assert that only a lord who is in fact a prince is fully entitled to diplomatic representation. But his references relate his judgment to his general doctrine of the delegation of the imperial authority to the governors of provinces and cities, and his main line of reasoning is clear.[3] The practice of the 1350s would scarcely have permitted a more definite statement.

Eighty years later, though the theoretical statement had been elaborated, it is still not much more definite, perhaps because practice was still far from clear cut. Noblemen like John of Gaunt and Louis of Orleans sent formally accredited ambassadors who were received at royal courts, by sovereign republics like Venice, and on occasion even by the pope, with as much solemnity as if they were the envoys of crowned kings. And there was still a sense in which the delegates to an imperial diet, or those of a metropolitan see to the Roman curia might be regarded as ambassadors. The theorists, therefore, were not led to try to distinguish a single definite class of diplomatic principals but, instead, to establish a rough gradation of dignity among all the powers and authorities who might, under at least some circumstances, be entitled to some form of diplomatic representation. Consequently, the emphasis falls on the classification of diplomatic agents and the beginning of a more precise terminology to describe the different grades.

Here we may begin to take for a guide the first textbook of diplomatic practice written in Western Europe. Its author, Bernard du Rosier, was provost (he was later to be archbishop) of Toulouse. He had lectured for years at Toulouse on the civil and the canon law, written copiously on subjects legal, moral and theological, and served his university, his archbishop and his king on diplomatic missions. He may have been on one when he finished his 'Short Treatise About Ambassadors' on Christmas Eve, 1436, at the court of the King of Castile. He meant the work as a handbook of practical advice for diplomats.[4] It is invaluable now for the light it throws on the diplomatic practice of its time, and for the assumptions, political and legal, on which that practice was based.

About nomenclature Rosier says brusquely: *Legatus* and *ambaxiator* are two words for the same office, the one used by classical antiquity, the other of more recent origin. Formerly all diplomatic agents were called *legati*, but now the term is most properly applied only to the cardinal legates of the Holy See. Minor officials, once also called *legati*, are now called 'nuncios' and 'procurators' according to their functions. But those whom the greater secular princes, the governments of some cities, and the three estates of certain realms employ on their major business are called ambassadors.

The greater secular princes, the governments of some cities and the three estates of certain realms — it would have been impossible when Rosier wrote to define the class of diplomatic principals more exactly. It would still have been hard a century later. Certainly no one in Rosier's time questioned the right of the Duke of Milan or the Duke of Brabant to send and receive ambassadors, though they held their fiefs of the Empire. If the sovereignty of Venice was unchallenged, that of Florence and Genoa was less certain, yet it would have been hard to distinguish between them in point of diplomatic status. And not only the diets of Poland and the Empire sent and received ambassadors, on occasions, independently of their princes, but so did provincial estates like the assemblies of the Hansa and those of the Basque provinces. The Swiss continued to do so throughout the fifteenth century, though their sovereignty was still not generally recognized. In time, the number of these anomalies lessened and the list of diplomatic principals became easier to draw. But by the 1430s it was already accepted that only the greater European powers were entitled to employ diplomats of the highest rank.

About the correct name for these diplomats, Rosier was not so much wrong as premature. The term he preferred, 'ambassadors', though it had been in use since the thirteenth century, was not accepted as quickly or as universally as he expected. The humanists' taste for elegant latinity gave '*legatus*' a revived currency. Down through the middle of the seventeenth century, in some official documents and in most Latin books, ambassadors were still *legati*. Meanwhile the Italians had found another term less barbarous than '*ambaxiator*', and throughout the Renaissance diplomatic agents, sometimes of the highest rank, were frequently referred to as 'orators'. But in all the vulgar tongues some form of the word 'ambassador' became increasingly common, and in usage increasingly restricted to the major diplomatic agents of the major powers, just as Rosier had said.

For the minor business of the great princes and for all the business of other persons or corporations conceded any diplomatic rights practice had developed and theory recognized two classes of agents, nuncios (*nuntii*) and procurators. Both, in the exercise of their functions, were regarded as diplomatic officers, and were entitled to at least some of the privileges accorded ambassadors.

About the definition of these two classes theory was perfectly clear. A nuncio was a messenger, speaking with the voice of his principal. He might be a great nobleman, a herald, the representative of a corporate body, or a simple courier. In any case, his function was the same. It was to deliver a message or to grace a ceremony as the representative of his employer. He had no power to negotiate anything, and when his message was delivered or his symbolic act performed his mission was over. A procurator, on the other hand, had no symbolic representative function, but he could negotiate. He was a person armed with specific legal powers to represent the interests of his principal, or to arrange on more or less fixed terms a particular piece of business. His name and general function derived from Roman law and survive today in the proctors and *procureurs* of certain courts. 'A procurator speaks always in his own person though in his lord's name; a nuncio speaks in his lord's person, never of himself' was the way the textbooks put the difference.[5] Theorists found no difficulty in telling nuncios from procurators, and both from ambassadors.

But alas for clarity, and alas for the historians who have tried to reduce this part of late medieval practice to order. Both terms became involved in confusion. It was not so bad that the papacy which had begun to restrict the term *legatus* to cardinal legates *a latere* took to calling its next ranking diplomats 'nuncios', as it does to this day. Everyone knew that papal nuncios, then as now, corresponded roughly in rank and function to secular ambassadors, and since the diplomatic practice of Rome was always peculiar to itself, its different terminology was not hard to bear in mind. But a '*nuntius*' is a messenger, and some chanceries had long described and long continued to describe an envoy charged with a special message as a nuncio. Sometimes, with a love of sonorous reduplication which modern foreign offices have not quite thrown off, they called him 'legate, orator and nuncio' all in one breath. And since a distinguished envoy carrying a message may also be provided with powers to conclude an agreement, 'procurator' often got added to the string of titles. Down to the seventeenth century most ambassadors were styled 'ambassadors and procurators', until the more resounding term 'plenipotentiary' finally drove 'procurator' out of use.

Confusing as all this seems now, it does not seem to have confused anybody at the time. The full-fledged diplomatic envoy who was also described as a nuncio was not therefore mistaken for a herald or a simple messenger. The greater dignity covered the less. And the ambassador who was also a procurator was a very different sort of officer and stood on a different footing from the lawyer holding an act of procuration from a client, even though the lawyer might be a bishop, and his client a king, and his procuration a watching brief for all the ecclesiastical interests of a great realm at the papal court. In fact, it was exactly at Rome where procurators were most common that the distinction between them and ambassadors was most sharply drawn. Simple procurators, no matter how important their clients, or how distinguished their own station, always ranked below ambassadors, and for some occasions enjoyed no diplomatic status whatever.

Of one characteristic and picturesque class of quasi-diplomatic officers the canonists and civilians took no account, except by implication as one kind of nuncio. Yet no sketch of late medieval diplomatic institutions should omit some mention of the heralds and their subordinates. The second estate was loosely united by ties of chivalry in a society coextensive with Christendom. However vague and rudimentary those ties may once have been, by the fifteenth century they had been elaborated, rationalized, formalized and written down in books for the use of an increasingly literate aristocracy. The laws of chivalry prescribed the proper conduct of the feudal class in peace and war, regulated precedents and the etiquette of intercourse in all situations undetermined by direct feudal obligations, and laid down the tabus to be observed and the courtesies to be extended. The custodians of this code, and the agents of formal intercourse under it, were heralds.[6]

Since the main business of the feudal class was war, it was chiefly in war that the special machinery of heraldry, its pursuivants, trumpets and parleurs was conspicuous. In the formal summoning of besieged places, in the arrangement of truces, parleys and the ransoming of prisoners these minor officials were supposed to act. Royal heralds and kings-at-arms were, by the fifteenth century, deemed the most appropriate bearers of solemn warnings, ultimatums and defiances. But also, in the learned elaboration of heraldry which was part of the ornate pattern of chivalry in decadence, heralds claimed for their colleges a fanciful descent from the Roman *fetiales*, and for themselves a prior lien on all diplomatic functions. 'It is the business of those greater messengers who are called heralds-at-arms', says Nicholas of Upton, a fifteenth-century English authority on heraldry, 'to negotiate peace and matrimonial alliance between princes, to visit foreign kingdoms and regions and to confer honours . . . and to bear the messages of their superiors, faithfully and without softening their import.' In a model oath for heralds, Nicholas asks them to swear to carry out all negotiations entrusted to them 'in truth and plainness . . . and so to behave that your lords suffer neither by your indiscretion to others nor your reserve toward him'.[7] Salutary advice for ambassadors which shows that Nicholas, at least, expected heralds-at-arms to serve in that capacity.

So, occasionally, they did, though not, apparently, before the fourteenth century and not, on the whole, very often. When heralds were used to conduct negotiations, as Henry V used Arundel Herald in a mission to Portugal in 1413, as Henry VII twice used Roger Machado, Richmond Herald, and as Maximilian of Austria used Toisson d'Or, the qualities of the man rather than the appropriateness of the office seem to have determined the choice.[8] A herald's credentials and instructions were just like those of any ambassador, so that the fact that a few heralds happened to serve as ambassadors is without particular significance. In general heralds lacked the training, the experience, the social position and character to make successful ambassadors. A dignified appearance at a public ceremony and firmness in making an unpleasant announcement were the most that could be expected of them.

In spite of the writers on heraldry, heralds never enjoyed greater privileges and immunities than were extended as a matter of course to all ambassadors. Sometimes less. Heralds acting for other than royal persons or without diplomatic credentials were at best simple nuncios, and the minor officials of heraldry when lacking credentials were usually not granted any diplomatic status. The treatment of heralds, like the treatment of other diplomatic officers, was beginning to follow a formal legal pattern reflecting the development of a hierarchy of diplomatic principals.

CHAPTER III

DIPLOMATIC PRACTICE

THE occasions for sending ambassadors, says Bernard du Rosier at the beginning of his little treatise, are daily increasing, and because of the pressure of public events seem likely to go on doing so. This is 1436. The intense English diplomatic activity initiated by Henry V had hardly slackened, and was now being countered by revived French efforts which had recently triumphed at the Congress of Arras which Rosier may have attended. The king of Castile, having settled his difficulties with Portugal, was at the moment negotiating with the princes of Navarre and Aragon on the one hand and with the Granadan Moors on the other. Over Italy was woven a complicated net of diplomatic intrigue. The ambitions of the Emperor Sigismund, the conflicting claims to the kingdom of Naples, the reviving temporal power of the papacy, and the bitter, triangular struggle of Milan, Venice and Florence all spun threads which were shuttled back and forth by busy envoys. And, as generally happens when diplomatic tensions are prolonged, the personal interviews of sovereigns and full-scale public congresses were giving place in the 1430s to the sustained activity of working diplomats.

The business of the diplomat is multifarious, says Rosier,[1] and the occasions for sending ambassadors are as numerous as the kinds of advantages to be obtained. He lists them: 'to pay honour to religion . . . and the imperial crown, to protect the rights of kingdoms, to offer obedience . . . to confirm friendships . . . to make peace . . . to arrange past disputes, and remove the cause for future unpleasantness . . . to reprove tyrants and bring rebels back to their obedience . . .' and so forth. Roughly, one may divide the whole list of occasions into two categories: embassies of ceremony ('to pay honour . . . to confirm friendship', etc.) and embassies of negotiation ('to make peace . . . to arrange . . . to remove', etc.). Similarly one may divide the missions into two general types: ordinary embassies sent to pay a compliment or negotiate a dispute at a single court and then to return, and circular embassies, ordered to visit a number of courts in turn. Both main divisions admit combinations and overlapping. An ambassador might be sent to a particular court, but be instructed to pay compliments at others on his way, or he might be sent ostensibly on a visit of ceremony but really to initiate some negotiations. Fifteenth-century practice supplies abundant illustrations of all the varieties of embassies Rosier lists and all their possible combinations.

Both the archives and the legists comment amply upon Rosier's next two points. Having accepted a mission, an ambassador should prepare to start promptly. And in return for his diligence his government will see to it that he is generously provided for. Both points seem to have been counsels of perfection. All over Europe the delays of ambassadors in starting on their missions were the cause of frequent complaint and not infrequent diplomatic misfortune. And one reason for these delays was often the difficulty of meeting initial expenses. It was the common practice of Christendom to pay ambassadors a stipend — usually quite modest — on a *per diem* basis. It was also accepted in law and in practice that an ambassador was entitled to the ordinary expenses of his journey and to indemnity for losses incurred in it.[2] Once he had presented his credentials, his ordinary living and that of his suite would be, it was assumed, at the expense of the receiving government so that his *per diem*, plus expenses, made up a reasonable remuneration. But commonly the *per diem*, or most of it, was not payable until the ambassador's return, and there was no clear rule about initial expenses, in Rosier's time or a good deal later.

Yet for a formal embassy, these expenses, the horses and horse furniture, the liveries for the servants, the provisions and bedding and plate and hangings and the like were often extremely heavy, and it was sometimes hard to disabuse treasury officials of the idea that individuals entrusted with diplomatic missions ought to pay for the honour conferred. Rosier strongly rejected this point of view; no ambassador, he said, should set out unless he is sure of being adequately provided for. Possibly when he wrote he still had an unsettled bill against some principal's treasury; a good many of his contemporaries had. And a good many diplomats continued to have, in spite of wise maxims like Rosier's, and of generations of complaints and remonstrances.

Once they are ready for their mission, says Rosier, ambassadors ought to take their departure in a solemn and public manner so that their prestige may be increased, the fame of their coming fly before them, and the powers to whom they are sent may be the more ready to receive them. Rosier is recommending the Roman practice. The departure of papal legates *a latere* was regularly accompanied by the greatest pomp and ceremony. At secular courts similar publicity was less frequent, but still often used, especially for embassies of great consequence. It did more or less serve the purpose of notifying those concerned of the mission's destination. Notification by any other means was, on the whole, unusual. Prior inquiry as to the acceptability of the ambassador at the court to which he was to be sent was definitely not customary for a long time to come.

At the final public audience before their departure, ambassadors were usually handed the documents necessary for their mission, their credentials, their instructions and perhaps their powers. But it would be presumably at some prior and less public conference that Rosier advised all envoys to have their instructions orally explained to them. In oral conference, questions can be asked and doubts resolved. Against the danger of ambiguous instructions, whether oral or written, Rosier warns in terms so emphatic as to leave little doubt that he had either suffered himself from such pitfalls or seen colleagues fall into them. In fact, the records of fifteenth- and sixteenth-century diplomacy show no more common cause of confusion and failure in negotiation than such ambiguities, sometimes deliberate, probably, since ambiguity is one way by which makers of policy may mask their own indecision.

Once started, Rosier advises, the embassy should travel with reasonable speed, but without undignified haste and in a manner marking its public function. Until it reaches its destination the embassy is on an easy and informal footing, during which time juniors will take pains to relieve their seniors of the disagreeable tasks of travel, and the elder and more experienced members may beguile the journey by instructing their juniors in the duties expected of them. This easy reliance on travelling time to get the embassy into shape reminds one that under medieval conditions of travel, a party journeying 'without undignified haste', might spend weeks, even months, on the way.

On arrival the embassy must expect to make a solemn entry.[3] The court to which they are destined will send to greet them, at some distance from the place appointed for their reception, 'persons of a rank and distinction appropriate to the position of the ambassadors and the solemnity of the embassy'. This phrase is the only reference to the whole subject of diplomatic precedence to be found in Rosier's treatise. The rank of the ambassadors and the solemnity of the embassy are the joint criteria for determining the degree of ceremony with which a particular mission is to be treated, the solemnity of the embassy being judged in turn by the importance of its sender and the importance he attached to the mission, as Rosier elsewhere makes clear, so that princes are urged to emphasize really important missions by choosing persons of high social position as their chiefs.

The normal special embassy of which Rosier was writing was, in fact, unlikely to raise any very complicated questions of precedence, if only because it usually would not encounter the ambassadors of other powers. But where such conflicts did occur, the rank of the head of the mission was almost as strong a card as the rank of his principal. Roman ceremony observed a rough gradation among the monarchs of Christendom, but that a count or duke should walk behind a simple gentleman, or an archbishop behind a canon was too shocking in a feudal society to make any fixed precedence purely on the basis of the rank of diplomatic principals practicable, even at the papal court.

The persons of appropriate rank sent to welcome the embassy were expected to escort them, after a dignified delay, in a ceremonial public procession into the presence of the ruler to whom they were sent. This 'solemn entry' of a special embassy was one of the oldest and most widely used customs of European diplomatic intercourse. We hear of it, in the reception of papal legates, as early as the twelfth century. It continued to be observed in the age of Louis XIV. Its origins are certainly Byzantine, going back to those ceremonies with which the emperors on the Bosporus sought to impress the barbarians. But Western Europe had made it its own, and leavened the original hieratic stiffness with something of the chivalric courtesy of the prelude to a tourney, and something of the gaiety of a carnival. Throughout the Renaissance the ceremony increased in splendour. The welcoming committee would often be headed by a great magnate — a peer or a grandee, perhaps even by a prince of the blood. The streets might be hung with banners and garlands, and the ambassadorial procession in its most splendid apparel would advance to the sound of music (really solemn embassies carried their own trumpeters), of clanging bells and booming cannon. The citizens might oblige with a pageant in appropriate allegory, fountains might run wine, and certainly the whole affair would wind up with a stately public banquet.

Before the banquet, however, would come the ceremonial audience. The escorting magnate would conduct the ambassador into the presence of the chief of state, and the ambassador would hand over his credentials, the formal official evidence of his ambassadorial character. He might carry no other documents, and quite frequently did carry no other meant to be exhibited, but every ambassador had to be provided with credentials. Before 1400 the form was fixed. The document is on parchment, in Latin, engrossed in the best chancery style, and sealed with the seal of state. It greets the recipient by all his titles and is signed with all the titles of the sender, but the text between is commonly no more than a few lines, the sense of which is to beg the recipient to give full faith to the bearer (usually named) in what he shall say on behalf of the signer. Sometimes a specific subject is mentioned, more often not. Usually there is an elaborate complimentary close. By Rosier's time all the principal chanceries of Europe had in their formularies model credentials showing how each of their neighbours should be addressed, and most legal textbooks laid down the general rules to be observed.[4]

Rosier dismisses the solemn entry with a few generalities about the desirability of an honourable public reception, and he assumes that his readers are familiar with credentials. He reserves his space for comment on the next step in the proceedings, the ambassador's first formal address to his host. Custom required the ambassador, as soon as he presented his credentials, to say why he had come. Custom, before 1400, had already made of this first address an exacting exercise in Latin eloquence. In Italy, Latin eloquence in the new humanist vein had already become one of the respectable weapons of statecraft. If the eloquence and pathos of the ambassador's Latin style and the effectiveness of his delivery did not really influence the success of his embassy, at least it was an Italian literary fashion to say that they did. But even in the outer transalpine darkness, where diplomats divided their discourse after the barbarous fashion of the schoolmen and mangled their Latin grammar, ambassadors were not let off the task of this first formal oration which, skirting delicately around the real business of the mission, was supposed to cover the emptiness of its subject matter with a profusion of resounding words. Bernard du Rosier, though his Latin is not without reminiscence of the poets, was certainly no humanist, but he takes the initial oration as seriously as if he were. In the fifteenth century ambassadors had to.[5]

For embassies of ceremony, the ritual of the solemn entry and the formal reception and address, followed perhaps by attendance at some further ceremony, a marriage or a christening or the ratification of an alliance, might be the whole of an ambassador's task. Rosier assumes, however, that readers will be more interested in embassies for negotiation, whose real work begins when the reception is over and the ambassadors settle down with their opposite numbers to thresh out the business in hand. Yet we need not pause long over his advice about the tactics of negotiation. Translated from the clichés of the fifteenth century to those of the twentieth, what Rosier has to say might have been said by Andrew D. White, or Jules Jusserand or Harold Nicolson. Students in foreign service schools in Rome and Paris, London and Washington are reading in their textbooks much the same generalities at this moment.

One must be as clear as possible in exposition, but one need not say everything one has in mind at once before feeling out the opposite point of view. One must listen attentively, and look especially for points of possible agreement; these it is usually desirable to settle first. One must adjust one's methods to circumstances, and be prepared to make all concessions consistent with the dignity and real interests of one's principal and the clear tenor of one's instructions. One must press steadily and persistently but patiently towards an agreement, remembering that the more quickly a just solution is arrived at, the more valuable it will be, since time is always an element in politics, and undue delay may, in itself, be a kind of failure. But one must always be polite and considerate of one's colleagues, not prod them, or irritate them unnecessarily, not make a fuss over trifles, not allow oneself to be carried away by the vain desire to triumph in an argument or to score off an antagonist. Above all one must not lose one's temper. One must remember that the diplomat's hope is in man's reason and good will.

If all this says more about the value of patience, truthfulness, loyalty and mutual confidence, and less about bluff, bedazzlement, intrigue and deception than might be considered appropriate for the century in which Machiavelli was born, perhaps it is not the less realistic on that account. Scholars and literary men often seem more given to the inverted idealism of *realpolitik* than working diplomats. Even Machiavelli himself was not in practice Machiavellian. Rosier may really have believed, along with other experienced diplomats, that, in the long run, humdrum virtue is more successful than the most romantic rascality.

About the procedural framework of negotiations Rosier is sketchy, but it is possible to fill out his allusions from the reports of ambassadors of his own and later periods, and to identify in his comments the routine steps of the diplomatic conference. When he gets to work, the ambassador meets, usually, with the official to whom, at his formal reception, his credentials were passed by their addressee, and the ambassador's first task is to explain, this time simply and without oratory, what his credentials mean; what he asks, and what (at least in part) he is prepared to offer. Then the other side, after consideration and at another meeting, may be expected to state its position, and it is appropriate for both sides to begin to ask some questions.

The most searching questions asked ambassadors were generally about their instructions. Written instructions, telling ambassadors what their major objectives are and how they must try to attain them, what they may concede and where they must stand firm, appear quite early in the history of Western diplomacy. They do not have the public character of credentials. Originally, and down through the fifteenth century, they were, theoretically at least, for the ambassador's eyes alone. Thus, though signed by the ambassador's principal, they do not commit that principal to anything, and most chanceries, not regarding them as public documents, had no fixed form for them. In France, Castile and the Italian city states, instructions were quite often in the vulgar tongue.

It was not long before ambassadors began to be asked to produce their instructions. The tenor of the instructions, after all, would show more quickly than anything else whether agreement was possible, and if ambassadors were sincere they ought to have no objection to proving that they were. The point was a ticklish one, for, of course, the instructions would also show the extreme concessions that the ambassadors could make

Instructions were private documents, and there was certainly no obligation to produce them. Rosier proposes the solution usual at his period. Ambassadors might offer to read aloud sections of their instructions, but should not let the actual papers out of their hands. Further than this they should never go without specific authorization. With proper authorization, however, they might, at need, give copies of a part, or even of the whole, or, in extreme cases, even surrender the original, though never without getting a notarial record of the transaction. Rosier does not mention what was becoming an increasingly common dodge in negotiation, the issuance of two sets of instructions, one to be exhibited or even handed over as a token of confidence, the other to be closely guarded and never alluded to, but to furnish the real guidance. By the sixteenth century, double sets of instructions were completely customary.[6]

Communications, in the 1430s, were so difficult, and chains of post stations so few and unreliable, that one might suppose that ambassadors, once started on an embassy and furnished with instructions, would be practically on their own. Nevertheless, Rosier's advice makes it clear that the known instances in which distant embassies sought and obtained supplementary instructions, sometimes on several successive occasions, each time at the price of weeks of delay, were not really exceptional. It was a regrettable necessity, Rosier felt, and one calling for all sorts of special precautions, but immensely to be preferred to a hasty and unauthorized conclusion, and still more so to a failure to come to any terms. If there was one thing of which Rosier was certain, it was that the most tediously prolonged conference, ending in the most lame and partial agreement, was preferable to a diplomatic rupture and no agreement at all.

Whatever the outcome of the negotiations, Rosier assumes, the ambassadors will return home with no more than a report of their mission and a draft of any agreement they have succeeded in reaching. In most major negotiations this was usual. No matter how many months' work the ambassador had put in on the draft of the treaty, no matter how much painful scrutiny and endless wrangling had been survived, and no matter how closely the final terms corresponded with the ambassador's instructions, what he carried home was still only a draft, which, if it proved acceptable to his home government, would be formally ratified, after due notice, at a public ceremony timed to coincide as nearly as possible with the public ratification by the other party. Only then would the treaty be in force. Everyone clearly understood that no ambassador could bind his principal in virtue merely of his credentials, no matter how magniloquently phrased, or of his instructions, no matter how specific or how sweeping. To make his signature to an agreement worth anything, the ambassador had to be holder of a specific mandate, a grant of power like a power of attorney, executed in due form.[7]

Powers, like credentials, are public documents. In the fifteenth, as in the sixteenth and seventeenth centuries, they were in Latin, on parchment, phrased in the accepted formula of the chancery which issued them, and sealed with the state seal. Unlike credentials, powers are extremely specific. Usually they authorize the bearer to affix his signature to a particular text, a copy of which he has with him, without any change whatever. Less often they indicate the possible changes or the essential terms. Less often still they empower the holder to sign any agreement which he considers consonant with his instructions.

When ambassadors were armed not merely with credentials and instructions but with powers, whether limited or full, the production of such powers, their careful examination, and the taking of notarially attested copies by all concerned were routine preliminary steps. But even when powers were found to be without flaw, and even when they authorized their holders, not merely to discuss and concede and draft, but actually to sign and ratify, governments generally preferred subsequent formal ratification by the principals, in their own persons or in that of one of their great officers of state. For really major treaties, grants of full

powers in the preliminary stage of negotiations were rare throughout the fifteenth century. For great affairs, powers, when given
at all, were so hedged about with qualifications as to provide not
much more than a basis for discussion. But for minor matters,
full powers were not infrequently granted. The same ambassador
might have several sets, relevant to particular issues, to be used
or not as he saw fit.

Having concluded negotiations, embassies were expected to go
home promptly. Whether successful or not, Rosier says emphatically, the ambassador should never depart without taking formal,
public, courteous leave. The less successful he has been and the
more strained relations are at the time of his departure, the more
important for him to salute his hosts in a friendly fashion and make
an unruffled and dignified exit, returning with the same public
calm and affability he used in arriving. On his return he should
complete his embassy with a full report, delivered at or after a
public reception which, again, Rosier thinks, should be pleasant
and honourable even if the mission has been entirely unsuccessful.
Here and throughout, the main point is perfectly clear. Diplomatic failures should be minimized and successes emphasized, not
to serve the prestige of the agent or his principal, but because the
grand object of diplomacy is peace. And if an agreement cannot
be reached, peace is best served by keeping open the hope of
agreement in the future.

If we have lingered over Rosier's treatise it is partly because so
much of what he described remains the same throughout the two
centuries of change with which this study is concerned. Had
Rosier been transported from the court of John II of Castile to
that of Philip IV at Madrid, or had he been able to attend the
Congress of Westphalia instead of the Congress of Arras, he would
have very soon found his bearings. In the legal and theoretical
writings of the seventeenth century, though he would have been
shocked by some of the arguments, he would have understood
most of the points at issue. He would have recognized the same
basic diplomatic documents, credentials, powers, instructions,
and been able to settle down into a routine of negotiations not
basically unfamiliar. In the new attitudes they brought to the
objects of diplomacy the intervening changes were, indeed,
revolutionary, but much of the old structure of habit and custom

endured, substantially unchanged. Even the modern student may find behind the wall of Rosier's archaic language not a few patterns of procedure still in use, and not a few maxims and precepts still applicable today.

CHAPTER IV

DIPLOMATIC PRIVILEGES AND IMMUNITIES

FOR any modern reader the most puzzling part of Rosier's little book is undoubtedly his remarks on ambassadorial privileges and immunities. They are brief. Perhaps, having lectured for years on legal questions, he had written about the subject at length elsewhere.

Many others certainly had, and throughout the rest of the fifteenth century others were still to do so, sometimes in special treatises, sometimes in scattered paragraphs. Later, enough of this legal literature found its way into print so that we can still satisfy ourselves that Rosier was not exaggerating when he said that the rules and principles governing the treatment of ambassadors were most familiar to all experts in the civil and the canon law. And we can reassure ourselves that whatever may be puzzling in Rosier's views is not due to any discrepancy between them and the best legal opinion of his day.[1]

At first glance Rosier's discussion seems clear enough. Ambassadors, he says, are immune for the period of their embassy, in their persons and in their property, both from actions in courts of law and from all other forms of interference. Among all peoples, in all kingdoms and lands, they are guaranteed complete freedom in access, transit and egress, and perfect safety from any hindrance or violence. These privileges are enshrined in the civil and the canon law, sanctioned by universal custom and enforced by the authorities of states. Those who injure ambassadors, or imprison them, or rob them, who impede their passage, or even abet or approve such acts are properly regarded as enemies of mankind, worthy of universal execration. For whoever interferes with ambassadors in their public function injures the peace and tranquillity of all.

The legists from Bartolus on supplement Rosier with more specific rules than there is space for here. To strike or injure an ambassador or restrain his liberty is an offence punishable by death. An ambassador cannot be sued in any court, nor may any writ lie against him for any act committed or debt contracted before the beginning of his embassy. He cannot be made subject to reprisals for the acts or debts of his countrymen. He is exempt from all taxes, tolls and customs on goods or property necessary for his mission. He is entitled to support from the public treasury wherever he may be. All authorities, ecclesiastical and secular, are bound to protect and assist him in every appropriate way. An ambassador enjoys these privileges and immunities from the day he takes up his mission to the day he lays it down, including periods of transit through the territories of states not mentioned in his credentials. And the immunities of an ambassador extend to all regular members of his suite.

All this seems as emphatic and unambiguous as the best modern doctrine, and as useful in providing ambassadors with every necessary safety and facility. In one respect at least, the assertion of the ambassador's right to maintenance at the expense of governments other than his own, it goes further than we would go today. Nor did any of the legists indulge in unrealistic assumptions about the enforcement of diplomatic law by the emperors or the popes. Canonists did usually say that violators of ambassadorial immunities ought to be excommunicated. But, like Rosier, the legists chiefly relied for the enforcement of their rules on the existing secular authorities of actual states, and beyond them on the pressure of a public opinion which derived its strength from the general harmony of sentiments throughout Latin Christendom.

In other words, like the twentieth century, the fifteenth was obliged to get along with an international law based on custom and convention and on the instinctive respect of rulers and governments for what all men recognized as the law. There was nothing stronger to rely on. And, although the fifteenth century was a violent and anarchic time, the reliance was not in vain. The pressures and sanctions on which the legists counted did operate, on the whole, to enforce their rules. With remarkably few exceptions ambassadors, and even minor diplomatic agents, did enjoy the privileges and immunities to which theory said they were entitled. And further scrutiny shows that among the relatively few exceptions there were some which were not really exceptions at all.[2] For about these matters, the general harmony of sentiments turned on a view of society now so remote that it is easy for us to mistake for complete illogic, logic based on premises so different from our own.

The illogic begins to appear in what seem obscurities and contradictions in the rules. An ambassador could not be brought into court for any act committed or debt contracted before the beginning of his embassy, but his conduct while an ambassador might expose him to the full penalties of the law in the land where he was serving. For certain kinds of debts contracted while he was on mission, he might be sued and his goods distrained. From punishment for crimes of fraud and violence committed while ambassador, his status gave him no immunity. And for a whole list of political crimes, espionage, conspiracy, treason and the like, he might be tried and sentenced by the prince to whom he was accredited, just as if he were one of that prince's subjects.

This is so alien to our modern notions of diplomatic immunity that it is not surprising to find scholars describing this aspect of late medieval jurisprudence as 'formless', 'chaotic' and 'absurd'. If an ambassador is to be subject to the courts of the country where he is serving, if his political acts are to be judged by the government to which he is accredited, how can he be said to enjoy any effective immunity whatever? So it becomes reasonable for a well-informed writer to conclude that 'before the middle of the seventeenth century there was, properly speaking, no international law of diplomacy at all'.

In the sense that, properly speaking, 'international law' is that set of conventions and agreements governing the relations of sovereign, autonomous nation-states, each a law to itself and its own highest end, the judgment is indisputable. It is also a tautology. But to men who thought of themselves as living in a common society, under the rule of a common law, the precepts of the jurists made excellent sense. There was no more reason to let an ambassador's immunity save him from the penalty for murder or treason than to let a judge or a tax-collector escape punishment for fraud or extortion just because the law gave him special protection in the exercise of his office.

And who was to enforce the laws governing an ambassador's conduct except the prince of the country where the ambassador was serving? In the commonwealth of Christendom secular authority was divided among a number of princes. Each was expected to enforce not merely the municipal law of his own realm but the common law of the whole community. In practice, that meant the applicable sections of civil and canon law as interpreted in the light of custom by the leading authorities of the day. In some cases questions might arise as to which law ought to be applied, but there could be no question about diplomatic cases. Ambassadors were protected by the civil law and were therefore subject to it. In cases involving diplomatic agents, jurisdiction lay with the highest court administering the civil law, that is to say, with the prince's court.

That was the basic assumption about jurisdiction over ambassadors. It was still held, only a little shaken, at the beginning of the seventeenth century. The assumption about the kind of behaviour which might expose an ambassador to the judgment of a prince's court was equally clear and simple, though even more foreign to our modern style of thinking. The law was intended to give the ambassador every privilege and immunity necessary for the performance of his office. It was not intended to protect him in the abuse of those privileges and immunities for other ends, any more than it protected the tax-collector who practised blackmail, or the judge who perverted his authority to favour his friends and revenge himself on his enemies.

The key to the doctrine about the limits of ambassadorial immunity lay, therefore, in the prevailing concept of an ambassador's function. Bernard du Rosier states and re-states it in half a dozen different ways. His warnings and exhortations are likely to be dismissed by the unwary reader as that lip service to an empty idealism which, we have been told, was characteristic of the Middle Ages. But this would be a grave injustice. Rosier was just putting into popular language the legal doctrine about an ambassador's function:

'The business of an ambassador', he says again and again, 'is peace . . . An ambassador labours for the public good . . . The speedy completion of an ambassador's mission in the interest of all . . . An ambassador is sacred because he acts for the general welfare.' And near the beginning of his treatise he defines the important limitation on ambassadorial immunity. Ambassadors must never be sent to stir up wars or internal dissensions, to plot the seizure of other people's property (it is clear he means the territories of other princes), to foment rebellion or schism, or to organize pernicious (read aggressive) leagues or illegal conspiracies. 'The office of an ambassador is always for good, never for discord or evil . . . and the ambassador of evil, coming for a bad purpose brings evil upon himself and will come to a bad end.' In other words an ambassador who used his office for other than its proper ends forfeits his immunity, and is liable to punishment at the hands of an offended prince. And the proper end of his office, the proper function of the ambassador, is to serve the general welfare, by promoting peace.

The jurists were making the same point when they said, in succinct chorus, 'the ambassador is a public official'. In the twentieth century we are so accustomed to thinking of a public official as a man on the pay roll of a particular governing body, with obligations only to the government which pays him, and status only within its jurisdiction, that it comes as something of a shock to realize that all these writers, from Bartolus down into the sixteenth century, were talking about a much larger public. When they said that peace, which is an ambassador's business, is a public good, they did not mean the good of a particular state or pair of states. At the very least, the public good of which they spoke was that of the Roman Republic or the Commonwealth of Christendom. And since some of them, anyway, were quite specific in insisting that the privileges of ambassadors extended equally to infidels, we may not be exaggerating if we take it that they meant not just the Commonwealth of Christendom, but of the Commonwealth of Man.

Perhaps the notion that such a community could command anybody's ultimate allegiance does not sound quite so fanciful today as it did fifty or even twenty years ago. Nevertheless we must recognize a certain stubborn optimism in the jurist's assumptions. Bernard du Rosier and his colleagues were surely not unaware that diplomacy, as practised in the first decades of the fifteenth century, sought less than the noblest ends. They knew quite well that the embassies shuttling back and forth across Europe in their day were rarely in the service of universal peace. Probably they knew also that it had never been much different. Probably they knew that they were putting the ideal higher than the possible, in the hope that men might thus be pricked into climbing a little higher.

If they had posed the problem in those terms, they could have alleged that the tactics of idealism deserved considerable credit for whatever progress towards civilization Latin Christendom had made between the tenth century and the fifteenth. But they would not have posed the problem so, because the alternative would not have occurred to them. In the Latin West idealism was not a policy deliberately adopted, but a basic moral assumption. Man was not the less bound to strive eternally towards perfection because he knew in advance that his best unaided efforts could scarcely bring him measurably nearer to it. The gulf between aspiration and achievement was a part of God's ordering of the universe. Like other creatures, princes and republics were prone to sin and error. That did not impugn the validity of the norms by which their conduct must be judged. It had not yet been suggested that in these matters society might accomplish more just by expecting less.

And, in fact, as far as the laws of diplomacy were concerned, fifteenth-century assumptions were not so unrealistic as they seem. In an age of anarchy and violence, diplomats did actually enjoy to a remarkable extent the privileges and immunities prescribed for them by the jurists. And if the maxims of the schools did not much influence the policy of princes, probably they did restrain the conduct of ambassadors. Some men, perhaps many, must actually have felt the moral force of the propositions advanced. Those who did not would still have known that the law would sanction and public opinion would approve their condign punishment if they violated the accepted standards and were caught in the act.

To the limitation on diplomatic immunity elaborated in the fifteenth century, only one alternative proved to be open. That was the cynical rule, later adopted, than when ambassadors were caught in conspiracy or espionage they could not be punished on the spot but only sent home 'for punishment'. In other words, no government can be expected to do justice when its own vital interests are involved. And a crime committed in the interests of one's country and in obedience to higher authority is not a crime at all.

Even had the fifteenth-century jurists hit upon any such formulation, they could not have accepted it. It would have been unworkable in practice and repugnant to the sentiments which provided the law of nations with its strongest sanctions. The fifteenth-century climate of opinion was not yet prepared to tolerate the view that no man has any moral responsibility higher than his duty to his country. People still clung to the idea that the object of diplomacy ought to be peace, instead of being resigned to regarding it as simply the lesser of two evils, the pursuit of the objectives of war by other means. The fifteenth century was no more ready to accept the sacred egotism and moral irresponsibility of the sovereign state than our society accepts the sacred egotism and moral irresponsibility of the sovereign individual.

Yet the very increase in diplomatic activity which stimulated Rosier and his contemporaries to elaborate the accepted theory was a warning of impending change. One may date the beginning of the new time from the battle of Nicopolis, or of Agincourt, from the fall of Ceuta, or of Constantinople, from the Council of Constance or of Basle, from the martyrdom of John Huss or of Joan of Arc, but somewhere within the lifetime of Bernard du Rosier the forces which were to make the modern world began decisively to overbalance the old.

Chief among these forces was the new territorial state with, as a notable weapon in its arsenal, the new diplomacy. As Rosier wrote his little treatise, the Italian city states, more self-conscious and more precariously balanced than the rest, were experimenting with unprecedented diplomatic techniques. Before Rosier laid down his pastoral staff at Toulouse, resident ambassadors were established, a revolutionary change in practice which finally forced so complete a shift in theory that the medieval law of diplomacy was almost forgotten.

PART TWO

THE ITALIAN BEGINNINGS OF MODERN DIPLOMACY

CHAPTER V

THE RENAISSANCE ENVIRONMENT

DIPLOMACY in the modern style, permanent diplomacy, was one of the creations of the Italian Renaissance. It began in the same period that saw the beginnings of the new Italian style of classical scholarship and in the same areas, Tuscany and the valley of the Po. Its earliest flowering came in the same decade in which Massacio announced a new art of painting on the walls of the Brancacci Chapel and Brunelleschi began the first Italian Renaissance building in the cloister of Santa Croce. Its full triumph coincided with the full triumph of the new humanism and of the new arts, and under the same patrons, Cosimo de'Medici, Francesco Sforza and Pope Nicholas V. Thereafter, like other creations of the Italian Renaissance, the new diplomacy flourished in Italy for forty years before it was transplanted north of the Alps, and acclimatized in one country after another of Western Europe.

The new diplomacy was the functional expression of a new kind of state. It is simple and easy to say that this new kind of state, 'the state as a work of art', was in turn a primary expression of the creative spirit of the Renaissance. That classic generalization has supplied the foundation for most of what has been written in the last century about Renaissance diplomacy.[1] It does make easy a vivid distinction between the newer style of diplomacy and the older; otherwise it is not very useful. What we see when we look at Italy between 1300 and 1450 is the rise of a number of new institutions and modes of behaviour, among them a new style of diplomacy, all leading to something like a new concept of the state. To label this bundle of ways of acting and thinking and feeling 'the Renaissance State' is unobjectionable. To treat the label as if it were an entity, and say that it was generated by another entity, the spirit of the Renaissance, is explanation only in terms of mythology. It might make better sense to say that the spirit of the Renaissance (whatever that might be) had, among its causes, the evolution of the new state. In this gradual evolution, separate institutional adaptations to changes in

55

the political climate, and consequent acceptance of appropriately changed modes of feeling certainly preceded the finished concept.

The political climate of Italy began to change in the eleventh century. Some of the institutional adaptations, then, are far older than anything we usually call the Renaissance. When the reformed and reforming papacy first defied the German emperors, forces were set in motion which finally burst for Italy the feudal ties in which all the rest of Europe long remained entangled. The energies of the new Lombard and Tuscan communes were set free. By the aid of those energies the papacy tamed the violence of Barbarossa and survived its mortal struggle with Frederick II. By their aid the popes triumphed, and the Guelph party shattered with revolutionary violence the last props of German feudal and imperial dominance. Except for the overshadowing papal and Angevin power, the burghers of Lombardy and Tuscany were left masters of their own political future. By the early fourteenth century, the decline of the Neapolitan kingdom and the failure and humiliation of the papacy cleared the board.

After the popes withdrew to Avignon, Italy was a political vacuum, a gap in the medieval system of hierarchically ordered duties and loyalties. The vacuum had to be filled by the political inventiveness of Italians. After the Emperor Charles IV's subsidized excursion to Rome to collect the imperial crown like a tourist's souvenir, the party war-cries of Guelph and Ghibelline lost meaning. When, in another twenty years, the legates of Avignon re-established the temporal sway of the papacy in central Italy, it was the great Guelph republic Florence which, with eloquence and gold, with hired arms and the new weapons of diplomacy, fought the papal forces to a standstill. The temporal authority of the popes could only be re-admitted to Italy if it accepted equality with those purely temporal powers which had grown up under its shadow.[2]

It was one of the paradoxes of the papal revolt against the emperor that it produced the first, and for a long time the only, purely secular states in Christendom. Everywhere else temporal powers were masked and sanctified by religious forms, by priestly consecrations and unctions with holy oil, just as they were at once buttressed and confined by fundamental laws and ancient constitutions, and elevated and immobilized by their position as keystones in the intricately interlocking arches of European feudalism. But in Italy, power was temporal in the strictest sense of the term. It was naked and free, without even the most tenuous connection with eternity. Fundamentally it was illegitimate, the unanticipated by-blow of a clerical revolt and thus an anomaly in the ordered hierarchy of divinely legitimated rights. Its theorists might dream of republican and imperial Rome. Its custodians might occasionally buy themselves an imperial or a papal title to turn an immediate profit. But they knew that the key to power was force. Thus, in Italy the struggle between the two heads of Christendom cleared the ground for the planting of the first omnicompetent, amoral, sovereign states.

The pragmatic and provisional nature of power made all temporal authority quite literally temporary authority. It depended on the ability of the rulers to compel by force an unhabitual obedience, and on the voluntary allegiance of enough citizens to permit the use of force against the rest. The insecurity of their tenure made the rulers, whether tyrants or oligarchs or dominant factions of the burgher class, alert, uneasy, self-conscious. They had to be sensitive to every threat from within or without. Just 'to maintain the state', just, that is, to keep the current government from being overthrown, was a grave, continuous problem. Because the state, in the realistic sense in which Renaissance Italians used the term, that is, the government, the persons or party actually in power, was always beset by enemies. There were implacable exiles, the leaders of the faction out of power, prowling just beyond reach. There were rival cities, eager to make a profit out of a neighbour's difficulties. And there were usually secret enemies conspiring within the gates.

Therefore the state, depending for its survival on power, was compelled constantly to seek more power. It was ruthless to anomalies and inconsistencies which a more stable, traditional authority might have seen with indifference. And it widened its boundaries when it could. Because the state (that is, the government) could not count on the automatic, customary allegiance of its citizens, it had to win and hold that allegiance by intensifying the community's self-consciousness. It had to serve, or appear to serve, at least some of the interests of at least some of its people.

The shortest way to these objectives was by war. War dramatized the state. War focused loyalty by identifying opposition with treasonable comfort to those who were plotting to plunder the city's treasures and bring low her liberties. War, if it injured the trade of a competitor, strengthened a monopoly, or cleared away an obstructive toll, might actually benefit the interests of the merchants who were always worth conciliating, even when they were not themselves in power. And successful war, if it resulted in the conquest of a neighbour, or the wiping out of some enclave within one's boundaries, actually increased the power of a machine which fed on power.

So warfare between city and city became endemic all over northern and central Italy. Only commercial giants like Venice and Genoa could afford to wage their wars on the sea lanes and shake half the peninsula with their quarrels. Mostly the war was with the nearest independent city, a convenient day's journey or so away. Thus Perugia warred with Arezzo, Florence with Siena, Verona with Padua. But whether the distances were more or less, whether the cities were tyrannies or republics, great or small, war became the health of the state.

It was also its most dangerous disease. More even than the factional quarrels of the ruling classes and the mounting unrest of the urban proletariat, the endemic wars of Italy threatened its communes with the loss of their hard-won liberties. Even the richest and strongest cities found long-continued wars debilitating. And in the end, victory and defeat were almost equally dangerous. If defeat threatened the return of the exiles, victory risked the seizure of power by a successful general.

The chief danger, however, was complete subjugation. Big cities ate smaller ones. The boundaries of the victors widened ominously towards one another. From 1300 on, the number of independent communes dwindled. Florence took Arezzo and then Pisa, Milan absorbed Brescia and Cremona, Venice annexed Verona and Padua. And these victims had been powerful cities, the conquerors of their smaller neighbours before they were conquered in their turn. Unlikely as it seemed that any one of the rivals could succeed in devouring all the others, no city was strong enough to feel really secure. Under jungle law, the price of survival was incessant alertness. One method of providing for this alertness and of countering the dangers of constant war was found in a new style of diplomacy. It was one of the most characteristic adaptations of the Italian cities to their growing pressure upon one another.

These pressures were intensified, just as the internal development of each state was hastened, by the scale of the peninsular environment. The growth of states of a new kind in Italy was fostered by a favourable ratio between the amount of social energy available and the amount of space to be organized. In any attempt to account for the precocity of Italian Renaissance political institutions, and particularly for their precocity in diplomacy, this point is second in importance only to the peculiarity of the psychological environment of which we have been speaking.

At the beginning of the fifteenth century Western society still lacked the resources to organize stable states on the national scale. On the scale of the Italian city state it could do so. Internally the smaller distances to be overcome brought the problems of transport and communication, and consequently the problems of collecting taxes and maintaining the central authority, within the range of practical solution. The capital wealth and per capita productivity of the Italian towns may not have been very much greater (it was certainly somewhat greater) than that of the more prosperous regions north of the Alps. But the relative concentration of population and the restricted area to be administered enabled the Italian city states to find the means necessary for the ends of government to an extent long impossible to the sprawling, loose-jointed northern monarchies. In consequence, not only was the natural pull of each capital intensified by the regular activities of paid officials, but the whole state was able to mobilize its forces with rapidity and ease rarely possible beyond the Alps.

In external relations, scale had a double effect. The comparative efficiency of the new Italian states (in part a function of their limited areas) enabled them to pursue the objectives of their foreign policy with greater continuity and agility than Europe could show elsewhere. At the same time, the presence within the limited space of upper Italy of armed neighbours, equally efficient, agile and predatory, made continuous vigilance in foreign affairs a prime necessity.

North of the Alps the greater spaces to be overcome made the clash of foreign policies less continuous and less menacing. A Philippe le Bel, an Edward III, a Henry V might be just as aggressive, ambitious, and unscrupulous as any Italian tyrant, and such a king might be capable of summoning from his realm a spurt of energy comparable in intensity to the best Italian effort and, of course, enormously more formidable in size. But such bursts of energy proved sporadic. Because they had not yet succeeded in organizing their own internal space, the feudal monarchies were incapable of really sustained exertions, and the more they were driven towards it, the more likely they were to sink back into regional indifference and factional strife. Meanwhile, the relatively vast and unorganized spaces of transalpine Europe cushioned political conflicts.

'Vast spaces' is scarcely an exaggeration. We are accustomed to thinking of space as having shrunk in our day. We are vaguely aware that Moscow is nearer to Chicago now than London was to Paris in Napoleon's time. But we are not so aware that space has been shrinking, though at a slower rate, for a good many centuries, and that in terms of commercial intercourse, or military logistics, or even of diplomatic communication, European distances were perceptibly greater in the fourteenth century than in the sixteenth, and remained greater in the sixteenth than they were to become by the eighteenth.[3] In the fourteenth and fifteenth centuries, the continental space of Western Europe still impeded any degree of political organization efficient enough to create a system of continuous diplomatic pressures. Rulers might indulge themselves in foreign adventures out of vainglory or greed or spite; they were not yet compelled to continuous vigilance and continuing action beyond their own frontiers by constant, unavoidable pressures.

It was otherwise in Italy. In upper Italy, by about 1400, space was becoming completely organized; political interstices were filling up; the margins and cushions were shrinking, and the states of the peninsula were being obliged by the resulting pressures to a continuous awareness of each other. Italy was beginning to become such a system of mutually balanced parts in unstable equilibrium as all Europe was to be three hundred years later, a small-scale model for experiments with the institutions of the new state.

For this model to work freely, one other condition was necessary: a relative isolation. For more than a century, from about 1378 to 1492, Italy did enjoy that condition. The schism of the papacy, the impotence of the Empire, the long misery of the Hundred Years War, the recurrent anarchy of the Iberian realms, produced all round Italy a series of crises and conflicts which diverted European pressures from the peninsula. Not that Italy was ever long free from the intrusion of some foreign adventurer in quest of a crown, a lordship or a subsidy. Not that there was ever a decade in which some Italian power was not intriguing to call in a foreigner in order to gain for itself some local advantage. But the foreign intrusions were all on what one may call an Italian scale. None of them threatened more than briefly to become unmanageable, or to alter radically the peninsular balance.

The final result of this long immunity from serious foreign threats was to make Italian statesmen insensitive to the difference in scale between their system and that of Europe, blind to the fact that the tallest giants among the Italian states were pigmies beside the monarchies beyond the Alps. They grew rashly confident of their ability to summon the barbarians when they might be useful and send them home if they became embarrassing. Thus, in the end they failed to understand the catastrophe that overwhelmed them. But the immediate result of the absence of severe outside pressures was to set the states of Italy free for their competitive struggle with one another, and so to intensify their awareness of the structure and tensions of their own peninsular system.

Mainly it was these tensions that produced the new style of diplomacy. Primarily it developed as one functional adaptation of the new type of self-conscious, uninhibited, power-seeking competitive organism. But relatively secondary factors had some influence: the character of Italian warfare and the trend of upper class Italian culture.

Warfare in Italy had changed as busy, pecuniary-minded citizens turned over more and more of the actual fighting to professional soldiers. These were recruited from the more backward regions of the peninsula and commanded by generals who were, in effect, large-scale contractors. Wars waged by mercenary troops under generals mainly zealous for their own professional reputation tended to be less bloody and less decisive than the earlier clashes of citizen militias, though still painfully expensive. War became more rational and, therefore, if less glorious, more civilized.[4] But for this very reason, as campaigns became more and more a series of manœuvres for political advantage, conducted by relatively small bodies of not always trustworthy professionals, the management of wars made increasing demands upon statesmanship. Success now depended less upon the brutal shock of massed force than upon vigilant and agile politics. The diplomat was needed to supplement the soldier.

At the same time the dominant elements in Italian society began to set a higher value on a form of contest in which their leading citizens, not mercenary strangers who might change sides for the next campaign, were the champions. Business men were delighted by the skills of the diplomat, the nimble anticipation of the next move on the chess board, the subtle gambit which could trip a stronger opponent, the conversion of an enemy into a partner against some common rival, the snatching of victory from defeat by bluff and persuasion and mental dexterity. These qualities were surely more admirable than the brute valour of the condottiere. Diplomacy was for rulers; war for hired men.

It was also natural for the ruling groups — merchants and professional men — most of them with some legal or notarial training (the practical basis of a humanistic education) and most of them experienced in the haggling of the forum and the market place — to believe that words might be as potent as swords. The faith of the merchants and the politicos in the efficacy of diplomatic and forensic persuasion as an auxiliary to or substitute for military force was probably heightened by the reviving interest in classical literature. In turn, no doubt, this faith strengthened the new humanism and helped to give it its prevailing bias towards public rhetoric. The real effectiveness of this form of psychological warfare no one can hope to estimate now. Certainly public opinion among the educated classes was more or less susceptible to propaganda, and certainly, from the time of Petrarch and Cola de Rienzi onward, there was an increasing tendency to try to manipulate this opinion by literary means.[5]

One may be permitted to doubt that an oration by Coluccio Salutati really fell into the scales of political decision with the weight of a thousand horse, but the straight-faced ascription of such a remark to Salutati's most formidable antagonist reminds us of the norm of Renaissance judgment. In that judgment the importance to the state of the diplomat's power of public persuasion, of his ability to deliver a moving formal speech or compose an effectively argued state paper, was at least equal to his utility as an observer, reporter and manipulator of events. In both his aspects, as public orator and as secret negotiator, the fifteenth-century Italian tended to value the successful diplomat with or above the successful general. Not because 'the business of an ambassador is peace', but because the diplomat, like the general, was an agent for the preservation and aggrandizement of the state.

CHAPTER VI

PRECEDENTS FOR RESIDENT EMBASSIES

THE pressures of the Italian system led to the invention of a new kind of diplomatic officer, the resident ambassador. Before the end of the fifteenth century, resident ambassadors, unknown elsewhere in Europe, were common throughout Italy. They had become the chief means by which Italian statecraft observed and continually readjusted the unstable equilibrium of power within the peninsula. They were at once the agents and the symbols of a continuous system of diplomatic pressures. And they had proved their worth as one of the most potent weapons of the new states in their unremitting struggle for survival and for the power on which they fed.

As weapons in the struggle for power, resident ambassadors began to be employed by the other states of Europe in about 1500. They have been the most characteristic officers of Western diplomacy ever since. They differentiate our system strikingly from any other we know about elsewhere. Naturally, therefore, scholars have inquired what prior suggestions could be found for this striking invention, and not unnaturally, the answers have been various.

Perhaps it would be as well to say here what is meant by a resident ambassador. He is, to put Wotton's wry epigram into English and disregard its English pun, 'a man sent to lie abroad for his country's good'. He is a regularly accredited envoy with full diplomatic status. But he is sent — this is the significant departure — not to discharge a specific piece of business and then return, as Bernard du Rosier assumed all ambassadors would be, but to remain at his post until recalled, in general charge of the interests of his principal. For the period before 1648 it is not sensible to impose any third requirement. Not all resident embassies were reciprocal. And not all residents were called 'ambassadors', though whenever there are enough documents it is easy to tell whether they enjoyed that status.

Most sixteenth-century writers about diplomacy were still puzzled and embarrassed by the mere fact of resident ambassadors. When, towards the end of the century, the humanists finally agreed on an account of their origins, the genealogy was fanciful. Some of the provisions of Roman law concerns those *legati* sent by the provinces to represent them at the capital. Some of these *legati* were obliged by their business to remain in Rome for years. 'Certainly,' said the humanists, who thought no institution respectable unless it had a classical ancestor, 'anyone can see what happened. When the empire fell, the barbarian kings of the succession states continued to maintain the *legati* of their provinces at the papal court. These were the first resident ambassadors.'

The explanation has not the slightest basis in historical fact, but it continued to survive in the textbooks for a long time. Even today most writers walk warily around it by excluding Rome from any generalization about the history of residents. In many respects, of course, the diplomatic relations of the papacy were quite unlike the relations of secular states with one another. But resident embassies are a secular institution, and the Roman curia played only a slight rôle in their development. There were no resident ambassadors at the Holy See before the 1430s, or at least there is no discernible trace of any. Their appearance at Rome in the fifteenth century was a consequence of the general development.

Two more recent suggestions connect the origin of the system with Rome. A nineteenth-century German canonist thought he had found the first resident ambassadors in the resident representatives maintained by the popes at Constantinople from the sixth to the middle of the eighth century. These officers, called *apokrisiarii* or *responsales*, were in charge of the business which the see of Rome still had with its then temporal overlords, the Eastern emperors.[1] During the same period the patriarchs of Alexandria, Antioch and Jerusalem maintained similar representatives at Constantinople, also for ecclesiastical business. The popes stopped sending any before 750. Certainly nobody in the eighth century thought of such officers as ambassadors. Probably nobody in the fifteenth century remembered them at all.

In the early 1900s another German scholar pointed out that the procurators sent by James II of Aragon to Rome at the end of the thirteenth century actually discharged most of the duties later expected of resident ambassadors.[2] This seems a more plausible precedent. Besides performing their normal legal function, the

Aragonese procurators negotiated diplomatic business, and regularly reported to the king the latest developments in Italian politics. For at least a decade they constituted a continuous series. More recently a brilliant study has drawn attention to a whole line of procurators representing the kings of England at Paris in the early 1300s. It suggests that these procurators were prototypes of the resident ambassador, and that similar procurators at the papal court at Avignon, 'became the first permanent diplomatic representatives'.[3]

These instances are interesting for their parallelism in certain respects to the first phase of the establishment of resident embassies, and for their differences in others. Both thirteenth-century examples show a prolonged period of negotiation between two powers with common interests, between the king of Aragon and Pope Boniface VIII, because of their alliance against Frederick of Sicily, and between the English and French kings because of their efforts to solve the problems of their feudal ties without resort to war. Both the Aragon of James II and the England of Edward I and Edward II displayed an unusual degree of diplomatic activity. Both left in their archives evidence of the precocious development of record-keeping and other foreign office techniques necessary for the conduct of continuous diplomacy. These are among the conditions which, nearly a century and a half later, seem to have favoured the development of resident embassies.[4] Both England and Aragon, by maintaining procurators at the courts of their partners, did take what looks like the first step in such a direction.

The differences, however, are equally striking. In both countries the burst of diplomatic activity flagged and died away. After the transfer of the papacy to Avignon, the kings of Aragon were not always represented at the curia, and, when they were, their procurators rarely had any but the usual ecclesiastical business. After the 1330s England had no procurators in Paris, and a little later none at Avignon either. There is no evidence that the early experiment was remembered two hundred years afterwards, or that it had any influence as a precedent.

It scarcely could have had, since the very act of sending a legal procurator meant the acknowledgement of a superior legal jurisdiction. Legal procurators were officers attached to a court of law, representing the interests of clients with suits at its bar. If the king of England had not been, in his dignity as duke of Aquitaine, subject to the jurisdiction of the *Parlement de Paris*, he would have sent no legal procurators to France. Of course, not only kings but cities or corporations or individuals sometimes sent such procurators to the papal court. In the English and Aragonese instances confusion is easy because both groups of documents mention two kinds of procurators, legal ones, residing near a court of law, and envoys with powers to conclude diplomatic transactions. But the diplomatic procurators were not residents, and the resident ones were not diplomats.[5]

This does not deny that resident legal procurators were sometimes useful to royal diplomacy. Apparently the Aragonese ones were in the 1290s, and later, after 1450, when most of the major powers were beginning to maintain permanent resident procurators at Rome, some of these church lawyers had occasion to report political news to their clients and even to meddle in diplomacy. In the 1480s England and Spain were represented at Rome by individuals who were accredited both as ambassadors and as procurators.[6] So it is fair enough to say that their procurators at Rome gave transalpine powers their first experience of permanent diplomatic representation and, in a sense, their first resident ambassadors. But by the 1480s resident ambassadors were commonplace among the secular states of Italy. Whatever really influential precedents for the new institution there may have been, must have been available, therefore, in previous Italian experience.

One of the chief functions of the resident ambassador came to be to keep a continuous stream of foreign political news flowing to his home government. Long before 1400 the Italian city states had the opportunity to appreciate the value of such news to makers of policy. It came to them from two sources, from the consuls of their merchant communities abroad, and from the resident foreign agents of their bankers.

From the twelfth century onward Italian merchants began to cluster in colonies in the chief commercial cities of the Levant and to organize themselves under the jurisdiction of consuls. The consuls were often elected by the members of the community and were primarily judges or arbiters of disputes among its members and the official representatives of its interests before the local authorities. From the first, however, the home governments of the colonists participated in this colonial organization and sent out officers with various titles to supervise and direct it. Later the consuls themselves acquired a more official standing and were frequently appointed by the governments of their native cities and directly responsible to them. In a sense they represented not just the interests, say, of the Pisan merchants at Acre, the Genoese at Constantinople or the Venetians at Alexandria, but the whole power and dignity of the Pisan, Genoese and Venetian republics.

Strictly speaking, consuls were not diplomats. Their status depended not on the general principles of international law but on special treaties with the powers on whose territory they were. But they did in fact perform some of the services later performed by resident ambassadors. Although any really important message or negotiation would be entrusted to a special embassy, consuls did sometimes deliver messages on behalf of their governments to the local authorities, sometimes, therefore, to reigning princes. Sometimes they did negotiate on behalf of their governments. In some places they had positions assigned to them at public functions. And the consuls of some republics, those of Genoa and Venice, at least, were expected to report regularly news of political as well as of commercial interest.

For Venice, anyway, a case might be made for her consuls having been the precursors of her resident ambassadors. One Venetian representative abroad, the *bailo* at Constantinople, performed both consular and diplomatic functions in the fifteenth century. Other consuls were sometimes given special diplomatic credentials. And all the surviving evidence indicates that by the latter part of the fifteenth century regular consular reports to the Venetian Senate had become a long established custom. Apparently the Venetians themselves thought there was a close connection between the two institutions. When, in 1523, the Venetian ambassador was recalled from England, the Senate voted that, until he could be replaced, the interests of the republic should be confided to the Venetian consul at London, 'according to the custom of former times'.[7]

Even before Venetian consuls appeared in European cities, the merchant bankers of Lombardy and Tuscany had begun to maintain permanent resident representatives, the medieval equivalents of branch managers, at the courts or in the commercial centres where they did most business. Since much of that business was loans to sovereigns, the access of banking agents to the prince and his council could be as easy as that any diplomat enjoyed. In the correspondence of these agents the political news must often have been the most profitable part of the letter. When the bankers thus represented were members of the ruling oligarchy of their city, or the trusted clients of its tyrant, the reports of their agents could supply the basis for political action, and the conduct of the agents themselves might be guided, by political motives. When the banker reported to was himself the actual, if unofficial, ruler of his city — when, for example, he was Cosimo de'Medici — the diplomatic function of his foreign branch managers might become very considerable indeed. After 1434 it was progressively harder to distinguish between the resident representatives of the Medici bank and the political agents of the Florentine state.[8] But this is a late instance.

Before 1400, the tyrants and oligarchs of northern Italy must already have learned all that experience with consuls and branch banks had to teach. The earliest Italian resident diplomatic agents are to be found well before that date. They were not called 'ambassadors' at first or entitled (as we shall see) to diplomatic honours and immunities. But they were received in the cities where they resided as the actual agents of their masters, and were charged with most of the duties later discharged by resident ambassadors. In northern and central Italy between 1380 and 1450 this kind of semi-official resident agent became increasingly common. Towards 1450 several of the earliest official residents of whom we have any certain notice began their careers as members of this ambiguous class, among them that Nicodemus of Pontremoli upon whom the consensus of recent writers has thrust, on somewhat slender grounds, the distinction of being the first resident ambassador.[9]

We shall probably never be able to lay down with certainty every step in the period of transition before 1455. Many records have vanished. Those which survive are largely unpublished and inadequately explored. Nor is it likely that any number of documents would enable us to assign with confidence respective weights to the influence of such antecedents as procurators, consuls and banking agents on the invention of resident ambassadors. But the main outline of the story is clear. The new institution was Italian. It developed in the hundred years before 1454. And whatever suggestions, possible antecedents, and analogies may have offered, the development was, in the main, an empirical solution to an urgent practical problem. Italy first found the system of organizing interstate relationship which Europe later adopted, because Italy, towards the end of the Middle Ages, was already becoming what later all Europe became.

CHAPTER VII

THE FIRST RESIDENT AGENTS

JUST as Lombardy in the eleventh century saw the earliest and most vigorous city republics, so after 1300 it became the area where the struggle to organize Italian political space was most acute. Where full-fledged city republics had first arisen, popular governments were the first to give way. Under the pressure of internal conflicts and external wars, the distracted cities of Lombardy early began to sacrifice their liberties to tyrants, and the concentration of power in the hands of a single ruler hastened the development of centralized, bureaucratically administered territorial states. At first such states were still crude, shifting and unstable. But where once thirty-six communes had joined to defend their liberties, before long a half-dozen despots competed for power. It is in the surviving records of these nascent dynasties that we find the first steps towards the new diplomacy.

It may be that the Gonzagas of Mantua actually were more politically alert than their rivals. The precarious position of their little wedge of strategically important territory driven in among more powerful competitors required special vigilance. Or it may be that we know more about their diplomatic activity simply because the Mantuan archives are relatively well-preserved. At any rate, the first resident diplomatic agent of whom we have any published mention served Luigi Gonzaga, 'Captain of the People of Mantua', at the Imperial court of Louis the Bavarian before 1341.[1] Luigi may also have had an agent at Ferrara. The emperor and Ferrara were the two allies he relied on to help him keep his slippery grasp on power. It is unlikely that his agents with either carried what their century would have regarded as diplomatic credentials. It is possible that they were not such isolated instances as they now appear.

The Mantuan archives also furnish our next and much more fully documented instance of resident diplomatic agents.[2] Between 1375 and 1379 Ludovico Gonzaga of Mantua and Bernabò Visconti of Milan were each represented at the other's court by a resident agent. We know about this only from an incomplete file of the letters of the Gonzaga agent, master Bartolino di Codelupi, preserved at Mantua. From these we can gather that Codelupi and his opposite number behaved much as resident ambassadors did a hundred years later. They negotiated details of policy (including a marriage alliance) and kept their masters informed, the two chief duties of resident ambassadors for a long time to come. In two other ways they resembled the resident agents of the transitional period. Although they were the publicly recognized representatives of their respective lords, they were certainly not styled 'ambassadors' and almost certainly not regarded as having any diplomatic status. And they were certainly not exchanged simply out of mutual courtesy or in token of peaceful relations. They were frankly the liaison agents of two temporary partners in the struggle for power. For many years no residents were sent for any other reason.

From the fragmentary record it is impossible to say how long the liaison between Milan and Mantua continued. It probably began before 1375. It may have lasted until 1390. But as the great lord of Milan, Giangaleazzo Visconti, grew more powerful, swallowing up first one and then another of his rivals, and as the lords of Mantua became more suspicious and alarmed, the connection was broken. This, too, is characteristic of the period of transition.

The reunion of the Visconti holdings under the great Duke Giangaleazzo,[3] and Milan's subsequent expansion eastward across Lombardy and southward into Tuscany and the Romagna mark the first major political crisis of the Italian Renaissance. If any single Italian city was to emerge from the dog-eat-dog struggle as the ultimate victor, the creator of an Italian kingdom, Milan, by its proud history, its impressive resources, and its geographical position, seemed chosen. The Milanese territory contained the richest Italian fields and, besides its populous industrial capital, a number of important smaller cities. It was compact and knit together by easy communications. It had a shadowy memory of the Lombard crown. It had even a vague sense of cultural unity, outweighing its separatist traditions by at least as much as the separatist traditions of Lucca and Pisa and Siena outweighed their Tuscanism. Most important of all, perhaps, it had no natural frontiers, or none nearer than the Alps, the Adriatic, and the Apennines, across which it drew the daily breath of its commerce.

Thus the rulers of the Milanese were committed by geography to a policy of aggression indistinguishable in the view of the merchants and craftsmen of their towns and even of the petty lords and peasants of their *contado* from a policy of defence. Perhaps the need felt by the Lombard burghers for strong leadership may explain the political success of the Visconti tyranny quite as much as the cunning and ruthlessness which were marked Visconti family traits. Whatever the cause, the Visconti had acquired, by the days of the great duke, a prestige, an autocratic authority, and a regular, reliable revenue which lifted Milan altogether out of the class of petty tyrannies and faction-torn republics. Giangaleazzo could plan and undertake the orderly piecemeal conquest of Italy, while at the same time constructing within his expanding frontiers the outline of the first 'modern' state.

One says 'modern' for want of a better word. Today national states are strong as against one another in respect to their total usable economic and human resources; they have been developing in that direction, now, for some time. But before the French Revolution, states found their chief strength in money. Giangaleazzo may have been the first ruler to formulate for himself Louis XIV's dictum that 'Victory lies with the last gold piece'. He would have meant, of course, as Louis XIV must have meant, the last available, spendable gold piece. If Giangaleazzo was confident of his ability to wear down and absorb his neighbours, it was certainly not because Milan, as rich as it was, was richer than the rest of them put together. It was probably not as rich as Venice or very much richer than Florence. It was because the duke of Milan had the spending of the Milanese revenues, while the officials of Florence and Venice could spend no more than their governing merchant oligarchies would allow. The gold of Giangaleazzo was to that of his rivals as an army on a war footing is to a half-mobilized reserve.

In a history of diplomacy the point is worth emphasizing. In no department of government is a steady dependable revenue free from embarrassing controls more important than in the conduct of foreign affairs. Spectacular necessities, wars and weddings and pompous special embassies, may find special sources of supply, but the daily drain of a well-staffed chancery and of permanent resident embassies is unlikely to be met, until such expenditures are sanctioned by custom, except by governments with ample funds and little need to account for them.

Milan was probably the first Italian state to be capable of sustained diplomatic action. The same resources which made Giangaleazzo strong enough to frighten Italy with his mercenaries gave him the means of transcending the spasmodic behaviour of medieval rulers, and laying the lines of a permanent foreign policy with large objectives stalked patiently, year by year. It may have been an appreciation of his advantage quite as much as any temperamental antipathy to the risks of war which led Giangaleazzo to prefer diplomacy whenever possible. Certainly diplomacy brought him his least expensive and most profitable victories.

The great duke was his own foreign minister, but under Pasquino Capelli, his secretary, and later under Francesco Barbavara, his chamberlain, an organized chancery performed at least some of the functions of a modern foreign office. It seems to have drafted official documents, prepared instructions for ambassadors, collated reports from different parts of Italy, acted as a buffer between the duke and foreign envoys, and begun the systematic keeping of records, without which a coherent foreign policy is inconceivable. Those records were lost when the Castello of Milan was razed by enthusiastic republicans in 1447, but the diplomatic web which centred in the Milanese chancery has left its traces in the archives of all the surrounding Italian states.

Giangaleazzo used diplomacy largely to divide and baffle his enemies and victims as a prelude, accompaniment and conclusion for each of his triumphant, aggressive pounces, and as a shelter behind which to gather strength for the next move. He was constantly sending and receiving special embassies, and built up something like a regular corps of veteran diplomats, most of them members of his 'secret Council' of foreign affairs, and most of them, apparently, legally trained. His solicitude for the law school at Pavia and his encouragement of humanistic studies are both connected with this aspect of his foreign policy.

In all this his behaviour was no different from that of such monarchs as Edward III or Philippe le Bel, but in addition he employed a number of resident diplomatic agents. We see their operations largely through the eyes of their enemies. They are likely to be referred to contemptuously as 'the duke's man here', 'the duke's agent', or 'familiar', sometimes 'the duke's spy'. No doubt some of them were spies, or at best agents with no official standing. But some of them must have had some sort of diplomatic status; for instance, the Visconti residents in Pisa, Ferrara, Perugia and Siena, who were all channels of official communication, and several of whom also served the duke on regular embassies. There is no evidence, however, of any reciprocal resident agents at Milan. Perhaps, like Louis XI, whom he resembled in other ways, Giangaleazzo did not enjoy close diplomatic observation. The final object of his policy was to secure, not allies, but subjects. Before death suddenly interrupted him, he had secured a good many.

The threat of Visconti domination aroused an almost equally intense diplomatic reaction. In particular, this is the period of the reorganization of the Florentine chancery under Coluccio Salutati, and of numerous Florentine embassies to Venice, to the states of the Romagna, to Rome, and even to France. But neither the Florentines nor the Venetians, the duke's two principal antagonists, seem to have employed resident diplomats to stiffen the shifting pattern of their alliances. That development awaited the second phase of the struggle with Milan.

In the interlude, while the Visconti dominions were divided and distracted, Florence finally scooped up Pisa, and the Venetians took Vicenza, Verona and Padua, effectively blocking off the lower valley of the Po, and establishing Venice as a major power on the mainland. Nevertheless, after Filippo Maria Visconti had reunited what was left of the Visconti patrimony, the initiative again lay with Milan. Filippo Maria inherited Giangaleazzo's chancellor, Francisco Barbavara, and Barbavara's foreign office. He got together an efficient set of ambassadors, and re-established a network of secret agents who were reputed to supply him with political information of amazing range and accuracy from all over Italy. He had his father's preference for diplomacy over war, and something of his father's skill in it, though he lacked his father's speed and daring, and attained nothing like the great duke's success. Yet his solidly organized state, his flexible revenues,

75

his able condottieri, his experienced servants enabled him to sustain a leading rôle in the Italian power struggle for a quarter of a century.

It seems likely that until his very last years Filippo Maria Visconti employed no resident diplomatic agents in Italy. Perhaps the fact that Giangaleazzo's residents in Pisa and Siena had subverted those republics and brought them under the Visconti yoke, made cities which had recovered or preserved their freedom reluctant to risk more Visconti embassies. Outside Italy, however, Filippo Maria's diplomacy was extremely active. He sent embassies to Aragon, to Burgundy, to Germany, and twice, on dubious missions, to the Turks. But the remarkable fact is that for more than seven years he maintained a resident embassy at the court of Sigismund, king of Hungary and Holy Roman Emperor elect. During most of this time Sigismund had a resident ambassador at Milan. For what it is worth, this is the first clear case of the exchange of regularly accredited resident ambassadors in history, or, more accurately, the earliest case thus far demonstrable.[4]

The verifiable dates for the Milanese embassy with Sigismund are May 1425 to July 1432. It may have begun somewhat earlier and lasted somewhat later. Of Sigismund's reciprocal orator resident at the Visconti court, we know only that he remained at Milan for at least seven years, that Filippo Maria used him as an official channel of communication, spoke of him as the emperor's ambassador and gave him place of honour at public ceremonies. About the Milanese envoys we are better informed. They carried regular diplomatic credentials and were accorded full diplomatic honours. They were rather frequently replaced, so that nine persons were accredited during seven years, but their missions were not so short as might be supposed, since normally there were two of them on duty at the same time.

The employment of two ambassadors for important special embassies was common in the fifteenth century, and the first two who presented their credentials to Sigismund and exhibited powers to negotiate an alliance look like such a pair. But before they completed their negotiations they were reinforced by a third ambassador, and they did not withdraw until they were replaced by two more. Thereafter there was always one and were usually two Milanese diplomats with Sigismund, replacements being made singly, to give greater continuity to the embassy. The tenor of their instructions and the assurances given Sigismund that they would not be withdrawn without replacement make it abundantly clear that this was not an overlapping series of special missions, but what was intended to be a permanent resident embassy.

In one important respect the exchange between Filippo Maria and Sigismund was true to the pattern of the period of transition. It was the result of an alliance. The business of the ambassadors was to co-ordinate diplomatic, and prepare for eventual military, action against a common enemy — in this case Venice. The exchange began just as Venice took sides with Florence in the war against Milan. When Sigismund lost interest in Italian adventures and the alliance between him and Filippo Maria fell apart, the embassies were discontinued.

Filippo Maria's anxiety for the alliance of Sigismund illustrates not so much the weakness of Milan as the increased strength of its antagonists. Italy was entering upon the penultimate phase of the organization of its political space. With the capture of Pisa in 1406, the republic of Florence had reached, not the natural frontiers of a Tuscan state, for Lucca and Siena and Piombino, all near and all coveted, continued to lie beyond her grasp, but the practicable limits of her expansion. Even those limits made her, on the Italian scale, a major power. Meanwhile the sea-borne republic of St. Mark's widened her boundaries on the mainland. To Verona and Padua and all that area of eastern Lombardy thereafter known as the Veneto, Venice added, about 1420, Feltre, Udine and the whole of the Friuli, carrying her frontiers to the eastern Alps, and swinging southward around the head of the Adriatic to dominate the Dalmatian coast. In point of territory, population and wealth Venice had become the most formidable of Italian powers.

The geographical position of Venetian strength was too eccentric, however, and the constitution of Venice too peculiar for her rulers to hope to unify Italy. The Signory was still greedy to snap up another city, particularly if it lay on one of their trade routes, and the menace of Venetian aggression furnished a recurrent theme of diplomatic correspondence throughout the fifteenth century. But Venice was not strong enough to conquer Italy, not strong enough even, barring some extraordinary upset, to conquer Lombardy. She was only strong enough to thrust hard against Milan, as Milan thrust hard eastwards against the Veneto and southwards against Romagna and the borders of Tuscany where Florence thrust staunchly back.

At the same time, the two southern states of the peninsula began to approach stabilization. The kingdom of Naples had been as anarchic as Scotland or Hungary, but Alfonso the Magnanimous, king of Aragon, grew stronger there each year after 1435, and in 1442 finally drove his Angevin rivals from the capital. For the next half century the house of Aragon ruled in the city of Naples and, after a fashion, in the kingdom, always able, though sometimes only just able, to overmatch their rebel barons, never able to expand their territories northward beyond the ancient frontier.

Meanwhile, more slowly, the Sovereign Pontiffs were beginning to reassert their authority over the states of the Church. The end of the schism and the triumphant installation of Martin V at Rome in 1420 were only a beginning. Most of the lordships which Martin V gave away to his relatives had to be taken back by force by the next pope who, in turn, was obliged to flee from the Vatican in 1434 before a briefly revived republic. But, beginning the next year, and using the characteristic methods of the Renaissance tyrant, Eugenius IV partially tamed Rome and subdued at least most of its immediate *contado*. Thereafter, though the more distant parts of the papal states continued to be a patchwork of petty semi-independent tyrannies, the popes, by virtue of their ability to compete for the services of eminent condottieri, and of their claims to suzerainty over most of central Italy, were able to play in Italian politics a rôle scarcely less important than that of a king of Naples or a duke of Milan.

Thus by the early 1440s Italy was dominated by five major states, Venice, Milan, Florence, Naples and the papacy, no one of them strong enough to make head against the other four, no two, as the combinations of the next decade were to show, decisively stronger than any other two. Here and there, sandwiched between the greater states in a pattern familiar to any student of later European politics, lay smaller ones, their independence precariously preserved by the mutual jealousies of their big neighbours. In a few areas, mostly in Romagna, Umbria and the papal

Marches, authority remained decentralized and fluid. But each decade saw political power in the peninsula crystallizing more definitely. While Filippo Maria was duke of Milan, although the Florentine and Venetian chanceries still raised the old battle cries of resistance to a universal tyrant, the Italian question was no longer what it had been in Giangaleazzo's time, how to achieve or to escape the subjugation of all to a single ruler. It was really how to allot the political space of the peninsula among the powers who seemed destined permanently to divide it.

For each major power, this meant how much could it add to its own territory without arousing the combined resentment of its rivals, and how much could it afford to concede. Each was beginning to recognize that no solution was possible on less than a peninsular scale. Consequently during the fourteen-twenties, 'thirties and 'forties, all Italy was involved in a rapid succession of crises and wars, and in a constantly shifting pattern of opposing alliances. In the thirty years following the Venetian intervention against Milan this series of peninsular-wide alliances spread resident diplomatic agents throughout the peninsula.

As might be expected, Venice, once launched on her career of continental expansion, took the lead in the diplomatic counteroffensive. Consequently most of the resident diplomats we know of during this period (other than Milanese) were Venetians. For the earliest, the evidence is inconclusive. At first, Venice had sought peace with Milan. During this time, from 1415 to 1425, it is possible that she maintained a resident agent at the Visconti court.[5]

About the next instance there is no doubt. In 1434 Venice, Florence and the papacy joined against Milan for the recovery, among other objectives, of two of the pope's towns and, some time before April 1435, Zacharias Bembo, an experienced diplomat, presented his credentials as Venetian orator resident at the Holy See. The date of his withdrawal is uncertain, but the weight of the evidence indicates that Venice thereafter had permanent diplomatic representation at Rome, except when the popes and the republic were actually at war.[6]

It is worth noting that Venice already had a procurator at Rome who continued to care for the legal business of the republic, as the 'Cardinal of Venice' continued to watch over Venetian interests at the higher levels of ecclesiastical policy. Bembo's mission, and that of his successors, were purely diplomatic. The Signory made a considerable use of him, regarded his presence at Rome as dispensing them from the necessity of sending special embassies, communicated through him to Pope Eugenius IV on all political matters, and expected from him regular budgets of news. Since the proof of a general negative is difficult, it would be bold to assert that Bembo was the first resident ambassador at the Papal See, and thus the founder of the first lasting resident embassy in history. But he certainly had no immediate predecessor, and the language of the Senate indicates that they regarded his appointment as an innovation. Nor had he, apparently, any colleagues. There is no trace of another resident ambassador at Rome during the 1430s. Rome in the 1430s, under Eugenius IV, was just beginning to recover its importance as a centre of political affairs.

Alliances in Italy, as later on in Europe, often tended to follow a kind of checkerboard pattern, and the Venetians were eager to ally with Milan's western neighbours, the duke of Savoy and the Marquis of Montferrat. The records of the Senate show Venetian envoys to both Savoy and Montferrat in the 1420s and again in the late 1430s and early 1440s, but we cannot be certain of a Venetian orator resident at the court of Savoy before 1447, or at Montferrat before 1450. The precise date for the beginning of neither embassy is ascertainable, but both seem to have enjoyed, after 1450, a normal measure of continuity.

Oddly enough, the two chief and most consistent allies against Milan were slow to exchange residents. In December 1447 the Venetian Senate declared that the republic could not conclude an alliance with France without consulting Florence, its ally for twenty-three years past. But at that time there was still, apparently, no Florentine resident in Venice to facilitate such consultation, and no Venetian resident at Florence. There was a Venetian consul who occasionally reported Florentine news, and Cosimo de'Medici's banking associates seem to have kept him abreast of Venetian affairs. But although at times the going and coming of special embassies had been so frequent as to constitute an almost continuous series, permanent channels of official communication were still not established. It was not until 1448 that the two republics finally exchanged residents, and this tardy exchange was soon interrupted by Cosimo de'Medici's dramatic reversal of Florentine policy, and a war in which Florence was aligned with Milan against Venice. Incidentally, although Florence had been the most active centre of diplomatic opposition to the Visconti for more than half a century, the ambassador sent to Venice, Dietisalvi Neroni, is the first Florentine resident of whom we have any certain record.[7]

Probably the relative slowness of the Florentine and even of the Venetian republics to make use of residents arose less from the natural conservatism of republican governments than from the constitutional difficulties of experimenting with the kind of semi-official representatives who had proved so useful to tyrants. A Visconti or a Gonzaga could send a trusted counsellor or confidential agent, provided with no more than a personal letter of introduction to a fellow tyrant or to some influential citizen. No matter how askance he might be looked at on his arrival, it would be highly embarrassing to refuse to let such an individual, ostensibly a private person, reside wherever and as long as he chose. Nor would it be particularly risky for his sender to 'disavow him, though in the meantime everyone would be perfectly aware whom he represented. Such agents could be appointed by an autocratic prince without consultation with anyone. They could be dispatched and recalled at will and paid out of private and unquestionable funds. They could receive their instructions directly from the prince, and report to him directly. They might even be given full ambassadorial credentials to be produced only if an emergency required it.

For the development of a new diplomatic tool, such flexibility was most convenient, but such a tentative, experimental technique was impossible for law-bound governments like Florence or Venice. Their foreign affairs were conducted by committees whose members were watchful of one another, and who were, collectively, more or less responsible to deliberative assemblies. The salaries and terms of office of their public officials had to be fixed by law, and their expenses to be met out of public appropriations. No mere private letter, nothing less than a properly sealed official document, could guarantee the right of any person to speak for Venice or for Florence. The republics could (and did) employ secret agents, just as they employed public ambassadors. But an ambiguous combination of the two rôles in one person was beyond their power. Therefore when Venice or Florence sent resident diplomatic agents intended to serve as channels of governmental communication, those agents had to be unmistakably official and formally accredited, and this naturally made the adoption of the new diplomatic tool a much graver departure from established custom.

It is creditable to the alertness and realism of the Venetian and Florentine ruling classes that they were as quick as they were to appreciate the advantages of the new device. Once they had done so, the further advantages of fully official, legal diplomatic representation were unmistakable. Had there been no constitutional republics in Italy, had all the major Italian states been ruled by tyrants, it seems likely that the transition from the semi-official agent to the fully accredited resident would have been much slower.

CHAPTER VIII

THE MILANESE WARS AND THE PEACE OF LODI (1444-1454)

IN the 1440s there began to form in certain Italian minds a conception of Italy as a system of independent states, coexisting by virtue of an unstable equilibrium which it was the function of statesmanship to preserve. This conception was fostered by the peninsula-wide alliances whose even balance of forces had ended every war of the past twenty years in stalemate. It recommended itself increasingly to statesmen who had accepted a policy of limited objectives, and had more to fear than to hope from a continuance of an all-out struggle. Cosimo de'Medici has sometimes been called the father of the idea of an Italian balance of power, and his most important political decisions were certainly in accordance with it. But its first practical expression was in the proposal of Filippo Maria Visconti, in September 1443, for joint action by Florence, Venice and Milan to end the war between the powerful condottiere, Francesco Sforza, and the pope, such action to be followed by a congress of the major Italian powers for the settlement of all outstanding political questions and the exchange of mutual guarantees.[1]

Historians have doubted Filippo Maria's sincerity. So did his contemporaries. His congress, when it finally convened, was poorly attended and came to nothing. Yet it may be that the last Visconti duke, tired out by thirty years of war and intrigue, ruling a people increasingly discontented, ringed by enemies and without a son to continue his line, was ready to exchange his unrealized ambitions for a more certain title to what he held, and to welcome a permanent settlement on the basis of the status quo. It was Italy that was not ready. Another decade of wars and negotiation had to pass before the five major powers could be prevailed upon to accept a scheme like Filippo Maria's.

This was the last decade (1444-54) of peninsular fluidity, the last decade of continuous struggle between constantly realigning coalitions over the entire peninsula. And it was also the last decade of tentative experiment with the new technique of permanent diplomatic representation. It saw the last important Italian use of the old device of the semi-official agent, made by Francesco Sforza, the last of the old-style tyrants to found a major dynasty, and before it closed it saw so wide an extension of the new official resident ambassadors that only a general peace was necessary to their diffusion throughout Italy.

The diplomatic crises of this decade all turned in one way or another about the rise of Francesco Sforza. His agents were among the most active diplomats. Each crisis was in some way involved with the great condottiere's chances of realizing the highest ambition of all great condottieri by making himself a ruler. Sforza aimed at Milan. Paid first by the duke of Milan, then by Milan's enemies, Sforza carved for himself a kind of principality in the papal states, and married, with something of the pomp of a princely alliance, Filippo Maria's natural daughter, Bianca. But his success aroused the jealousy not only of his suzerain, Pope Eugenius IV, but of his father-in-law, Filippo Maria, and of the formidable lord of Rimini, Sigismondo Malatesta. In 1445 these three and Naples joined forces to drive Sforza from his possessions in the papal states. One consequence of this league belongs to the history of resident embassies. Venice backed Sforza, and the angry pope declared war on the republic and ordered the Venetian resident to withdraw. Milan promptly took advantage of the breach. The duke sent his secretary, Marcolino Barbavara, as his own resident ambassador to Rome, another step in the spread of the new system.[2]

Sforza was hard pressed, lost town after town, and found himself reduced to a losing defensive. His only hope was in support by Venice and Florence. Without their co-ordinated efforts in his behalf, he would certainly share the fate of earlier over-ambitious condottieri. Whether the closer diplomatic liaison between the two great republics at this time may have been due, in part, to Sforza's influence with his old friend Cosimo de Medici we can only conjecture. All we know is that Sforza, anxious to persuade his allies to an all-out effort and, no doubt, even more anxious to have the earliest possible warning if either of them planned to desert him, sent, early in 1446, two semi-official diplomatic agents to reside in Venice and another to Florence. Of the agents in Venice we know only that they did act, until August 1447 and perhaps later, as channels of communication between Sforza and the Signory.[3] Of the agent in Florence, Nicodemo Tranchedini da Pontremoli, we know a great deal more.[4]

Nicodemo da Pontremoli has long been mentioned as 'the first resident ambassador outside of Rome' and mere repetition has ensured his name an eminence scarcely deserved. Whether or not Francesco Sforza could have sent a fully-accredited ambassador to Florence before 1450 when he became duke of Milan, there is no evidence that he did so. Nicodemo da Pontremoli was well known, indeed, to be Sforza's confidential agent, and was on intimate personal terms with many individuals high in the Florentine administration. But primarily he was Sforza's liaison man with Cosimo de'Medici. It was to Cosimo that Nicodemo communicated Sforza's views, leaving Cosimo to present them to his compatriots as he thought best. It was Cosimo who informed Nicodemo of Florentine political decisions, and whose views Nicodemo reported to his master. And Cosimo, of course, was not the lord of Florence, nor even in public charge of the city's foreign affairs. He was merely the republic's most influential private citizen. During the first four years or so of his residence in Florence, therefore, Nicodemo must be counted a member of that transitional class of semi-official diplomatic agents already known in Italy for almost a century. Later, after Francesco Sforza was duke of Milan, Nicodemo did become the regularly accredited orator resident of Milan at Florence. He continued in that post for seventeen years, proving himself among the ablest and most useful, as he became by far, in continuity of service, the senior, of all the resident ambassadors in Italy. It is for the length and distinction of his diplomatic career, not its priority, that he deserves to be remembered.

Or perhaps he should be remembered most for his share in the diplomatic revolution of 1451. The decision to ally Florence with Sforza against Venice was Cosimo's. We shall never know how much that decision was influenced by a broad vision of an Italian system, and how much by personal motives, pique at Venetian tactlessness, fear of losing the money already lent to Sforza, and the preference of a politician who was advancing towards absolute power for dealing with a despot rather than with a republic. At Florence, anyway, Nicodemo's part in bringing about the reversal which saved his master was second only to Cosimo's. Few resident ambassadors have ever enjoyed as close a relationship with a ruler as Nicodemo's with Cosimo. In persuading the Florentines that a revived duchy of Milan under Sforza would be less dangerous than the expansion of Venice, Nicodemo and Cosimo worked hand in hand. The decision meant abandonment of an alliance which had been the corner-stone of Florentine policy for a generation. It meant the beginning of a new and doubtful war; for Venice had hoped to add Milan itself to her conquests and was furious at Sforza for forestalling her. It also meant that Cosimo intended to use Florence as the makeweight of an Italian balance, and was thus adopting by implication Filippo Maria's policy of saving the status quo.

The war that followed, the war of the Milanese succession (1452-54), again saw the peninsula divided between two fairly equal leagues, their operations this time co-ordinated by a great extension of the system of diplomatic residents.[5] As soon as Cosimo had persuaded his fellow citizens to ally themselves with Sforza, Dietisalvi Neroni, who had gone to Milan with an embassy to congratulate the new duke on his succession, was instructed to remain there as fully-accredited resident.[6] About the same time Nicodemo da Pontremoli's ambiguous status was regularized. These two provided the permanent liaison between the chief partners of an alliance to which Genoa, Bologna and Mantua soon adhered. Before the end of 1452 Florence had a resident orator in Genoa and another in Bologna, while Sforza had established embassies in both cities and in Mantua as well. Genoa and Mantua, at least, seem to have reciprocated. Meanwhile the former allies of Milan under the Visconti, Naples and Siena, joined the Venetians. Venice promptly sent a resident ambassador to King Alfonso at Naples and another to Siena. She already had residents at the courts of Montferrat and Savoy, and she continued to maintain permanent diplomatic representation with all four major allies throughout the war. Siena sent her first resident to Venice in 1451 and another to Naples three years later. The King of Naples was less forward. Even as late as 1454 he had no resident ambassador except at Rome, not even one in Venice.[7]

Among the more important peninsular powers, only the papacy, Ferrara and Lucca managed to stay neutral during this war, and the chief of these neutrals, Pope Nicholas V, deliberately set himself to provide a diplomatic link between the two warring leagues. The Jubilee of 1450 had seen more embassies of ceremony than ever before in the history of Rome. As the crisis over the Milanese succession deepened, a good many of the Italian embassies left at least one of their members to enjoy the unrivalled advantages of the Holy City as a diplomatic listening post. Almost as soon as war broke out the pope began, through these diplomats, and through the Venetian and Milanese residents, efforts at mediation. These efforts, in turn, drew new embassies to Rome, and before long most of the chief Italian powers had accredited resident orators to the papal court. Thus, by 1454, each warring league was linked by exchanges of residents among its adherents, and the major members of both leagues had residents at the court of the principal neutral. It needed only a general peace to complete the pattern.

Peace delayed until 1454. Everyone, except perhaps Alfonso of Aragon, was really tired of the war, but the two alliances involved so many long-standing claims and ancient vendettas, so many conflicts of interest or prestige, that the peace congress summoned by Nicholas V got hopelessly snarled. Perhaps without external pressures Nicholas's project might have proved as abortive as Filippo Maria's had been a decade earlier.

This time, however, such pressures were not lacking. Two threats hung over Italy more persuasive than papal eloquence. The French had joined the Sforza-Medici alliance, and the horde of rapacious, battle-hardened French veterans who brought the savage methods of the Hundred Years War to Lombardy frightened their allies almost as much as they did the Venetians. It began to seem to everyone advisable to keep the French out of Italy. The pope was alarmed by an even more serious threat. Constantinople had fallen. The Turk was pressing towards the Adriatic. All Christendom was in danger. Everyone expected the next blow to fall on Venice or on Naples.

Even so, it took all the tact of a tactful mediator to achieve as much as a separate peace between Venice and Milan. But from this separate peace, the Peace of Lodi, quickly grew the first general pacification of Italy, the Most Holy League. It was entered into, with the full concurrence of Pope Nicholas V, by the three chief northern belligerents, Florence, Venice and Milan, for the purpose of stabilizing the status quo and guaranteeing existing Italian powers against aggression from within or without the peninsula.

The solemn treaty was signed at Venice, August 30th, 1454.[8] It concluded a defensive alliance for twenty-five years, with provisions for subsequent renewals. The signatories promised to defend each other's territories in Italy (neither Milan nor Florence cared to undertake the defence of the Venetian overseas empire) against any and all aggressors, and for this purpose agreed on a schedule of military forces which they were severally to maintain, and a programme for joint military action in case of emergency. Each signatory reserved the right of its allies to be included.

So far the Treaty of Venice seems no different from a good many previous Italian treaties. But the remaining provisions show that its negotiators had wider views. All three signatories agreed to try to persuade the pope and the king of Naples to adhere to the league. A specific invitation was extended to each of the Italian neutrals to adhere also, and a general clause declared the alliance open to all states within the boundaries of Italy. The signatories renounced the right to make any treaty prejudicial to the league, or not sanctioned by its members, In case of war or the threat of war, all members were to consult immediately, and all subsequent negotiations were to be jointly conducted. Any member who attacked another was immediately to be expelled and disciplined by common military action. The grand object was to guarantee permanent peace within the closed Italian system.

The first response of the Italian powers aroused the rosiest hopes of the humanists. The pope, who had been sympathetic from the beginning, announced his adherence at the first dignified moment. The other powers of Italy, allies and neutrals, were so quick to join that the signature of Naples, somewhat sullenly affixed the following January, was the last. In theory, the organization of Italian political space was complete, and the status quo was permanently guaranteed.

For the development of the system of resident ambassadors, the Most Holy League was crucial. So far, resident diplomatic agents had been exchanged between allies to help co-ordinate action against a common enemy. The end of the alliance had meant the end of the embassies. Except for the embassies at Rome, most of which in 1454 were only a few years old, and one which Sforza had just established at Ferrara, there were no resident embassies with neutrals. By 1454, the peninsula-wide pattern of alliances had led to a great extension of the system among the two coalitions, but after the general acceptance of the Most Holy League it would have been perfectly possible for rulers to hold that alliance with everybody was equivalent to alliance with nobody, and to call their ambassadors home. Instead, perhaps partly because there was some vague notion of a general war against the Turks, the opposite view was adopted, and the exchange of residents was extended. Extremely rare in 1440, resident ambassadors were commonplace throughout Italy by 1460.

One plain implication in the basic treaty may have fostered this development. It called for immediate consultation among the signatories on any threat of war, but provided no machinery for such consultation. Whether or not the drafters, several of whom had been residents themselves, actually expected that a system of resident ambassadors would be utilized, the experience of the previous decade had proved how much an exchange of residents did, in fact, facilitate consultation in emergencies. And, although the league was never employed against the foreign enemy it chiefly contemplated, the Turk, many people thought it might be. In such an emergency, particularly if the attack was launched suddenly with the connivance of some disgruntled member of the league, a network of resident ambassadors might prove invaluable in spreading the alarm and co-ordinating counter-measures.

There may, of course, have been other reasons for expanding the new system. Italian statesmen had learned in a period of shifting alliance that one use of a resident ambassador with an ally was to gather information about the strength and intentions of a potential enemy. They had learned also that any enemy, if one knew when and how to bid, might become a partner. Although they had all ratified the solemn declarations of the League of Venice, the statesmen of the four powers had each sound reasons for supposing that the other three had not really renounced all thought of future aggrandizement, since each knew his own state had not.

Nor can the petty tyrants and smaller republics have felt entirely secure in the promises of their larger neighbours. Renaissance Italians had not had our experience of five centuries of power-politics, but they already had a very limited confidence in international agreements. Most of them believed that if the lamb had to lie down with the lion, or even if one wolf lay down with another, a wise animal kept one eye open. The decades preceding the Peace of Lodi had proved the value of a system of resident diplomatic agents in the struggle for survival and for power. It was characteristic of the age that the conclusion of a universal league for the maintenance of peace and the mutual defence of the status quo was made the occasion, not for abandoning the new weapon, but for improving it. Automatically, the new states provided first for their own safety and advantage. By nature, they could not do otherwise. The state, by the law of its being, could think only of itself.

CHAPTER IX

THE CONCERT OF ITALY (1455-1494)

THE State could think only of itself. The natural egotism of a political organization with no higher end than its own self-perpetuation and aggrandizement may come nearer to explaining the diplomacy of the 'concert of Italy' than all the more complex explanations subsequently elaborated.

What needs to be explained is that although the situation in 1454 called for a policy of unity, all that was achieved during the next forty years was a policy of tension. Internal and external realities demanded some sort of Italian confederation. The geography of the peninsula and the sense of the cultural unity among its ruling class provided the necessary strategic and psychological base. The Most Holy League concluded at Venice explicitly recognized the need and outlined the answer. But neither within nor without the peninsula did the league perform its expected function. Instead of the stable equilibrium of confederation, Italy arrived only at an unstable balance of power, a precarious counterpoising of the conflicting interests of jealous, sovereign states.

The first crisis after 1454 set the pattern. Alfonso of Aragon and Naples, called the Magnanimous more on account of his generosity to men of letters than for any quality of his statesmanship, had sullenly refused to let the peace of 1454 settle one of his Italian quarrels. He was at odds with Genoa over Corsica, and he attached to his adherence to the Most Holy League the unilateral reservation that the Genoese be excluded.

Thereafter, relations between Aragon and Genoa steadily worsened. The stubborn Genoese, although they alone were left at war with the common Italian enemy, the Turk, would not abandon Corsica. Throughout 1455 there was a situation which was not quite war but was certainly not peace. In the Corsican coastal towns there was sporadic fighting, the naval forces of both powers intervening. Catalan galleys (were they the galleys of the king?) raided the Ligurian coast. Genoese corsairs (were they actually in the service of the republic?) seized and plundered

Catalan and Neapolitan shipping. When twelve months of fumbling and insincere negotiations broke down, Alfonso flung at Genoa the fleet which, with the aid of special church taxes, he had been fitting out at Naples for the crusade against the Turks. In his campaign against the only Christian champion on the seas he even swept along a squadron of the pope's own galleys entrusted to his command.

Against the Neapolitan attack the Genoese appealed to the league. A special place in the treaty had been reserved for Genoa. It had adhered promptly, and by the plain terms of the league and the common law of Christendom it was entitled to protection. By the pens of their humanists the Genoese appealed to Italian public opinion, and through their resident ambassadors to the pledges and interests of the powers. They found sympathy, but no useful support. The Venetian senate declared against having anything to do with the Genoese question. Cosimo de'Medici made mild remonstrances, but did not wish to offend Naples. Francesco Sforza of Milan tried to reason with Alfonso, and even sent a paltry two hundred infantry to reinforce the Genoese, but he was generally supposed to be more concerned with snatching the lordship of Genoa for himself than with meeting his treaty obligations. Only the pope sounded as if he might be in earnest, and his chief censure fell on Alfonso's cynical use of a papal squadron in his unchristian war. None of the major powers was prepared to risk the wrath of a strong neighbour for the sake of a weak one. Finally the Genoese grew weary of bearing the burden alone and gave their city into the protection of the king of France, so that the net result was to bring back French intervention, and to keep the south in a turmoil for the next six years.[1]

All this, it should be noted, was in 1456-58, while Mahomet II was still in the spring tide of his victories, when the signing of the Most Holy League was fresh in men's minds, when the See of St. Peter's was occupied by a pope who was deeply sincere about the war against the Turks, and when those two veteran statesmen, Francesco Sforza and Cosimo de'Medici, Genoa's recent allies, were ruling her two most powerful neighbours. The inefficacy of all this to prevent a flagrant breach of the peace makes it almost unnecessary to inquire how the league worked thereafter.

In the next thirty years, in fact, Italy saw five more wars among

Italian powers, lasting on the average two years apiece, while for more than twenty years the Turkish menace did not lessen. Relentlessly the Genoese and the Venetians were pushed out of their holdings in the Levant. Twice the Turkish armies raided deep into Friuli, and, when Venice was forced to conclude a disastrous peace, a Turkish squadron seized and garrisoned Otranto in the kingdom of Naples, and maintained for thirteen months a thriving market for Christian slaves on Italian soil.

Never in all this time was there an effective anti-Turkish coalition. All the pathetic eloquence, literary skill and diplomatic finesse of Pope Pius II could not muster for the crusade, which in desperation he undertook to lead in person, a force one-half as formidable as had been manœuvring in a domestic quarrel in Calabria the summer before. Even the Genoese and the Venetian fleets, fighting in the same waters against the same enemy, failed to co-operate. For each republic, satisfaction at a set-back to a rival balanced, or over-balanced, alarm at the progress of the common foe.

As for the other states, they were too busy watching each other and jockeying for position to have time for the Turks. In the preambles to public documents and in formal ambassadorial orations the objective was always the peace of Italy and the security of Christendom. The enemy was always the Infidel. But in the ambassador's confidential instructions the objective was much more likely to be profits of some salt pans, or the tolls of a hill town, and the enemy was always a good deal nearer home.

The enemy most frequently envisaged, the power whose ambition, so her neighbours thought, had most often to be checked, was Venice. In territory and resources the most powerful of the Italian states, Venice, on the whole, did come off best in the manœuvres of the period, adding in Italy a town here, a strip of territory there to balance, at least partially, losses in the Levant. But although some historians since have called the Venetians the main menace to the Italian balance-of-power, it would be hard to convict them of being, in fact, the chief disturbers of the peace. They did not actually begin any of the six wars between the Peace of Lodi and the French invasion, and in four of the six they must be held guiltless of having instigated or seriously abetted the original aggressor.

93

Of these six wars, two, Alfonso's unmagnanimous attack on Genoa and the War of Ferrara, were frankly wars of aggression. The other four, on the surface at least, were civil wars in which the Italian states were led to intervene. Actually, each of the six wars had its roots in the unstable, illegitimate nature of political power in Italy, the same trouble which filled the intervals between them with recurrent crises. And in each war, as also in the many crises which almost led to war, the conflicting ambitions of the greater Italian states were a major factor.

In all this Venice was not guiltless. She connived at a mercenary general's blow at Florence in support of an exile faction. She accepted Pope Sixtus IV's invitation to attack Ferrara. And in other crises the Venetians proved themselves skilled fishers in waters which sometimes they themselves had helped to trouble. But in forty years the Venetians caused less disturbance in Italy than Pope Sixtus IV, by his vengeful irritability and obstinate determination to make princes of his worthless nephews, did in eight. In general, though they were stronger and more successful, the Venetians were neither greedier nor more unscrupulous than their competitors.

Nevertheless, a judgment on the diplomatic history of this period does properly hinge on an analysis of Venetian policy. For in Venice alone among the Italian states political power was legitimate and stable. The Venetian republic harnessed its aristocracy to civic duties, serving no family's dynastic interest or individual's mania for fame or power. Venetian institutions were the organic growth of centuries, and aroused in her citizens something of the same pride and reverence and instinctive loyalty felt in later times by Englishmen for theirs. Venice alone among the states of Italy was without dangerous internal factions, and could rely on the allegiance of her subject cities and on the gentry of her *terra firma*.

Of the four other major powers, the papal states were a crazy patchwork of feudal lordships and petty tyrannies, ruled, nominally, by elderly elective sovereigns who, even when they did not devote their brief reigns to the aggrandizement of their families, could count on little genuine loyalty and pursue few connected policies. The other three were all illegitimate despotisms, that in Florence thinly masked; those in Milan and Naples naked and brutal. In them, as in the minor states, political power was achieved by violence, cunning and good luck, and retained by the same means. To this basic insecurity of political life historians have sometimes attributed certain characteristics of Italian Renaissance diplomacy, instability, cynical disregard of obligations, greedy opportunism and ruthless grasping after petty gains.

Now Venice did not share this basic insecurity. Yet its policies, if steadier than those of its rivals, had no higher or more generous aims, and stooped to the same means. Above the welfare of Italy or Christendom, above any considerations of religion or morality, the rulers of Venice preferred — could not do other than prefer — the self-preservation and aggrandizement of their own republic. Venice is thus the limiting case which defines the necessary character of the diplomacy of the age.

Since the resident ambassadors were tools of this kind of diplomacy, servants of the sacred egoism of their respective states, the only kind of unity which they could foster was a unity in wary hostility, a unity of continuous tension. The very presence of this permanent corps emphasized the continuous pursuit by the governments they served of selfish and conflicting objectives. Their covert pressures in pursuit of these objectives, their mutual watchfulness, and the constant possibility which their existence afforded of sudden changes of alliance, unheralded by the goings and comings of special envoys, tended to keep the strain from relaxing. The sensitivity with which they registered and transmitted every change in the political atmosphere, every hint of impending crisis, heightened the awareness of tension.

Yet the efficiency of the residents in detecting each shift in the relationships of power, in alerting their governments and in facilitating realignments which restored the balance, did help preserve the precarious equilibrium. Sometimes, as in the Milanese crisis of 1476, the attitude of the major powers was so promptly registered by their ambassadors that fishers in troubled waters were deterred, and war was averted. Sometimes, as in the war of the Pazzi conspiracy, although an attack was actually launched by a coalition counting on victory and profiting by surprise, the energetic reactions of the residents quickly set up a counter coalition which restored the even balance of the struggle. Sometimes, as in the War of Ferrara, the vigilance of diplomats

95

enabled the threatened powers to organize adequate counter-measures before the attack. In general, though the network of residents helped to spread each war throughout Italy, it helped each time to limit the intensity of the conflict and to prepare the way for a negotiated peace.

So for forty years, by virtue of the mutual jealousies of its balanced states, by a politics of continuous tension, and by the help of its new diplomatic machinery, Italy did enjoy a kind of uneasy peace. Although scarcely a year was without some sort of crisis or potentially dangerous intrigue, although, at times, the whole system seemed on the brink of disaster, disaster was each time averted. Wars were less destructive than they had been, absorbed less of men's energies, and consumed less of the social income. No major towns were sacked; no desperately bloody fields were fought. And for three years, almost, out of four there was no fighting anywhere in Italy worth a historian's serious attention.

Those forty years saw the amazing flowering of the Italian, particularly the Florentine genius. It seems likely that without that mild, genial springtime some of the finest fruits of the Italian Renaissance would never have ripened at all. And it may be that had the separate city states been unable to preserve their independence, had Florence been conquered by Milan, for instance, or both been swallowed by Venice or by Naples, some of those fruits might not have ripened either. All we can say with certainty is that the preservation of the balance of power within the peninsula did create one part of the actual environment of the Italian Renaissance. If the politics of tension came, finally, at a grievous price, tension was not without its immediate rewards.[2]

The success of the Italian system depended, of course, on its isolation. The peninsular balance of power was too delicate not to be upset by any major foreign intervention. And yet, one of the consequences of a policy of tension was that foreign influence could never really be excluded. As long as the Italian powers watched each other from potentially hostile camps, it was a practical certainty that some of them would look for outside support.

Milan led the way. From being the strongest and most aggressive of the Italian powers, the duchy, under Francesco Sforza, had become the weakest and least stable. Sforza saw the French house of Anjou established in Genoa and preparing to attack his ally, Naples. The French house of Orleans had a claim to Milan itself. And the half-French house of Savoy, on his western frontier, was allied with his recent enemies, the Venetians, now uncomfortably close to the walls of Milan. It hardly needed the advice of Cosimo de'Medici to persuade Sforza to turn to France.

As long as he lived he cultivated a French alliance, beginning with an intrigue with the Dauphin, conducted through a confidential agent, and continuing with a series of fully accredited resident ambassadors after the Dauphin became Louis XI of France. For some years after Francesco's death his son continued the connection, so that there was a Milanese resident ambassador to France from 1463 to 1475, the first embassy of the kind at the French court from any Italian state, and during most of the 1460s, the only resident embassy established beyond the Alps.[3]

In the main, the objectives of the Milanese alliance with France were prudent and sensible: the undercutting of Angevin pretensions in Naples and the checking of Orleanist ambitions, French acquiescence in the independence of Genoa, and French discouragement of a Savoyard rapprochement with Venice. In return Louis XI got money and mercenaries and a welcome flow of political information. Since Louis was glad to bridle the houses of Anjou and Orleans, and too busy at home to have time for Italian adventures, the Milanese were not obliged to make more dangerous concessions. But had Louis been less occupied or less prudent, Milanese assurance to him that he could, when he liked, 'give laws to Italy' might have been less than wise.

The next Milanese diplomatic adventure certainly was so. Francesco Sforza's rash son, Galeazzo Maria, shifted his alliance from France to Burgundy, partly because he had not the patience to endure French snubs, partly because he feared that the Venetians would succeed in persuading Louis' rival, Charles the Bold, the great duke of Burgundy, to tip the Italian balance in their favour.

Venetian relations with Louis XI had been as bad as those of Milan had been good. In 1463 Venice apparently intended to establish a resident embassy to France, but their ambassador had been harshly ordered to go home and had not been replaced. A second attempt in 1470 met with equal rudeness.[4] Meanwhile

Venetian commercial relations with Bruges were so close that although Venice would have been glad enough to be on good terms with France, it could not afford to be at odds with the powerful duke of Burgundy, count of Flanders, and so lord of Bruges. In 1470, therefore, the senate accredited a resident ambassador to the court of Burgundy who was honourably received and was soon reputed to enjoy great influence.[5]

By 1473-74 it looked as though Venice had picked the winner. King Ferrante of Naples imitated the Venetian example and sent first a solemn special embassy and then a resident to Burgundy. And in February 1475, Galeazzo Maria, who was almost as suspicious of Naples as he was of Venice, and was at once frightened and dazzled by Charles the Bold's growing reputation, unwisely followed suit. The Milanese ambassador in France was recalled without replacement, and simultaneously a resident was accredited to Burgundy. Outside Italy residents were still sent, according to the older custom, only to actual or desired allies.

That Milan had blundered became apparent almost at once. The Milanese ambassadors were just in time to report Charles the Bold's disastrous campaigns in Switzerland and the preparations of his allies to desert him. Too late Galeazzo Maria attempted to reverse his play. He made inept overtures to France, but Louis XI, though he had no immediate intention of punishing Milan's defection, had no further use for its support, and refused to permit the new Milanese ambassador to remain as resident.[6] The assassination of Galeazzo Maria and the death of Charles the Bold before Nancy left Milanese diplomacy in chaos.

The power whose extra-Italian diplomacy ultimately profited was Venice. The Venetians had been shrewd enough to discontinue their resident embassy at the Burgundian court in 1475. In 1477, while Louis was still smarting from the Milanese desertion, the Venetians sent him a special embassy which negotiated so skilfully that it was able to return with a treaty clearing up most of the disputes which had embroiled Venetian relations with France for twenty years. There were no significant political clauses in the treaty, but there seems to have been an understanding that a Venetian resident would be acceptable, since in the summer of 1478 one was dispatched to the French court.[7] When he came home in 1480, his successor was immediately appointed, and thereafter whenever there was a break between the departure of one resident and the arrival of the next the ambassador's place was supplied by the secretary of the legation, so that the embassy was in fact continuous. During the 1480s it was the only really permanent embassy outside Italy. The commercial and political advantages to Venice were considerable.[8]

Whatever counterpoise there was to Venetian influence in France was supplied by Florence, mainly by the personal diplomacy of Lorenzo the Magnificent. Frequently during the unofficial principate of Lorenzo, special embassies journeyed to France to assert the unswerving loyalty of the city of the lilies to the royal fleur-de-lis, but Florence maintained no resident in France, and Lorenzo's real diplomacy did not depend upon sentiment, nor act, as a rule, through official ambassadors. Throughout the 1480s Lorenzo's chief agents, the most trusted sources of his political information and the confidential transmitters of his actual views and pressures, were not diplomats but merchant bankers, representatives in France of the Medici bank. The fragments of their correspondence which have been published suggest that, in spite of his great reputation as a diplomat, the magnificent Lorenzo was given, in statecraft as in banking, to assuming rash commitments. It may have been fortunate for his fame that he did not live to see his bills come due.[9]

Looking backwards from the dark days of the invasions, however, Italians saw the age of Lorenzo the Magnificent bathed in a golden sunlight of serenity and moderation. In fact, its wars had been neither bloodless nor lacking in wanton destruction. But compared with the horrors which foreign armies had since brought to Italy the old wars seemed like harmless and amiable tournaments. In fact, its diplomacy had been neither prudent, nor far-sighted, nor well-advised. It had always failed to face the larger issues, and had often tempted grave dangers for the sake of petty gains. But, for a while, it had worked. So when, after 1494, each fresh effort of Italian diplomacy ended only in a fresh disaster, men sighed for the wisdom and dexterity of their fathers. In retrospect the precarious Italian balance-of-power seemed a miraculous device, which, in the right hands, might have prolonged the golden age who knows how long. In judging the statesmen of that age, men forgot the rash gestures, the chilling anxiety, the desperate contortions, and remembered only that the equilibrists had stayed on their tight-ropes.

Actually, in the forty years after the Peace of Lodi, Italy owed its freedom from foreign invasion less to statesmanship than to sheer good luck. More than once the politics of tension precipitated a crisis which invited foreign intervention. But no power was ready to intervene. The invasion of Italy waited, not for a change in Italian leadership, but for the great powers of Europe to complete their internal tasks. Once they had done so, no such wisdom as Lorenzo the Magnificent and his contemporaries had ever displayed could have postponed catastrophe for long. On the contrary, once France and Spain were ready to face each other in the Italian arena, they were sure to find Italian diplomats proclaiming that the lists were open. The selfish policies pursued for forty years made it certain that it would be so.

CHAPTER X

THE MACHINERY OF
RENAISSANCE DIPLOMACY

In the last half of the fifteenth century medieval diplomatic
institutions were successfully adapted to the uses of the new
Renaissance state. In that period Italian diplomats built the
traditions and acquired the professional dexterity which later
aroused the admiration and imitation of the rest of Europe. By
the 1450s all of the major states of the peninsula had set up
organized chanceries which required written reports from their
agents and kept copious records. Each of these chanceries was the
centre of a network of permanent embassies which provided a
constant flow of information and channels of official intercourse
with important neighbours.

Until the records of this diplomacy have been calendared, or at
least adequately catalogued, it will be impossible to write about
its machinery without many reservations. We cannot, for instance,
determine any series of the resident ambassadors sent or received
by any given power. There is no reliable list even of the Venetian
or Florentine residents, or of the Italian ambassadors in Rome
between 1450 and 1500, although such lists could certainly be
established by the same sort of co-operative effort which has
produced similar lists for all Europe after 1648.[1] Until this is
done, it would be idle to attempt to trace the representatives sent
to and by the minor powers, interesting as this might be. But the
general pattern of diplomatic representation can be recon-
structed, just from published materials, in more detail than would
be useful here.

In the first place, all four of the greater secular states had
established permanent embassies with each other. Naples, the
laggard, had a resident in Venice by 1457, and one in Milan
before December 1458. Thereafter only open war interrupted
this reciprocal representation among the four. For the minor
powers the pattern was highly variegated. Each major power
usually maintained agents with minor states in its immediate
sphere or strategically useful to it. Each often received resident

envoys from them in return. In many instances, however, these exchanges were interrupted by one side or by both, and frequently they were not reciprocal. Venice might have a resident at the court of Savoy, although there was no Savoyard ambassador at Venice, or receive one from Rimini without returning the compliment. At some times, Siena had a resident at Milan, at others not. And, in general, although the pattern among the major powers did not vary, that for the secondary states changed often.

During all this period the right to send or to receive ambassadors, special or resident, was still vague. It remained about equally vague throughout Europe until the middle of the seventeenth century. The choice by any state of those to which it sent residents was dictated, just as in Europe much later, by policy, or convenience, or particular custom. The sending or receiving of resident envoys was not taken to be a mark of respect or a prerogative of sovereignty.

The network of resident embassies did not, of course, replace older means of diplomatic intercourse. In addition to the general credentials with which residents were armed, special powers were necessary for the negotiation of even minor agreements and, partly because distances in Italy were not great, such powers were usually entrusted to special envoys more fully informed about the current views of their government. Even announcements and compliments of more than routine importance were often conveyed particularly. Important negotiations or ceremonies always called for full-scale special embassies with several ambassadors and, whenever a congregation of notables gave opportunity for competitive display, large and glittering retinues.

Now and then princes were their own ambassadors, and for these occasions there were no set rules. They might be conducted with the greatest pomp or with the greatest informality. Personal interviews between the heads of states have always had obvious advantages. When they turned out well, as for instance, Lorenzo de'Medici's interview with Ferrante of Naples in 1480, they gave the outcome a look of special solidity and the successful prince an increment of that prestige so important to a Renaissance tyrant. But such interviews were risky, and politicians began to see that one of their chief risks — the fanfare of attendant publicity which advertised failure as surely as success — extended also to solemn special embassies. Unobtrusive special envoys or the still less conspicuous residents were safer.

All these officers, resident as well as special, had, of course, full diplomatic status. Both classes were spoken of in the vulgar tongue as ambassadors. Both were received with the formalities due to their rank and that of their sender. Both were entitled to lodging and entertainment at the expense of their hosts. Both were accorded the privileges and immunities which custom prescribed.

So far, the new style of diplomacy had not affected the classification of agents. It had, however, begun to add new subordinate officers to the accepted categories. Among these, the commonest was the resident's secretary. Medieval embassies composed of several ambassadors frequently included a secretary either separately accredited or mentioned in joint credentials. It was his duty to assist his more distinguished colleagues with the drafting of papers, the examination of documents, the taking of attested copies, and, perhaps, with general legal advice and the fruits of professional experience. In France, especially, it became customary to assist the great nobles and high ecclesiastics to whom solemn missions were entrusted with a secretary, who was, as a rule, a legist and a royal counsellor. French secretaries were separately appointed and accredited, and ranked with, though after, their colleagues as full fledged ambassadors. In virtue of their abilities, training, and connection with the court they were often, in fact, the leading spirits of their embassies. No other country accorded the secretary quite so prominent a place. In Italy, where rank was not so often separated from talent and education, the advancement of a subordinate officer to ambassadorial standing aroused amused comment.[2] But Italian special missions with more than one full ambassador often included an accredited secretary appointed and paid by the state and directly responsible to it. The same practice was known in the Iberian kingdoms and in England.

When an ambassador went alone on a special mission, however, he customarily took with him only his own servants. This personal entourage shared, of course, the ambassador's immunities and privileges in so far as their services were necessary to the embassy, but they had no separate status, and no direct responsibility to their government. If the ambassador took a personal secretary with him, that was his affair. Since resident ambassadors were sent singly, their secretaries also, at first, were just their personal servants.

By the 1460s, however, the Venetians were providing secretaries for certain of their resident ambassadors, and at about the same time the Florentines began to apply to their more important permanent legations the rules about secretaries already laid down for major special embassies. Thereafter, the secretaries of Florentine and Venetian resident embassies were separately appointed by the state and separately paid. They were expected to report directly to their signories, and were separately accredited so that in the absence or incapacity of the ambassador they could continue to carry on his duties. The Venetians even adopted the sensible device of leaving the secretary at his post for a time after his chief was replaced so that the new ambassador could profit by the secretary's experience.[3] No other Italian state developed the secretary's office as highly, but before the end of the century separately appointed and accredited secretaries were the rule in the chief resident embassies of all four major powers.

Except for secretaries, fifteenth-century Italian governments added no separately appointed officers to the staffs of their residents. As had been and continued to be the case for special envoys, the terms of a resident's appointment laid down the number of men and horses he was expected to take with him. (The usual stipulation was ten or twelve men with six or eight horses.) These included, as a rule, the ambassador's equerry and body servants, his cook and grooms and lackeys, and perhaps two or three young men of somewhat higher social station who could act as gentlemen ushers, messengers, and couriers. The ambassador was free to increase this entourage if he had the means, though not to diminish it below the stipulated minimum. All these persons were the ambassador's personal appointees, paid out of his stipend or his private purse, directly responsible to him alone, and without status except as members of his suite.

The increased work and responsibility which fell upon the residents did introduce, however, one or two further modifications. It was natural that government couriers sent to the resident with information and instructions should return with his latest dispatches. Chanceries anxious for a constant flow of news increased this service until, to judge from random samples, most of the residents' dispatches must have been carried by government couriers, separately provided with what we should now call diplomatic passports.

In addition, as the importance of resident embassies increased, so did the number of young men of good family who wanted to go abroad with the resident. When such young men were strongly enough recommended by important members of the government, the recommendation was tantamount to appointment, and though these gentlemen aides did not correspond officially with their governments, they did communicate with influential friends. In Florence, in 1498, these posts were made official and salaried. Their holders were elected by the Signory and responsible to it, and were accredited and regulated just as if they were senior diplomats. Apparently the decree of 1498 was not fully carried out, but its framers seem to have been conscious that the work of the resident embassies required a division of labour and that supplying junior aides for this purpose gave an opportunity for educating future diplomats. It may not be entirely fanciful to see in this Florentine experiment the first step towards modern diplomatic attachés.[4]

In the new system one major power was exceptional. Whether they felt that the reciprocal exchange of residents was beneath the unique dignity of their office, or simply because the pope could hardly lack, in Italy, for agents, for informants or for means of communication, the Roman pontiffs received resident ambassadors but sent none:[5] Nevertheless, although its importance in this respect was recent, Rome was, after the Peace of Lodi, the nerve-centre of the Italian diplomatic system. Before the end of the pontificate of Nicholas V, Venice, Naples, Florence, Milan, Savoy, Genoa, Siena, Mantua, Lucca and Ferrara all had resident orators at the papal court. That is the full list of the major and secondary powers, and a greater concourse of important residents than could have been found in any other Italian capital. Several of the petty princelings of Romagna and the Marches usually also had agents at Rome, striving for recognition as ambassadors.

Under Nicholas V (1447-55) and Calixtus (1455-58) a number of diplomats had simply remained at Rome in indefinite prolongation of the formal embassy of obedience, customary upon the elevation of a new pope. Their status was, in consequence, ambiguous. Pius II, forgetting (or perhaps remembering) the arts whereby he himself had risen, felt that there were far too many ambassadors, and shortly after his accession threatened to degrade to the rank of proctor all envoys who remained in Rome more than six months. Innocent VIII repeated this threat, but neither pope carried it out, and nothing discouraged the increasing concourse of residents at Rome. Before long Pius II, himself, found how useful this corps of diplomats could be for spreading important announcements, or initiating new lines of negotiation.[6] Anyway, he lacked the one means that might have been effective in cutting down their numbers. It had ceased to be customary for ambassadors to be entertained at the pope's cost. Princes who sent residents to Rome expected to have to pay their expenses.

From the 1460s on, then, Rome became what it was long to remain, the chief training school and jousting field of diplomacy, the listening post of Italy, the centre, above all others, of high political intrigue. Here were felt the first tremors of every Italian upheaval; here a whispered word in the corridors might be of more consequence than the clash of arms in Calabria or Piedmont. To Rome, therefore, the Italian states sent their most accomplished diplomats, their most promising juniors, and their handsomest and best supplied legations.

That these ambassadors were, for the most part, laymen in a city of priests may have contributed something to their growing *esprit de corps*. The papal practice of addressing them collectively, of assigning them places together at all important ceremonies, and of issuing, from time to time, regulations for their common governance, probably contributed more. At any rate, it is at Rome, and during the Renaissance only at Rome, that we find the first signs of something like an organized diplomatic corps, developing a rudimentary sense of professional solidarity, exchanging social courtesies, codifying their mutual relationships, and even, in certain emergencies, acting together as a body.[7] The example of such a body was certainly influential in the development along common lines of Italian diplomatic institutions. Meanwhile, although during most of this time there were no formally accredited resident ambassadors of the transalpine powers in Rome, many non-Italians were constantly visiting there, among them many diplomats on special missions and embassies of ceremony, so that one may assume that Rome was also the chief centre for the diffusion of Italian practice to the rest of Europe.

Most of the procedures, documents and usages of Italian Renaissance diplomacy needed, of course, no special agency of diffusion. They were a part of the common stock of medieval Christendom. In the very decades when the new diplomatic system was spreading from one end of the peninsula to the other, Martino Garrati da Lodi and Giovanni Bertachino could compile their collection of maxims about diplomatic law without mentioning any innovation or setting down a phrase which would not be as immediately intelligible on one side of the Alps as on the other. In the rules of ambassadorial behaviour, in the theory of diplomatic principals and the gradations of diplomatic agents, in the kinds of documents with which ambassadors were provided and in the privileges and safeguards which they could expect to enjoy, the Italian development made for a long time no perceptible difference.

Powers and credentials remained substantially the same, so did ceremonies and procedures. All the routine of the ambassador's departure, journey, reception, solemn entry, formal oration, subsequent negotiations, leave-taking and return, familiar to Machiavelli and Guicciardini after 1500, were already known to the Frenchman, Bernard du Rosier, as normal throughout Europe in the 1430s.

The significant differences which an observant foreigner in Rome might have noted would have been mostly refinements of known procedures due to more business-like Italian methods, or the development of the new techniques, directly connected with the one major invention, the resident embassies. Among these Italian innovations, any intelligent northern diplomat would have found a number well worth imitating. He would have been less likely to realize that these organized foreign offices with their auxiliary networks of permanent diplomatic agents and all the efficient devices they had invented were the concrete institutional expression of a profound change in the relations of political power, and of an accompanying reorientation in the minds and hearts of men.

CHAPTER XI

THE DUTIES OF A RESIDENT AMBASSADOR

THE changed attitude of late fifteenth-century Italians towards the duties of an ambassador, and the reorientation of
fundamental convictions and loyalties involved in that
change, emerge clearly from the first literary treatment of the new
diplomatic machinery. Its author, Ermolao Barbaro[1] was by
taste and training a scholar, a humanist. He had lectured on
Aristotle at Padua and exchanged epigrams and epistles with
leading lights of his literary set. He was also a scion of one of
those Venetian families expected to serve the state. His father had
held several diplomatic posts, among them that of Venetian
resident ambassador both at Naples and at Rome, and Ermolao
followed his father's footsteps. He served on a special embassy to
the emperor, and as Venetian resident in Milan. Then, in 1490,
while still a relatively young man, he was promoted to Rome, the
key post in Venetian diplomacy. He came as near as the custom
of the age allowed to being a career diplomat of a diplomatic
family.

While resident ambassador at Rome, Ermolao spent his
leisure in polishing, in the best Ciceronian tradition, a little essay
intended as advice to a friend entering the Venetian diplomatic
service.[2] He called it, chastely, 'De officio legati', since the office
of which he was writing had no other name in Latin respectable
enough to appeal to a fastidious humanist. But the duties he was
concerned with were those he was himself performing at the
moment, the duties of a resident. Clearly he thought them the
most important any diplomat could perform. He refused to adopt
any of the modern terms for the office, but he made his point quite
plain at the outset. 'Since declarations of war, and treaties of
peace and alliance are but affairs of a few days,' he says, 'I will
speak of those ambassadors who are sent with simple, general
credentials, to win or preserve the friendship of princes.'[3] All his
advice is directed to this new kind of ambassador. Although Italy
still saw many special embassies, and both he and his father had

served on some of them, all his illustrations are drawn from their experience as residents. Ermolao Barbaro is the first writer about diplomacy who even mentions resident ambassadors. He was the only one for a long time to recognize the prominence they had won.

Barbaro's essay has another significant distinction. It is the first writing about diplomacy to pass over in silence all the customary medieval phrases about an ambassador's office. He does not say 'An ambassador is a public official'. He does not say 'An ambassador labours for the common welfare'. He does not say 'The business of an ambassador is peace'. Instead he says quite simply: 'The first duty of an ambassador is exactly the same as that of any other servant of a government, that is, to do, say, advise and think whatever may best serve the preservation and aggrandizement of his own state.'[4] This is the voice of the new age.

For its preservation and aggrandizement, the state looked to its diplomats for two things, allies and information. When Ermolao said that he would speak of that class of ambassadors sent 'to win or to maintain the friendship of a prince', he was identifying residents by the customary opening phrase of their formal credentials. That phrase was a legacy from the earliest stages of the new diplomacy when residents were exchanged only between allies. In some such form as 'to conserve and extend the ancient friendship between our two republics', 'because of the loyalty and affection with which my father and I have always regarded the city of Florence', 'in order that your grace may be a partaker of all our thoughts as a friend and brother should', it remained in use even when the users were habitual enemies on the verge of an open breach. But at times resident ambassadors really were expected to help keep a restless ally in line, calm an unjust suspicion, or smooth over a threatened misunderstanding. When peace with a particular power best served the interests of his state, peace was still the business of an ambassador.

Beyond whatever personal charm and tact he could command, the resident of Barbaro's time had few means of influence. He could word the communications of his government as smoothly as their contents permitted. He could explain its actions as far as his instructions and wits would stretch. He could entertain prominent persons if his own purse were long enough. As a rule, he could not buy friends more directly. In Italy, though Venice was perhaps the most jealous, all the major states looked askance at one of their citizens taking a pension or gratuity, and the corruption of a really important officer of state was a tricky operation. It was not likely to be entrusted to a resident, who usually had no more funds than he needed for the normal petty bribery of gate-keepers and clerks. Those ambassadors who, like Ermolao Barbaro, had enough reputation to win friends by literary puffs, were fortunate. When it came to gaining the confidence of princes Barbaro had no better advice than some platitudes about virtue and integrity, and the judicious injunction not to pester the great unduly. Friendship among rulers followed the lines of high policy, and high policy was assumed to be beyond the power of a resident ambassador to alter.

If he helped to shape it, it was generally less by his conduct than by his observations, by the information he sent home. In the formative period of permanent diplomacy it was, apparently, as political intelligence officers that the residents demonstrated their usefulness most decisively. At any rate no clause is more certain to appear in their instructions than the injunction to report frequently and minutely everything of possible political importance. This injunction every ambassador who tried to be worth his salt took with the greatest literalness.

Nicodemo da Pontremoli reported frequently, shrewdly and, one would think, altogether adequately, but he was a casual and scrappy correspondent compared to some residents of the next generation. A really industrious ambassador wrote daily. One Venetian ambassador at Rome piled up a total of 472 dispatches in twelve months,[5] and if some of these are hasty notes of only three or four lines, others are detailed (as nearly as possible ver-batim) accounts of long conversations, or patient, laborious analyses of complicated political imbroglios, or bulging budgets of miscellaneous gossip; so that one wonders how he ever got time to do anything else than listen and write. This particular corre-spondence happens to be better preserved than most, but it was probably not far above the average in size for the Venetian service, and is certainly not a record. The Milanese and the Florentines were as copious as the Venetians.

Inevitably, a great deal of worthless stuff got into these long daily screeds. Endless accounts of pointless official conversations, elaborate bouts of verbal fencing in which neither side intended to say anything but each hoped to extract something from the inanities of the others. Long, circumstantial stories, built on hearsay and conjecture about intrigues which came to nothing, or existed only in the imagination of some informant. A miscellany of petty gossip, the backbiting and bickerings of official life, the public ceremonies and private scandals of the great and near-great. And often a journal of the ambassador's own activities, with a plaintive obligato about the absence or ambiguity of instructions, the delinquencies of couriers, assistants and colleagues, and (a recurrent theme) the ambassador's pecuniary embarrassment.

Sorting out all this must have been almost as much of a task for a fifteenth-century councillor as it is for the present-day historian. One is tempted to believe that, since they encouraged this loquacity, Renaissance politicians must have had not only an obsessive anxiety about the doings of their contemporaries, not only an almost pathological fear of being surprised, or anticipated or overreached, but also an insatiable appetite for mere gossip. But there was political wisdom in encouraging a constant, even if indiscriminate, flow of news. By making the mesh fine, fewer items were likely to escape because the man on the spot missed a significance clear enough to a minister who had the run of dispatches from all over Italy. And the advantages of a constant news service, the first really fresh, and fairly reliable news service which any European rulers had ever enjoyed, were worth the labour of sorting and evaluation.

By 1500, the rules for ambassadors' dispatches were much alike in all the major Italian chanceries. Whatever their literary quality they had to satisfy certain formal requirements. Immediately after the salutation, the ambassador was expected to note, first, official correspondence recently received, usually including pieces acknowledged in his last dispatch, and second, the date of that last dispatch, which was represented either by a summary or by an enclosed copy. Then followed the body of the letter, supported by transcripts of relevant documents. Then, before the formal close, came the place and date of the dispatch, often with the exact hour of sending so that the speed of the courier could be noted. At the very bottom of the sheet the ambassador signed. Later, this form was adopted throughout Europe.

Besides their regular dispatches, residents sometimes composed two other kinds of informative papers, reports and relations. Both became more frequent towards the end of the century. The report was a carefully prepared statement of the political situation at the ambassador's post, filling in the background, with special attention to the character and motives of the important persons and factions, summarizing recent developments, indicating future expectations, and sometimes suggesting possible lines of action. From residents such periodical reports provided the same sort of general survey of the progress of the mission and the observations and conclusions of the ambassador as governments were accustomed to receive from special ambassadors on their return.

In the Florentine service, where reports were most in use, the customary interval between them was about two months. Both for residents and special envoys, the Florentines regarded the report as the critical test of a diplomat's powers as an observer and analyst, and valued good ones as important aids to political decisions, expecting reports, because of their more considered drafting, wider scope, and analytical approach, to be both more reliable and easier to interpret than a series of hasty daily dispatches.[6] Before 1500, periodical reports began to be fairly common in Italian practice, either because governments requested them, or because ambassadors saw the advantage of supplementing their dispatches by these more careful and elaborate papers.

Originally a 'relation' was simply the final report customary from any ambassador on the completion of his mission. It was normally (in an earlier period, invariably) orally delivered, and, though its chief purpose was simply to describe the conduct and result of the mission, probably it often undertook to satisfy whatever curiosity its hearers could be assumed to feel about the court and the country whence the ambassador had returned. At Venice such relations to the Doge and Senate are said to have been required from the thirteenth century on. Similar ones were expected elsewhere throughout Europe. The less writing an embassy did during its progress, the more essential its final report was. In most countries, throughout the fourteenth and fifteenth centuries, final reports were everywhere presented, sometimes before a very select group, sometimes to a considerable assemblage. In the latter case wise princes followed the practice of Louis XI and first arranged privately what the ambassador's public relation would include.

The firm grasp which the Senate kept on the conduct of foreign affairs, and the consequent necessity for ambassadors to report formally and fully to a large body of their fellow-citizens was probably responsible for the special development of the Venetian relations. The curiosity of these Venetian merchant oligarchs must have been especially alert and various, so that ambassadors were encouraged to include a wider than usual range of topics, a sketch of the geography, past history, economy, government and customs of the country they had visited as well as of its current politics. The inclusion of such subjects made the relation of a resident even more interesting than that of a special embassy, and this, plus the fact that most senators never read the regular dispatches, must have led the Venetian government to continue to require public relations from their returning residents and to throw increasing emphasis on the ceremony at a time when the residents of other powers were being relieved of this responsibility. For the senators a formal relation was an intellectual treat, for the diplomat a challenge.

Some time in the fifteenth century the Senate began to reward any particularly able performance by ordering it to be written down and preserved in the archives for the benefit of succeeding ambassadors. Later, what had begun as a special distinction became an invariable rule. Hence arose that unique series of fascinating documents, the Venetian *relazione*, for manuscript copies of which contemporaries bid, even two or three years after their delivery, as high as fifteen gold pieces per hundred sheets, and without which all our histories of Europe in the sixteenth and seventeenth centuries would be the poorer.[7]

Outside the Venetian service the formal relation remained a much more restricted report, less and less often committed to writing, and of diminishing importance. Now and then, however, by way of emulation, diplomats of other powers were moved to try their hands at something like the Venetian model.

The collecting, processing and packaging of information were the resident ambassador's main task. He could rely on his secretary for the necessary copies and, as a rule, for the final drafting, either from dictation or from his own rough draft, of the actual dispatches. He could hope that the young gentlemen of his suite and perhaps his lesser servants might pick up scraps of gossip to supplement the news he gathered himself. Sometimes he was fortunate enough to receive valuable items of information from his fellow-countrymen resident abroad. But for the most part he had to rely on his own wits and industry to collect intelligence, and his own judgment to evaluate it.

Ermolao Barbaro particularly warns against stuffing out dispatches with rumours, inventions and prophecies, and concludes characteristically that an ambassador who tries to increase his importance by writing lies will only be ruining himself, since the truth will soon be known to the Senate anyway. The Senate wants facts. As to how to get them, Ermolao's best advice is to listen. The ambassador, he says, should not behave like a spy. (In Italy, Venice kept its rudimentary espionage distinct from its diplomatic service.) Nor should he appear to pry into what does not officially concern him. His father, he remembers, found it useful to interrupt with irrelevant remarks anyone committing a really interesting indiscretion, because the less you seem to want to hear, the more anxious people are to tell you. [8]

Ermolao has nothing to say about two other techniques of collection. Some residents bought information; some traded for it. But the first course had the same objection in the Renaissance as at later periods. One rarely got as much as one paid for. For the second, Venetian (and to a considerable extent Florentine) ambassadors were less well placed than the Milanese. Milanese, both resident and special ambassadors, were kept liberally supplied with general political news, culled from the reports of their fellows throughout Italy, apparently with the expectation that they could (as they often did) exchange these items for items they wanted. The republics usually gave their ambassadors less information, and were more suspicious of this kind of informal collaboration with the diplomats and officials of other powers. Even for the Milanese, however, the chief means of collecting intelligence must have been, as it has remained for diplomats ever since, just listening. Talleyrand was not the first to note that the art of diplomacy would become impossible if more people knew how to hold their tongues.

One is often impressed in reading Ermolao Barbaro with the timeless quality of what he says about the practice of the diplomat's profession. Much of it had already been said half a century before by Bernard du Rosier (whom Barbaro had not read) and would be said again in a decade by Machiavelli and in a century by De Vera (neither of whom read Barbaro), and later still by Wiquefort and Callières and other literary diplomats right down to the present. The intonation varies with the individual and his environment, but the essential substance remains unchanged. No matter with what air of discovery or paradox it is paraded, or with what personal experiences illustrated, it boils down to the same scanty residue of what seem like the tritest platitudes. So do the simple and difficult rules of any enduring human art.

Conspiracy, assassination, corruption, and chicane are not among the methods recommended by Ermolao Barbaro, or by any other Renaissance writer giving serious advice to diplomats. Nor, contrary to popular belief, were they among the ordinary tools of fifteenth-century Italian diplomacy. Such methods then, as since, were sometimes, though not often, successfully employed by governments to score a temporary success. But, as in any age, whatever their political result, they almost always ruined the reputation and therefore the future usefulness of the agent who used them. Intelligent men shrank from them as foolish and dangerous, even when they were willing to condone their immorality. There were some startling exceptions (exceptions may be found, also, in other periods), but in general the Renaissance diplomat understood that his job was to win and hold the confidence and respect of the people among whom he worked, since otherwise he could neither be believed himself, nor obtain the information which he sought. To the best of their ability, and as far as their instructions permitted, most fifteenth-century Italian diplomats tried to act accordingly.

On the whole, they were the kind of men from whom honourable and intelligent behaviour might be expected. They were not a restricted professional class, devoted to diplomatic careers, but a loosely defined group of public servants and prominent citizens among whom the honours and burdens of foreign service were distributed by a kind of rotation. Except for a sprinkling of magnates, usually employed only on the most important special embassies, they were mostly from what one might call the upper middle class, solid respectable burghers or petty gentry or junior scions of great families. They were rarely active merchants, soldiers more rarely still. Commonly they were men of substance well past their first youth, anxious only to acquit themselves well in the eyes of their prince or their fellow-citizens for the tour of duty expected of them, and so get home again to a known and comfortable routine.

Probably Ermolao Barbaro was somewhat above the average, both in birth and in education, but the average seems to have been high. Doctors of law were common among them; humanists and men of letters not rare. A good many came from illustrious families; a good many subsequently held high office, princely counsellors in Naples or Milan, state councillors in Florence or Venice. Among so many, there must have been some liars and profligates, some knaves and fools, but it would be as rash to take these as typical of their group as it would be to take the characters in *Mandragola* as typical of Florentine burgher society. Saintliness and genius were as rare among them as they are likely to be among any body of public office-holders, but, turning over the pages of their dispatches, one does not feel that they were inferior in character or intellect or sense of responsibility to their transalpine contemporaries or to the average run of working diplomats at subsequent periods.

This is worth saying with some emphasis, if only because the embittered pamphlet of a solitary man of genius has too often been allowed to describe the social and political atmosphere of half a century. Machiavelli's savage satire *The Prince* has been widely accepted as an objective picture of a society which had lost any sense of the moral foundation of political action. From such a position, it is a short step to believing that the cynicism and treachery which *The Prince* appears to recommend as a recipe for political success were actually characteristic of Machiavelli's contemporaries, and thence, another short step to the judgment that the failure of Italian diplomacy in the age of Machiavelli may be ascribed to the levity and amorality of its practitioners.

But what was occurring in Italy in the age of Machiavelli was not simply a break-down of moral standards. It was a profound transvaluation of current values, including the rise of the new political morality which Machiavelli preached. The way had been prepared for this new morality, for a long time, ever since the quarrel between popes and emperors had made a place in Christendom for the first purely temporal states, but the change came slowly. Only a generation before Machiavelli's birth, when Filippo Maria Visconti told an angry pope that, as for himself, he valued his soul more than his body, but his state more than either, the answer could still seem either a monstrous flippancy or a moral monstrosity. By the 1490s, by the time Machiavelli was beginning his political career, men of high moral seriousness, Machiavelli among them, could take Filippo Maria's response as a principle of political conduct. None adopted it more explicitly than Ermolao Barbaro. 'The first duty of the ambassador is the same as that of any government servant: to do, say, advise, and think whatever may best serve the preservation and aggrandizement of his own state.'

On this maxim, Ermolao repeats, the ambassador must meditate until he is wholly converted to its truth. As a Venetian, he must uphold the interests and policies of Venice against the world. Abroad, he must never speak slightingly of any of his countrymen or of any of their customs. He must bear himself in the eyes of the world as if the reputation of his country depended on his own. Above all, he must execute the orders and carry out the policies of his government, scrupulously and to the uttermost, no matter what they may be, no matter how completely they may contradict his political convictions or his personal sentiments. The ambassador can have no private views. He exists to serve the state.

Did Ermolao Barbaro, one wonders, a travelled aristocrat, a cultivated humanist, a freeman of the timeless and cosmopolitan commonwealth of letters, really feel this blind, exclusive patriotism? Or did he only find it prudent for a Venetian citizen and the servant of a jealous and watchful Senate to say that he felt it? It scarcely matters. The new omnicompetent, egotistic states were beginning to demand the external signs, at least, of this kind of total allegiance, and in making the expected gestures men were coming to feel the appropriate emotions.

The religion of patriotism has been found not without moral grandeur. Certainly no diplomat who practised it as Barbaro recommended could be said to lack integrity. And perhaps had the Italian states been larger, or had they had no larger neighbours, their diplomacy would not seem to us so fickle or so futile. But the diplomats, by the conditions of their service, could think only each of his own state, and the state, by the law of its being, could think only of itself. So, when the time of trial came, the skill and experience of the Italians, their desperate manœuvres and wavering jealous combinations proved as vain as once the selfish local patriotisms of the Greek city states had been against the might of Macedon and Rome. In Western Christendom the Italians had invented the first truly temporal states. They were to be the first to learn that all temporal power is only temporary power.

PART THREE

SIXTEENTH-CENTURY DIPLOMACY

CHAPTER XII

THE EUROPEAN POWERS

THE French invasion of 1494 ended the closed period of Italian Renaissance diplomacy with dramatic abruptness. Thereafter in the European arena and increasingly all over the world the major states struggled for power as in the previous two centuries the Italian states had done. In its earliest stages the greater struggle spread the new Italian diplomatic machinery throughout Europe as the age of modern diplomacy began. At the same time, the Italian power-system was wrecked for ever. By invoking foreign intervention, and invoking it successfully, Italian diplomacy destroyed in a decade its fifteenth-century achievement.[1]

Or so it seemed to later Italians, who blamed the statesmen of the 1490s, and particularly the usurping tyrant of Milan, Ludovico il Moro, for the catastrophe. But Ludovico's invitation to the king of France was only the occasion of the European wars. The cause lay deeper. Invitations to intervene in the peninsula had been issued before. They had been declined or, if accepted, had been without serious consequences, because the great powers were not ready. By 1494 they were nearing readiness and before long, invited or not, the pressure of the European power-system would inevitably have shattered its fragile Italian precursor.

Beyond the Alps the same forces had been at work which had produced the continuous pressures of the Italian sytsem. Their work was slowed by the greater distances to be overcome, by the more stubborn political habits of the people, and by the feebler pulse of commerce; and the result was deflected and skewed by a solider and more complex social organization. In the sixteenth century, the state-building forces were reinforced and distorted by new economic developments and by the recrudescence in new and violent forms of old religious issues. But the pattern which finally emerged was recognizable. What Italy had become in the years between the Peace of Lodi and the invasion of Charles VIl, all Europe was on the way to becoming.

In the fifteenth century, European states experienced a change of phase, like the crystallization of a liquid, like the changing of a gear. The fact is clear even if the values of all the contributing causes remain elusive. The tap-roots of the modern state may be followed as far back as one likes in Western history. One root runs back, indeed, to the cities of antiquity whereof the hazy images continued to provide some statesmen in every medieval century with an ideal model of authority and order. From the twelfth century onward each effort to realize, under the inspiration of that model, a civil polity on the scale of a Roman province seemed to have a better chance of succeeding than the last. In some parts of Europe, at least, each such effort actually added to the state some increment of unity and power. Yet each effort fell back defeated by the size and complexity of the problem, and states paid for each over-exertion by relapsing for a time into weakness and quiescence.

One thinks, for instance, of the strength of the French monarchy about 1300, and of its feebleness fifty years later. For that collapse many reasons have been offered — economic depression, the Hundred Years War, the Black Death. But one reason, certainly, was that royal power had over-extended itself. France was too big and too amorphous to be governed, given the resources of the age, from a single centre. In the outer provinces the king had to delegate authority. Unless the delegate had the means to be strong on the spot, he was futile. If he was strong, he made himself all but independent of the king and tended to turn his office into an hereditary fief. The experiment of using peers of the blood royal as governors and relying on family ties to hold the realm together worked worst of all. In England and Spain as well as in France the apanage system brought a return of feudal anarchy and a new blight of civil war.

Perhaps, on analysis, the earlier fifteenth century did show a real increase in the importance of the central government, since the aim of the great feudatories was now, not to be independent of the crown, but to control it. The more obvious fact, however, was that in the middle decades the chief monarchies of Christendom seemed to touch nadir. Under Charles VII and Henry VI, the sister crowns of France and England fell lower than they had been for centuries. It would be hard to name a king of Castile more powerless than that Henry whom his subjects nicknamed, for other reasons, 'the Impotent', and the contemporary kings of

Portugal and Aragon, though far abler, were almost as unfortunate. No German emperor ever seemed more futile than Frederick III, while in the Scandinavian north royal power sank steadily. A detached observer, scanning Europe in the 1460s, might excusably have concluded that the greater feudal monarchies were played out, and that the only political hope lay in such islands of relative peace and security as the Italian and German city states.

Yet the tide was turning, had, in fact, already turned. Nor was this merely another swing of the medieval pendulum. Just when order and centralized authority seemed everywhere routed there was a sudden rally. In certain areas this rally carried the central authority to decisive victory, and created the new monarchies with which the new European age began.

The cliché is that the bourgeoisie rallied round the kings to put an end to feudal anarchy. That can be said, usually with some accuracy, wherever kings proved strong at any time from 1100 on, but it cannot be the whole truth. The rally to authority was more marked in backward Castile than in prosperous, progressive southern Germany. It was at least as decisive in agrarian England as in the industrial Netherlands. But it does seem to be true that the second half of the fifteenth century saw a revival of economic activity after a long period of depression, and that this recovery made easier the task of the kings and prospered by their success.

Some of the factors in this recovery can be distinguished. New techniques in ship-building and navigation cut carrying costs and swelled the volume of European trade. Decade after decade Portuguese caravels pushed further along the edge of the dark continent and came back with slaves and gold dust and ivory for Lisbon, with ostrich plumes and guinea pepper and parakeets for the markets of Flanders, and with sugar, lately a rare drug, for the tables of the rich. And not only the Portuguese were learning to master the ocean. The new ships, bigger, handier, more seaworthy, were noted and admired at Hamburg and Lubeck, at Dieppe and La Rochelle, in the Basque ports and in the North Sea harbours, putting out from Bristol, anchoring in London river. Europe was already beginning to realize the profits of overseas expansion a long generation before a Genoese adventurer sailed from Palos, or Da Gama found his pilot at Melinde.

Meanwhile new techniques in mining increased the available currency, and new techniques in industry offered new commodities and enlarged the supply of old ones at a lower cost in human labour. As the mine shafts in Saxony and the Tyrol drove deeper to unworked veins of silver and copper, the pack trains of woollens winding across the Cotswolds grew longer, and the fairs at Leipzig and Geneva, Lyons and Medina del Campo flourished. Though the ancient towns, tied in the rigid straight-jackets of their guilds, complained of depopulation and decay, their suburbs and the open country buzzed with industry. From mid-century onward, spreading from the Rhine valley faster than any previous invention had spread, a new kind of machine, exploited by a new kind of capitalist, began to pour out the first standardized, mass-produced commodity, the printed book. Before long, the cheapness with which printing could multiply the written word would give the kings a new way to speak to all their people. At the same time, wherever water power could drive the hammers and lathes, wherever craftsmen could be assembled and iron or tin and copper be had, clamorous foundries were turning out the first efficient artillery, through which the kings spoke with a louder voice.

New techniques of transportation, of production, and of finance all contributed to the European recovery. The dying out of the Hussite wars in Germany, the Peace of Lodi and, at roughly the same time, the end of the long horror of the English wars in France, must have helped too. Was the rise in population, the first we can be sure of in the hundred years since the Black Death, a result or a cause? Probably both. And to the extent that despair and exhaustion led to a surrender of ancient liberties, and that the strengthened monarchies, by keeping internal peace, aided economic revival, despair and exhaustion may be said to have contributed also.

By the 1480s, four major territorial states had profited by the general forces of recovery and the special accidents of history. They faced each other in the European arena much as Milan, Florence, Venice and Naples had faced each other in Italy a half century before. Two of them were old enemies; France and England, hardened by their long duel, and each recently triumphant over internal dissension. Two were new power-aggregates:

Castile-Aragon and Burgundy-Austria, each the result of dynastic union.

The formation of those two new power-aggregates (we can scarcely speak of them as states) illustrates a characteristic growth-pattern of the European monarchies. In Italy, the city states had devoured their neighbours by the simpler forms of aggression. But the legalistic habits and traditional loyalties of five centuries of feudalism were so deeply ingrained in society beyond the Alps that mere conquests were hard to make and harder to keep, and even the greediest kings were eager to discover legal grounds for expansion. In the main, therefore, ruling dynasties laid province to province as the more successful landlords among their subjects laid field to field, by purchase and exchange and foreclosure, but chiefly by marriage and inheritance. Force was employed not to advance a rational interest but to support a legal claim. Wars over the titles to fiefs and kingdoms paralleled the battles which landlords waged against each other in the law courts. In consequence, the leading thread in the diplomacy of all this period was dynastic interest, and the leading power which emerged from it was one whose sprawling shape was determined not by geography, or national culture, or historic development, but by the irrelevant accidents of birth and marriage and death.

The primary nucleus of that future power was in lands we now call Austria, a cluster of Alpine lordships in south-eastern Germany which had fallen by one means or another to the Habsburg family. All lay within that decaying German kingdom which went by the pretentious name of the Holy Roman Empire, and several Habsburgs had already been elected to the imperial dignity before it was bestowed in 1440 on Frederick III. Nobody would have guessed then, or in the next thirty years, that from his time on only Habsburgs would be chosen emperors, and that Frederick's great-grandson would bestride Europe as no emperor had done since Charlemagne. Everything that depended on the gifts of a ruler — war, politics, diplomacy — went against Frederick. But death and marriage worked for him. The collateral branches of his house were extinguished, so that once more all the Habsburg lands came under a single head; his son married the heiress of the great duke of Burgundy.

The rise of Burgundy was itself perhaps the most spectacular instance of the success of dynastic politics. A younger son of the king of France, given by his father the Duchy of Burgundy, married the heiress of Flanders and Artois, the richest commercial and industrial region north of the Alps, and in three generations this cadet branch of the Valois had built themselves a territorial power which enabled them to patronize the emperor, defy and outshine the king of France, and generally appear the greatest uncrowned potentates in Christendom. The fourth duke of the Valois line, Charles the Bold, went too fast, and stirred up against himself not only the jealousy of France but all those stubborn resistances which aggressions too grossly illegal were then likely to arouse. At his death his own chief acquisitions were lost, and some of his inheritance, but his daughter Mary was still able to bring her husband estates nearly equal in area to present-day Belgium and the Netherlands. Equal, then, in relative wealth and power, to a good deal more.

As it should have passed to the son whom Mary of Burgundy bore to Maximilian of Austria, the Habsburg inheritance has a suggestive pattern. There were two main blocks of territory on opposite sides of Germany. The Austrian block stretched from the Bohemian quadrilateral to the south Slav lands and the eastern Alps. It guarded Germany against the Turks and controlled the trade routes which follow the Danube, and those which run southward into Italy. It was mostly mountainous, forest land, but rich in mines, and not without fertile valleys and tough, steady peasant infantry. The Burgundian blocks stretched along the North Sea, from the East Frisian islands to the English Channel, its land frontiers nowhere clearly marked except perhaps by the Ardennes. It faced south and west, stood guard against the French, controlled the greatest entrepôt of trade in northern Europe, and opened for Germany the roads of the ocean. It had the most highly productive industry (metals and textiles of all kinds), the most advanced agriculture, the most varied and thriving commerce, the greatest concentration of wealth north of the Alps. If its infantry were no longer as formidable as once they had been, its heavy cavalry were the only troops of their kind in Europe who were counted a match for the French. Between these two blocks lay smaller patches and bits of territory. Franche Comté covering the Belfort gap from the south-east, Breisgau on the Black Forest side of the upper Rhine, scattered holdings in Alsace and Swabia, a tenuous and broken chain. But their pattern suggested that it would be possible to link them up.

Even the mercurial Maximilian of Austria might have achieved something towards the linkage, and his descendants should have achieved the rest, particularly since Maximilian succeeded in handing on to them the imperial sceptre. For the Holy Roman Empire, though it was by no means as efficient a monarchy as France or England, was still, in 1500, a good deal more than just the ghost of the Roman Empire, crowned and sitting on its own grave. It was the only available political expression of the unity of the German plain, the source to which Germans looked for peace and order, as Frenchmen and Englishmen looked to their kings. Its central authority had been hamstrung by its constitution, but it still contained sentiments and institutions which might have helped the two masses of Austria and Burgundy to draw the empire into a unified whole.

Maximilian, however, had no steadiness of purpose. His son Philip predeceased him. And before Philip's son, Charles of Ghent, had succeeded there had been added to his Habsburg inheritance another, completely alien and distracting. Whatever might have been done towards linking up the segments of the Habsburg lands (as later the Hohenzollerns linked up the segments of their inheritance to make a greater Prussia), was lost sight of under the pressure of more urgent and, as it proved, irreconcilable demands. The chance which the blind accidents of birth and death had given, they took away too soon.

If the dynastic union of Burgundy and Austria sketched the framework of a state never to be realized, the union of Castile and Aragon blocked out one so familiar that it now seems inevitable. The marriage of Ferdinand and Isabella brought together the two main parts of what we have always seen on the map as Spain. Before Ferdinand's death, the conquest of Granada and of Spanish Navarre had given Spain its modern outline. But in 1469, when the doubtful heir to Castile married the barely established heir of Aragon, the future was not so clear. The rivers of Castile flow towards the Atlantic, those of Aragon towards the Mediterranean, and the watershed between them is perhaps the toughest natural barrier in the peninsula. For more than two centuries the two kingdoms had stood back to back, their path diverging. If one had had to choose, in 1469, two kingdoms destined to unite in a greater Spain, one would have said, going by all the tests of geopolitics, culture, and historic tradition, not Castile-Aragon, but Castile-Portugal. It could have been so until the arms and diplomacy of Ferdinand and Isabella decided otherwise. And even afterwards Spain continued to be tugged different ways by divergent drives. Castile wanted to go southward against the Moors, and then, still driven, like the Portuguese, by the unexpended energy of the crusades, westward into the Atlantic. In the same year that Granada fell, a new world opened to Castile beyond the ocean. But Aragon wanted to go eastward, across the Mediterranean to Italy, and so into the vortex of European politics. Before Columbus had returned from his second voyage, Gonsalvo de Cordova was already fighting the French in Calabria, and Aragon had dragged its greater partner into the first of those commitments which were to increase, at last, so disastrously.

Dynastic politics had contributed nothing to the establishment of the third power in the game of European diplomacy, unless the extinction of an old dynasty with traditional friends and enemies abroad may be taken as a contribution. England's only territorial unification in the fifteenth century had been in reverse. At the end of the Hundred Years War, England had lost not only the conquests of Henry V, but the whole Plantagenet inheritance in France, except the single fortress of Calais. In the following civil wars, not only every Plantagenet perished, but most of the greater nobility were wiped out as well. The first king of the new dynasty, Henry Tudor, seized power almost in the fashion of an Italian tyrant. But he consolidated his position by the consent of parliament, and by a marriage which gave his offpsring a reasonably legitimate claim to the succession. At home Henry VII was isolated by the depletion of the peerage; abroad, by the lack of foreign entanglements. He was the better able, therefore, to give England what it most needed, internal and external peace.

That the Tudors must be counted among the chief builders of the new monarchies, that, though they did their work with a difference, they made England a 'modern' state, for most purposes as efficiently centralized and flexible as any of its continental rivals, there is no question. But that their England ought to be counted among the major European powers of the day has often been doubted. It has been fashionable among English historians to say that England, at almost any period from 1485 to 1588, was 'a little country', 'scarcely more than a third-rate power', 'about on a level with Portugal and Denmark'. This is one form of Anglo-Saxon understatement.

It is true that in wealth and population England counted fourth among the Western powers, though it counted ahead of all but its three big rivals by a respectable margin. It is true that the prestige of the Plantagenet kings had derived largely from lost continental possessions and from the might of English bowmen who, in an age of gunpowder, no longer struck terror in their enemies. But there were offsets to the losses. England had always been a fortress with a wide moat, but it was ceasing to be the nook-shotten isle of Albion, thrust off in an odd corner of the world, and becoming a strategic base of great offensive potential, lying athwart one of the main sea roads of civilized traffic, a road every year more crowded with sails. At the same time, by the loss of its French dependencies, England had gained freedom of diplomatic manœuvre. Secure behind its seas, England could now take as much or as little of any war as it liked. No commitment was more than tentative, no alliance irrevocable, and at each new shuffle in the diplomatic game the other players had to bid all over again for England's friendship or neutrality.

England, Spain and Burgundy-Austria swung as it were in a kind of orbit around the first and greatest European power, France. Ever since Christendom began, the king of France had been, after the emperor, Europe's chief monarch. His kingdom, with its rivers that flowed, some to the Atlantic, some to the Channel and North Sea, some to the Mediterranean, its easy communications, its many towns, its smiling wealth of corn and vines, had always been the chief European kingdom. Now France was recovering from its most terrible ordeal. The colossus was gathering new strength.

In dynastic politics France enjoyed one great constitutional advantage. Its crown was strictly hereditary in the male line, and the apanages, the fiefs granted out to junior branches of the royal family, passed in the same way. The principle not only insured France against the accession through marriage of a foreign dynasty, it provided a double remedy for the dangerous practice of alienating provinces to provide for scions of the royal house. On the extinction of any cadet line, its apanaged fiefs reverted to the crown, and on the accession to the throne of any collateral heir, the lands of his branch returned with him. So in the reign of Louis XI, Guienne, ducal Burgundy, Provence, Anjou and Maine fell in, providing the main acquisitions of a king who, however much his statecraft was admired by his contemporaries, was successful chiefly by surviving his relatives. Later Louis XII brought back the great Orleans inheritance and kept the recent addition of Brittany, the last great independent fief, by marrying its heiress, the widow of his predecessor. At about that time the Venetian ambassador, speaking of the recent increase in strength of the French monarchy, put first among its causes the reconcentration of so many major fiefs in the hands of the king, so that while formerly there had always been some powerful vassal capable of letting in a foreign enemy or leading a feudal revolt, now there was no noble in France great enough to defy the crown.

In the game of power politics France had another constitutional advantage. For any considerable funds beyond ordinary expenses the kings of England had to go to Parliament, and the rulers of Castile-Aragon and Burgundy-Austria were even more hampered. In Castile, special subsidies had to be voted by a *cortes* not yet completely subservient to the crown, and the peninsular realms of Aragon, Catalonia and Valencia all had representative assemblies, sturdily independent and not generous. As for the provincial estates with which Maximilian had to dicker in the days when he was king of the Romans, regent of the Burgundian Netherlands, archduke of Austria and hereditary prince of the other Habsburg lands, their number almost defies counting. Maximilian's ill-success in dealing with them was the chief cause of his notorious poverty. But the Hundred Years War had convinced the French of the necessity of maintaining a regular army, and a regular army requires regular taxes. The Estates-General of 1439 had probably no intention of granting away for ever their power of the purse, but the same act which authorized a royal army supported by the *taille* worked out to place not only the collection of the *taille* but the fixing of its amount for ever in the king's hand. 'The French king taxes his subjects at whatever rate he pleases', Italian am-

bassadors used to write. That was not exactly true. When it came
to collecting the money, royal expectations often had to be modified. Nevertheless the main fact, that the king of France assessed
taxes according to his needs without consulting the estates of the
realm, set him apart from other sovereigns, and gave him, particularly in the conduct of foreign affairs, a dangerously greater
freedom of action.

But the chief advantages of France were its size and its central
position. For Western Europe at the beginning of the modern
period, France was the heartland. England, Spain, Italy and the
German Empire lay arranged symmetrically about it, so that
France commanded interior lines. And the heartland was also
the most populous kingdom. This is an age before exact statistics.
Any estimate of population as early as 1500 must be based on the
roughest of guesses. But we shall not be much more than a million
or so out of the way, plus or minus, if we give the king of France
at about that date some fourteen million subjects. That would be
more than four times as many as the subjects of Henry VII of
England; more than twice the population of Spain. The largest
organized Italian state, Venice, can scarcely have ruled more than
a million and a half persons. The Holy Roman Empire was more
populous than France, but its mass was politically inert. For troops
and taxes the Habsburgs had to rely almost entirely on their hereditary lands. We shall not go far wrong if we reckon France as almost
equal, in population and resources, to the next three European
powers combined.

None of the other European states counted for much, though
most of them were destined, sooner or later, to be sucked into the
vortex of conflict. The best organized, Portugal, had a population
of no more than a million and a quarter, and already it faced
away from Europe. Its energies were absorbed by the endless
crusade in Morocco, by the African discoveries, and, later, by
the empire of the Indian Ocean. Scotland, poor, backward,
scantily populated, politically feeble, had no policy beyond a
tradition of friendship for France and an automatic hostility
towards the English. The Scandinavian kingdoms were only
beginning to find the strength to shake off the domination of the
Hanseatic League. Poland, Bohemia, Hungary were all too dis-
turbed by internal conflicts or eastern pressures to exert more

than a fitful influence towards the West. Of the smaller powers within the empire, only the Swiss operated as a continuous factor in power politics, and they only because of the prestige of their mercenary infantry. From the Balkans and Anatolia, the Ottomans menaced the whole south-eastern frontier of Christendom, but in the first decades of the new diplomacy Turkish strength was rather a pretext than a motive or a make-weight. The power that polarized the field of European politics, playing the rôle that Milan had played in Italy a century before, was France.

CHAPTER XIII

THE FRENCH INVASION OF ITALY

A<small>LTHOUGH</small> the rôle which France played in alarming her
neighbours into concerted action, and so inaugurating
modern European diplomacy, much resembled that of
Milan in Italy a hundred years before, the analogy will not bear
pushing too far. The regular revenues and powerful standing army
which the French crown found at its disposal tempted it into
foreign adventures; but once the English had been expelled and
the Burgundian threat parried, France was driven by no such
necessity to conquer or be crushed, eat or be eaten, as had once
driven Milan. In the 1490s France was in no more danger of
being conquered by her neighbours than she was capable of
conquering any of the larger of them. Probably for this very
reason, because European political space was less organized and
the pressures of European power politics less acute, the French
monarchy lacked some of the nerves and sinews which had made
the Visconti state formidable.

For one thing, France had developed nothing comparable to
the Milanese chancery and diplomatic service. In part, the failure
must be ascribed to the temperaments of rulers and to the less
flexible structure of French administration. But in large part it
was because the mere size of France dwarfed and obscured the
significance of activities abroad and diminished for its rulers the
importance of foreign relations. Even Louis XI was only a partial
exception. Louis had observed the growth of Italian diplomacy,
and there were aspects of the game which always fascinated him,
the substitution of guile for force, the matching of wits, the far-
flung, fine-spun intrigues. But Louis was too suspicious, too
devious, and too parochial to grasp all the uses of diplomacy. He
could conceive of no negotiations not inspired by malice and conducted by deception. He made no use of resident ambassadors
because he never gave his servants that much independent
responsibility. In the end, Louis established no diplomatic
machinery or traditions of any use to his successors. In the first

generation of European power politics, France remained as laggard in diplomacy as she was froward in war.

Nor in the decade in which by invading Italy she began the age of modern European diplomacy had France any coherent foreign policy, either. She went to war simply because it was always assumed that when Charles VIII came of age he would go to war. What else could a young, healthy king with money in his treasury and men-at-arms to follow him be expected to do? War was the business of kings.

The reputable theory of the time recognized two main motives for it, honour and profit. Statesmanship consisted in finding an acceptable combination of both. Honour dictated war to avenge an injury, according to the code of the duello, or to make good a legal claim. Profits were reaped in booty, ransoms and indemnities, and above all in taxable conquests. The commonest political arithmetic throughout the Renaissance consisted in balancing the cost of a campaign (so many thousand men for so many months at such and such a rate) against the value of a province in terms of its annual revenue. Optimists were usually able to demonstrate that the war the king wanted was a good investment.

Practical statesmen recognized another motive for war, seldom explicitly avowed. It was a means of avoiding internal dissension, usually the nearest and sometimes actually the cheapest means. Outside Italy, all Europe was saddled with a class in possession of most of the landed wealth, most of the local political power, and most of the permanent high offices of state, who had no business except war and few peacetime diversions as attractive as conspiracy. Before it attained its zenith, the territorial state had no way of ensuring the allegiance of this class so effective as giving them some foreign enemy to fight. Leading the nobility and gentry to foreign conquests eased domestic pressures. Inevitably, writers compared the expedient to a judicious blood-letting which reduced excessive humours in the body politic.

As Charles VIII grew up, the French court was more and more thronged with clever Italians eager to prove to him and his counsellors that the theatre where all these motives for war, avowed and tacit, could find their fullest scope was Italy. There were exiled Neapolitan barons who had once raised the Angevin standard, promising Charles the crown of Naples in return for the restoration of their estates, suitably enlarged. There were exiled Genoese, ready to bring the French back to Genoa. There were Milanese exiles who pointed out that the duke of Orleans had the best legal claim to Milan. There were enemies of the Medici and enemies of the Borgias, with cloudy schemes for reforming Italy and the papacy as the first step towards a crusade.

The dreamers and schemers and malcontents drawn by the magnet of French power from every corner of Italy were symptomatic of the Italian malaise, the unstable, illegitimate nature of power in most of the peninsula. They might not have been effective in bringing down the French so soon, had it not been for a more serious manifestation of that malaise. One of the five great Italian powers, the power which should have been the most eager and most able to keep them out, invited the French into Italy.

Ludovico Sforza had made himself regent of the duchy of Milan. When the nephew in whose name he ruled came of age, Ludovico refused to surrender power. His nephew had the support of Naples, and Ludovico sought what support he could find. The other Italian powers would combine neither to repress Ludovico's usurpation nor to guarantee it. They waited, meanwhile pursuing the customary tactics of tension, carrying on the war of nerves, each against all, which was their usual alternative to military action. Ludovico's nerve broke. Too insecure to play a waiting game, he sent his ambassadors to offer Charles VIII his alliance and aid for the reoccupation of Genoa and the conquest of Naples. No doubt he flattered himself that when the barbarians had done his work for him, he could send them home as easily as he had summoned them. But this time the genie, so often invoked with impunity, really escaped from the bottle.

Ever since the summer of 1494, when the first clumps of French lances trotted down into the Lombard plain, people have puzzled over why Charles VIII accepted Ludovico's invitation. Even to contemporary eyes the operation seemed risky. Charles was leading his army the length of Italy to conquer its southernmost kingdom, leaving in his rear, across his line of communications, a half-dozen unbeaten and potentially hostile states. His servant, Philippe de Commynes, wrote in his memoirs that King Charles had neither the money nor the brains needed for such an undertaking. The only explanation for the Neapolitan adventure that

Commynes could arrive at was that the king was young and silly and had bad counsellors.[1]

Commynes's explanation is more plausible than the recent one that Naples was the objective because of French interest in the south Italian grain trade and the growth of French commerce in the Levant. One doubts whether even the cleverest or the stupidest of the Italian exiles would have suggested such a motive to the most mercenary-minded of Charles's counsellors. It would be a long time before kings fought for the profits of merchants. Until the rise of a new Venice at Amsterdam, only the tradesmen's republics of Italy and the Baltic fought over matters of trade. Nor did kings normally fight for the advancement of 'vital national interests', as those interests were later understood. Nineteenth-century French historians were particularly disappointed that the Valois kings allowed themselves to be distracted by Italian adventures from the task of rounding out 'the natural frontiers of France'. Certainly if any of the Valois had ever heard of those frontiers they gave no sign. For seventy years they pursued instead the mirage of Italian conquests, and Commynes's off-hand explanation of Charles VIII's folly will scarcely stretch to cover the whole period.

Louis XII should have been wise, if wisdom is the fruit of adversity. At least he was experienced, and the sagacity of his counsellors was much admired by contemporaries. But the first act of his reign was to invade Italy, in support of his claim to the duchy of Milan. In a few years more he had been sucked into the Neapolitan quicksand. He ended with no more land in Italy than when he had begun and much less credit. Yet the first act of his successor, Francis I, was to cross the Alps again. Forty years after, Francis I's son was still trying, and another French army was marching south towards Naples (how many had been lost there?) in cheerful disregard of an enemy in its rear. Only financial ruin and the crumbling of the French monarchy into anarchy and civil war stopped the vain effort which provides the leading theme of European diplomacy from 1494 to 1559.

Perhaps the French efforts were as natural, after all, as the constant attempts of a poplar tree to root itself in a drain. The territorial state seeks power as a vegetable seeks water and, quite aside from the twist imparted to French growth by traditional dynastic claims, Italy with its wealthy cities, its developed economy, its relatively weak states, was the most obvious reservoir of power, waiting to be absorbed and utilized by a growing organism.

The first French push demonstrated the vulnerability of the Italian system, and exposed the sham of the Most Holy League. That league had been solemnly reaffirmed in 1470, and referred to in many subsequent treaties. It was presumably still in force. But none of its members stirred to oppose il Moro's formidable guests or to defend their ally, the king of Naples. The Venetians were cautiously neutral. The Medici government in Florence collapsed. The pope had the interests of the Borgia family to think of. And the French sauntered through Italy with chalk in their hands to mark up their lodgings.

Too late the alarmed statesmen of Italy realized what they had done. Ludovico Sforza, said one rueful wit, was the man who turned a lion loose in his house to catch a mouse. Nobody was louder in blaming him than the pope and the Venetians, the two who had recently played on his fears with the least excuse, and whose veiled threats and menacing reserve had had the largest share in scaring him into inviting French intervention. But now he had done so, the only remedy anybody could think of was to call in the Spaniards to drive out the French.

CHAPTER XIV

THE SPANISH INTERVENTION

SPAIN was ready for the task. Neither the mysterious promise of the newly found lands beyond the western ocean, nor the crusade near at hand in Africa was so attractive to Ferdinand of Aragon as the ripe wealth of Italy. The resources of Spain were no match for those of France. But the Granadan wars had trained a tough infantry and able commanders who might find ways of coping with the apparently irresistible masses of French heavy cavalry. And, unlike their French rivals, Ferdinand and Isabella had not neglected the other arm of the new state. Even before the beginning of the Italian wars Spain, under Ferdinand's leadership, had begun to develop an active diplomacy and an experienced body of diplomats.

In the team of the Catholic kings, Ferdinand represented the Aragonese tradition, and a reliance on diplomacy had been practically forced on Aragon. It was a small kingdom, yet in the high politics of medieval Christendom it had played a major rôle. In Provence and Languedoc its kings had once held wide domains. These they had lost, but in compensation they had conquered the Balearics, Sicily, Sardinia, Corsica and, finally, Naples, though this last Alfonso the Magnanimous had willed away from the legitimate line to his bastard son. In all these gains and losses the enemy had always been French, and usually in superior force. In the long feud with France, diplomacy had succeeded for Aragon more often than war.

Before the Catholic kings were sure of Castile, the renewed power of the French monarchy under Louis XI called for new exertions. Louis stirred up trouble for Ferdinand's father in Navarre and Catalonia and took by force and fraud the counties of Cerdagne and Roussillon, last remnants of the Aragonese domains in Languedoc. In Castile, Louis backed Isabella's enemies. Later, in 1481, Louis inherited not only Provence, facing Aragon across the Gulf of Lions, but the Angevin claim on the kingdom of Naples. Everywhere Ferdinand felt himself and his house menaced by the French.[1] Whatever Isabella's motives may have been, if Ferdinand worked incessantly at strengthening the Spanish monarchy, centralizing authority, building, in the long Granadan war, the beginnings of a regular army, it must have been largely because he looked forward to coming to grips, some day, with France.

While Ferdinand was still only heir apparent of Aragon, and his consort Isabella was scarcely sure of Castile, Ferdinand persuaded her to renounce the traditional Castilian policy of friendship with France, in retaliation for Louis XI's support of her enemies. Between 1475 and 1477 Ferdinand and Isabella sent a series of envoys to England, Italy, Germany and the Netherlands, offering a Castilian alliance 'to all those powers destined by necessity to be perpetual enemies of France'.[2] The amateurish effort was disturbing enough to lead Louis XI to recognize the new rulers of Castile and buy them off with a treaty. Ferdinand's first essay in European diplomacy accurately prefigured the shape of his later policy.

In the breathing spell afforded by the treaty with Louis XI, Ferdinand began to experiment with diplomacy in the new Italian style. Aragon had long felt the tug of Italian politics, and even though the kingdom of Naples was now independent, under the illegitimate branch of the royal house, the legitimate branch, by virtue of its possession of Sicily and Sardinia, was still a quasi-Italian power. The Aragonese must have watched with special interest the development of the new Italian diplomatic institutions. As soon as Ferdinand succeeded to his father's crowns, he raised the Aragonese proctor at Rome to the rank of ambassador. The next year he sent a layman to Rome as a strictly political resident ambassador, and thereafter he was continuously represented by at least one resident in the city which he called, with a touch of awe, the plaza of the world.[3]

Perhaps he was over-represented there. During the War of Ferrara there were two Spanish ambassadors in Rome, resident and accredited to the Papal See, two others charged with a joint circular embassy to all the Italian powers, but also usually residing in Rome, and a constant coming and going of special envoys. Ferdinand may have been influenced by the medieval feeling that multiple embassies were especially impressive, or just unwilling to trust a single resident. Now and then the Aragonese ambassadors got in each other's way, but on the whole they functioned so efficiently that for fifteen years Ferdinand felt he needed no other resident embassy in Italy.

As long as the French did not cross the Alps, as long as the war of Granada lasted, Spanish diplomats in Italy had no mission except to support Ferrante of Naples, advance Spanish prestige when possible, and help maintain the uneasy balance of peninsular power. But the French danger was never far from Ferdinand's mind. Camping in the Sierra Nevadas, pounding at the Moorish strongholds with his new artillery, slowly clearing the passes that led southward, Ferdinand kept looking back, over his shoulders, towards the north.

If Ferdinand had hoped that France would be less formidable under the regent, Anne de Beaujeu, than it had been under Louis XI, three events in the summer of 1485 showed him his mistake. The leader of the feudal opposition, Louis, duke of Orleans, submitted to the regent. With French aid, Henry Tudor made himself king of England. And the fall of the duke of Brittany's anti-French minister, Pierre Landois, seemed to foreshadow the success of the French drive to absorb the last great feudal dukedom into the royal domain.

Even if he could have persuaded Isabella to turn back from the crusade, Ferdinand would have understood the folly of attempting to defend Breton independence with Spanish arms. But he was eager to encircle and hamper the French as much as he could and to make any possible profit out of French embarrassment. The threatened increase in French power stirred him to a fresh diplomatic effort.[4]

The first step was obvious. Maximilian of Austria, widowed of his Burgundian heiress, hoped to marry the heiress of Brittany. Some time in the winter of 1487-88 Ferdinand and Isabella sent their councillor, Juan de Fonseca, to Maximilian in Flanders. Fonseca bore the offer of a Spanish alliance against France to ensure Breton independence. More fatefully, he bore the instructions to discuss cementing the alliance by marriages between Maximilian's children and those of the Catholic kings. Fonseca's credentials were those of a special ambassador, but he remained several years at Maximilian's court, one of those ambiguous transitional figures not infrequent in the beginning of the new diplomacy.

At the same time Ferdinand sent Don Francisco de Rojas to Brittany to encourage the party of independence and co-ordinate prospective military efforts. For such a mission, a soldier and a gentleman, a man of ancient lineage with experience of the Granadan wars, seemed more appropriate than a wily canonist and industrious royal councillor like Fonseca. Rojas was a fully accredited ambassador, sent to remain at the duke of Brittany's court 'as long as your grace pleases', an ambiguous phrase which makes him almost a resident, in intent, if not in effect.[5]

But the keystone of the diplomatic arch was England. Until he began to read Fonseca's dispatches, Ferdinand may not have known how feeble Maximilian really was, how the title of king of the Romans imperfectly masked an empty purse and a scanty following. But geography and history demonstrated that English bases were essential for operations in Brittany. Against the will of the lord of the English Channel, Spain and the Netherlands not only could not make a successful war in Brittany, they could not even keep in touch with each other. So, the Catholic kings sent another councillor, Dr. Rodrigo Gonzales de Puebla, to Henry VII.[6]

De Puebla was instructed to proceed cautiously. The value of England to Ferdinand's schemes was unquestionable, but the solidity of Henry Tudor's position was not. Until Dr. de Puebla had explored the English situation his own status was left so ambiguous that the English appear to have doubted whether he really was an ambassador. His mission was attended by none of the pomp usual to formal embassies, no solemn entry, no full-dress court reception. It could hardly have been otherwise, since the chief return he could offer for English alliance was formal Spanish recognition of the Tudor dynasty.

Nevertheless, the mission so begun was the beginning of a long career, and the first step in establishing one of the chief centres of Spanish diplomatic action. De Puebla was to remain in England, with only one three-year interruption, for more than twenty years. In that time he took a great part in laying the foundations of Anglo-Spanish relationships, and in establishing the traditions of what was to be, for almost a century, the oldest, most nearly continuous, and, on the whole, most important Spanish embassy outside of Rome.

For de Puebla judged that the Tudor king was solid enough on his throne to be a valuable ally . When Henry VII made the price of alliance the betrothal of his infant son to a Spanish princess, De Puebla urged acceptance. As soon as he could persuade his masters, De Puebla escorted an English embassy to Spain, saw a treaty signed for the marriage of Arthur, Prince of Wales, to Catherine of Aragon, and then hastened back to England to arrange details, encourage Henry's military preparations, prod his colleagues in the Netherlands, and generally act as chief liaison officer for the alliance to rescue Brittany.

If the negotiations of the 1470s suggest the diplomatic pattern of the earlier sixteenth century, the position about 1490 was a full-scale dress rehearsal. England, Spain and Austria were joined against France, with dynastic marriages being worked out between Spain and the two northern allies, and Spanish ambassadors, resident in fact if not in title, co-ordinating the alliance. Then, suddenly, the whole thing fell apart. Charles VIII married Anne of Brittany, and there was no longer any question of Breton independence. France made a separate peace with each of the allies, and each appeased monarch, pretending to think he had been deserted, resumed his freedom of action. Rojas left Brittany, Fonseca was called home from Flanders, and Dr. de Puebla, temporarily in Spain, did not go back to England. Even the marriage treaties were left in abeyance. The Breton question was too unimportant to polarize the European system. But a stronger magnet was to be provided. Charles VIII had made reckless concessions for peace in the north because he was in a hurry to go to Italy. There the full-scale power struggle was about to begin.

Even as he ratified the treaty which released Charles VIII for his Italian adventure, Ferdinand must have been thinking about another coalition against France. He had already sent Fonseca and a colleague back to Flanders to reopen the Habsburg marriage negotiations. Presently he reinforced them by Francisco de Rojas, whose real mission seems to have been to stick close to Maximilian wherever that errant monarch might go and talk to him about Italy. Dr. de Puebla was warned to stand by for England.

Meanwhile Ferdinand's caution and instinct for comedy suggested another development. With the remark that a treaty of eternal peace and friendship made closer diplomatic relations desirable, Ferdinand sent Don Alfonso de Silva, a distinguished veteran of the Granadan war, to the French court. De Silva told Italian diplomats that he had come to France as a resident. If so, he would be the first resident ambassador (outside Italy) not sent in the interest of maintaining an alliance, and an experiment on Ferdinand's part (the first non-Italian experiment on record) in using a resident ambassador to collect military intelligence.

If that was Ferdinand's purpose, it was only partially successful. De Silva was received at Lyons in a bustle of warlike preparations. He watched the French army defiling into the Alps, and the impressive parade of French might across Lombardy. But he never saw the great guns fired. At Pavia, Charles VIII, 'making small account of ambassadors as is the French custom',[7] summarily dismissed him, and after lingering indecisively for a while at Genoa, de Silva returned to Spain.

By that time, the triumphal French march down the peninsula was nearly over. The companies of men-at-arms had streamed across the Neapolitan frontiers, Ferdinand's Neapolitan relatives were on the point of flight, and Ferdinand's counter-stroke was preparing. An able captain who was to prove one of the shrewdest and most successful of Spanish diplomats, Don Lorenzo Suarez de Mendoza y Figueroa, was on his way to Venice with credentials as resident ambassador to the republic of St. Mark. At Rome, where two ambassadors, Medina and Carvajal, already stood guard, another envoy was waiting to present his credentials to Ludovico Sforza. And Dr. de Puebla was off to England. Each Spanish ambassador was instructed to urge his hosts to join the Holy League, of which the pope was to be head and Spain the right arm, a league to restore the independence of Naples and exclude the French from Italy for ever.[8]

The result was that famous treaty which the exasperated Commynes, the helpless ambassador of France to Venice, watched being celebrated along the Grand Canal in the first days of April 1495.[9] The new 'Holy League' looked much like the Holy League of 1455, concluded at Venice forty years before. The powers of Italy, under the presidency of the pope, banded together to protect each other in the possession of their territories, and to defend Italy against the Turk. (The ambassador of Bayazid II watched the signing from nominal concealment behind an arras, having been assured by the doge and the papal nuncio that nothing was intended against his master.) The league was to last twenty-five years. (It lasted nearly four.) And each signatory stipulated the contingent of troops he would contribute.

This time, however, the lists of signers was different. Maximilian, king of the Romans, was included, as suzerain of some fiefs south of the Alps. So were Ferdinand and Isabella, as rulers of the Italian islands of Sicily and Sardinia. When, a year later, Henry VII of England also adhered, any pretence that the new league was just an Italian affair was dropped. It was, in fact, a European-wide coalition against France, the first decisive drawing together of the major states of Europe into a single power system. Italian power politics were transferred to a wider arena.

CHAPTER XV

THE SPANISH DIPLOMATIC SERVICE

IF the Treaty of Venice of 1495 may be said to mark the beginning of modern European diplomacy, only Spain, among the major European powers, was ready at once to adopt the diplomatic machinery appropriate to the new phase. Ferdinand's experiments with resident ambassadors had convinced him of their usefulness, and he had plans which looked far beyond the mere ejection of Charles VIII from Naples. The missions he sent in furtherance of the Most Holy League fixed the outlines of his future diplomatic system. Each began a line of permanent resident ambassadors. With minor modifications, the posts they took up mark the key points in the Spanish diplomatic network for almost a century.

Each embassy was a link in the chain encircling France. There had been a Spanish resident in Rome since the 1480s. The arrival of Lorenzo Suarez de Figueroa at Venice established the second Spanish post in Italy, and Ferdinand found he needed no more there. The brief embassy to Milan was not continued, and none was established with pro-French Florence or semi-dependent Naples. Dr. de Puebla returned to England with credentials as resident early in 1495. Thereafter, the London embassy was continuous. Spanish diplomatic representation at the Habsburg court might be called continuous from an earlier period, but after 1495 Ferdinand always kept at least one accredited resident with Maximilian, and at least one other in the Netherlands.[1]

None of the smaller northern powers received a Spanish resident ambassador except, for a brief period, Scotland. None went to Portugal even, though the Iberian kingdoms were at peace, bound by dynastic ties, yet troubled by frictions in African and American waters. Resident ambassadors, as far as Ferdinand was concerned, were not sent out of courtesy or in token of friendship or to maintain and improve ordinary relations. Like their Italian prototypes of the early fifteenth century, they were the agents and symbols of an alliance.

With one partial exception, the five resident embassies at Rome,

Venice, London, Brussels and the migratory Austrian court, those necessary, that is, to his diplomatic encirclement of France, were the only ones Ferdinand thought it worth while to maintain. The partial exception was France itself. Because the two kingdoms were generally at war, or on the verge of war, no Spanish ambassador stayed very long in France, and it is impossible to be sure whether any ought to count as resident. But besides de Silva, Ferdinand sent three envoys who may have been meant as such: Don Juan de Galla (1501?-2), Don Jayme de Albion (1506-9?), and Pedro de Quintana (1514-15). Five years or so in twenty hardly make an embassy 'continuous', but that Ferdinand made even a gesture towards keeping a resident in France may indicate that the Italian feeling that resident embassies were normal in times of peace was percolating beyond the Alps.[2]

Slowly, however. For some time the other European powers did not even establish resident embassies with their allies. There was no English resident in Spain until 1505; none from either Habsburg court during most of Ferdinand's reign, and none from France at all until many years after his death. Of all the major competitors in the European power struggle only Spain, during the first phase of the Italian wars, set up a diplomatic network approaching in completeness the kind which the Italian 'great powers' maintained after the Peace of Lodi. The priority goes far to account for the prestige of the Spanish diplomatic service in the sixteenth century, as well as for the immediate diplomatic successes of the king of Aragon.

Not that the Spanish service ever reached an Italian standard of efficiency during Ferdinand's lifetime. The realms of the Catholic king suffered from more than the usual feudal decentralization, and Spanish administration overcame only gradually its unbusinesslike, essentially feudal habits. There was never a foreign office for the whole realm, and never a real foreign minister. The court was constantly on the move, swinging back and forth across Spain almost as far and often as the great transhumant flocks of sheep, and in a pattern less predictable. For writing their letters the sovereigns employed whichever chancery happened to be most convenient, and all his life Ferdinand kept the custom of his ancestors in regard to state papers. He carried them about with him, stuffed in leather-covered chests and when the chests got full abandoned them casually at whatever castle he happened to be leaving. So, in 1508, he could find no copy of the Treaty of Medina del Campo at his court, and twenty years later everyone hunted for months for the crucial papers about his daughter's second marriage in England. Like Louis XI, Ferdinand was too fond of secrecy, mystification and elaborate double-dealing to trust much to systematic organization.

One result of this lack of organization was that Spanish resident ambassadors were often dangerously out of touch with their home government. If the king was too busy to answer the ambassador's letter, or did not choose to do so, the ambassador got no answer. It was nobody's business to forward those budgets of news and advice on which fifteenth-century Italian diplomats depended so much. Every one of Ferdinand's veteran residents had the experience of waiting months for instructions or replies to urgent letters, and of feeling cut off and neglected, without any clear idea of what he was supposed to do.

This kind of neglect was quite apart from another practice of Ferdinand's. Not infrequently he deliberately deceived or misled his own ambassadors. Very often, through a fixed habit of distrust, he kept them in ignorance of negotiations directly affecting their own positions.[3] It must have been hard for even his shrewdest envoys to distinguish the silence of neglect from the silence of deception.

Often the royal silences were due neither to neglect nor to duplicity, but simply to stinginess. Ferdinand ran his diplomatic service on a slim budget, and though he came to appreciate the value of frequent ambassadorial reports and the advantages of prompt, co-ordinated action at foreign courts, he never got round to setting up an adequate courier service. A really good one would have been expensive. At one time, impatient for news of important negotiations, influenced, perhaps, by Italian precedent, and disregarding the difference between the distance from Rome to Naples and that from London to Toledo, Ferdinand ordered Dr. de Puebla to write and send daily. The ambassador in England calculated ruefully that to obey would mean at least sixty couriers constantly on the road. De Puebla had two in his own service, their pay sadly in arrears. Fuensalida in Flanders had two or three more who sometimes passed through England and picked up de Puebla's letters. In addition, there were usually about three royal couriers going back and forth from Spain, reaching Fuensalida first on the out trip if they came by land, or de Puebla first if by sea. With this skimpy service, not infrequently packets of letters arrived as much as six weeks apart.[4]

Parsimony hampered Spanish diplomats in other ways. Ferdinand spent practically nothing on bribing the servants of his rivals. North of the Alps standards were different from those in Italy. In Austria and the Netherlands, France and England, pensions and presents to noblemen and councillors were the most efficient emolient of diplomatic contacts. They were completely customary and without reproach to giver or taker. The French spent freely in such ways; the Netherlanders spent sagaciously; even the penniless Austrians promised largely. But Ferdinand supplied his ambassadors with no funds for such purposes.

Nor did he pay them either well or promptly, and his ambassadors' problems of subsistence were complicated by the fact that, unlike Italian residents in Italy, the Spaniards did not represent one side of a reciprocal arrangement, and consequently the governments of England, Austria and the Netherlands did not regard them as entitled, like special ambassadors, to lodging and entertainment. One of Maximilian's ambassadors crossed, on his way to Spain, his Spanish opposite number and suggested that they each draw the other's salary to save the inconvenience of transmission and exchange. Ferdinand did pay the Austrian, though a smaller stipend than Maximilian had promised; Maximilian never paid the Spaniard at all, and the whole affair ended in ill-feeling and inconvenience. Presently Maximilian's resident in Spain went home and was not replaced. That was the only time a reciprocal arrangement was even contemplated. The fact that Spanish residents had been so long at the major European courts before the exchange of ambassadors became common may account for the failure of the Italian manner of paying residents to be adopted elsewhere.

Ferdinand not only often neglected his resident ambassadors, sometimes deceived them, starved their courier service, and consistently underpaid them, but he distrusted them (unjustly) and set them to spy on and control one another. Several of Ferdinand's circular embassies had as one of their principal duties the collection of full reports about all the residents on their route. Ferdinand sent special envoys far more often than necessary, and frequently kept two residents with similar credentials at the same post. This rarely worked well. Fuensalida, for instance, spent most of his time in Flanders quarrelling with his colleagues, and the disputes between de Puebla and Don Pedro de Ayala, who shared the English post for several years, became the ill-natured jest of London.[5] The best Castilian negotiators were not well broken to double harness. They did not settle their disputes with drawn swords, but the clash of their flaming tempers reminds us that they were of the same race as the *conquistadores* who made the subjugation of two continents a mere incident of their civil broils. Had Ferdinand trusted his representatives more, his diplomatic service would have worked with less friction, and greater efficiency.

Nevertheless he was well served. The shrewd reports his ambassadors wrote and the skilful pressures they exerted prepared Ferdinand's most spectacular diplomatic successes and saved him from the worst consequences of his blunders. Perhaps he was skilful in picking men, or perhaps he was merely lucky in being king of a people whose genius was rising to concert pitch, so that it was easier to find men capable of just a little more boldness and persistence and address, a little more dogged endurance and devotion, than one had any right to expect. But the success of his diplomacy was far from being all luck. He knew how to take advantage of the mistakes and weaknesses of others; he knew also how to learn from his own. Not only was he the first king in Europe to appreciate the new diplomatic system, but, as he watched his foreign service at work, and as one European crisis after another increased his reliance on it, he remedied its weaknesses. Towards the end of his reign he began to have something like an organized foreign office. His courier service improved. His diplomats were better paid, and even paid more promptly. Probably he never completely trusted any of them, but he did keep them better informed, freed them of irritating checks and surveillance, gave them greater responsibilities. He was wise to do so. They were building, for him and for Spain, what was to be for a century and more the most impressive diplomatic service in Europe.

Before the end of Ferdinand's reign that service was beginning to seem, in one respect at least, more professional than its Italian models. As a rule Spanish ambassadors stayed much longer at their posts than was the Italian custom. In Italy the cultural homogeneity and political interdependence of the peninsula, the shorter physical distances and the ease with which a new ambassador could find his feet, all suggested a relatively rapid rotation in office in order to spread the burden of diplomatic service among a fairly large group. Once this habit was formed, it tended to determine the practice in the transalpine embassies of the Italian states as well. But when language and customs and internal politics were as strange as those of England and the Netherlands and Germany were to Spaniards, there were obvious advantages in keeping on as resident a man familiar with the country.

Whether he was moved by this consideration, or simply by the expense and difficulty of finding replacements, Ferdinand did tend to keep his residents fixed for considerable periods. No other ambassador stayed as long at the same post as de Puebla who, on two missions, spent eighteen of the last twenty-one years of his life in England, but several totalled nine years or more in one or more tours of duty in the same country. In addition, residents who had proved their ability at one post (or even sometimes had merely proved their loyalty) were apt to be assigned to another. Francisco de Rojas served at Rome, in Brittany, with Maximilian, and again at Rome; Fuensalida in the Netherlands and in England; Ayala in Scotland and in England; Caroz in England and Rome, and so forth, not counting ambassadors like Fonseca who were sometimes fixed in the Netherlands, sometimes trailing around Germany after the king of the Romans.

In consequence, again and again in the correspondence of three decades one encounters the same names. Probably not many more than a score of individuals wrote three-fourths of the reports which provided Ferdinand with his foreign information, and conducted nearly all his negotiations. When they were not on foreign duty Ferdinand made a habit of keeping these veteran diplomats about him, using them sometimes to talk to foreign envoys, sometimes to consult with his council (when they were not already members of it) on points of policy or technique, so that his foreign service acquired as a nucleus a small corps of professional experts.

In social position they were a mixed rather than a distinguished group. None were great noblemen, 'grandees', if one may use that term of an age when it had no exact meaning, although a number bore old and distinguished names. Others had risen in the Church or the law from among the middle-sized landowners and professional classes of the towns, or from more humble and obscure origins. The three sent out in 1487 may be taken as typical: Francisco de Rojas, the soldier, a gentleman, of ancient lineage and high connections if only moderate estate; Juan de Fonseca, the churchman, of a solidly established if recent family, a predestinate bishop; and Dr. Roderigo de Puebla the *letrado*, of distinctly lower middle-class origin, a man who had risen by his own ability to be *corregidor* of Ecija and a royal counsellor, but a vulgarian and, what was worse, a converted Jew, of whom it was asserted, though unjustly, that his father had been a tailor.

All these three were Castilians, and so were a surprisingly large number of Ferdinand's diplomats. The number is surprising; that is, in view of the past isolation of Castile from world affairs compared to the experience of the cosmopolitan lands of Aragon. It may be explained by the fact that it was easier to pay public servants from the revenues of Castile. Several of Ferdinand's veteran diplomats, however, were from Catalonia or Valencia, one at least from Majorca, and one or two from old Aragon. Only one element from Ferdinand's polyglot realms was lacking: there were no Italians. This is curious in view of the fact that Ferdinand had been King of Sicily as long as of Aragon, and more curious still when one remembers that the kings of France and England and Maximilian of Austria all employed Italian diplomats, not their natural subjects. Apart from the fact that Ferdinand's ambassadors were all Spaniards, however, it would be hard to find any common denominator of birth or education among them.

One experience they had in common. They had all worked in the royal administration, and at one time or another under the king's own eye. Most of them had at least some legal training, a number were royal counsellors, several were doctors of the civil and the canon law, and even the soldiers, like Rojas and Fuensalida, had served in other ways besides soldiering and were not without letters and learning.

SIXTEENTH-CENTURY DIPLOMACY

One emotion they seem to have had in common, loyalty to their king. Such abstract civic patriotism with overtones of classical antiquity as one finds in Ermolao Barbaro was a long time making its way beyond the Alps. Its surrogate in the European monarchies was a kind of chivalric, feudal loyalty to the person of the monarch, a loyalty raised to a new intensity, and strong, perhaps strongest, in those classes which had been exempt from feudal claims. 'My king', said Fuensalida, when Henry VII taunted him with Ferdinand's lack of money, 'does not lock up his coins in chests, but spends them on brave soldiers at whose head he has conquered and will conquer.'[6] This is perhaps no more than the ring of knightly pride. 'I place this object of His Highness', wrote Bishop Fonseca to Almazan, 'higher than the safety of my immortal soul.' (The object was to inveigle the Austrians into a new war with France which Ferdinand was starting in gross violation of his treaty obligations.) Fonseca was a trained theologian, an old man and, as far as one can gather, an honest one. He seems to have meant what he said.

CHAPTER XVI

THE SPREAD OF THE NEW DIPLOMACY

EVEN before the actual French invasion of 1494, the impending crisis had begun to spread Italian resident diplomats among the major courts of Europe. Ludovico Sforza of Milan had thought first that Ferdinand and Isabella might be willing to protect him against Naples, and had accredited a resident ambassador to the Spanish court in 1490. In the same year he sent to a Genoese merchant already living in London credentials as his resident ambassador to the court of Henry VII. By 1493 a long series of Milanese special embassies to Maximilian of Austria culminated in Ludovico's daughter Bianca Maria going to Germany as Maximilian's bride, and the establishment of a Milanese resident embassy at the Habsburg court. Already in 1492, as part of the arrangements for Milanese co-operation with the French enterprise against Naples, Ludovico had accredited a resident to the court of Charles VIII. So, when the storm broke, Ludovico could congratulate himself that with residents at all principal courts of Europe he was prepared to manœuvre as dexterously in Europe as his father Francesco once had done in Italy.[1]

Sooner or later the other major Italian powers were obliged to follow Sforza's lead. By 1493 Ferrante of Naples, aware of his danger, had sent resident ambassadors to Spain, England and Germany to counter-work the Milanese, and seek whatever outside help might be available against the French. For the brief period of its remaining independence, the kingdom of Naples had more or less continuous diplomatic representation at the courts of its three possible allies.[2]

Venice delayed until 1495. When the league against the French was signed at Venice that year, however, the Signory dispatched special ambassadors to its allies in Spain and Germany, and a few months later replaced them with residents. The Venetian resident embassy in England was not established until more than a year later, in November 1496, but from that time on Venice usually had permanent diplomatic representation with all of the major European monarchies.[3]

Florence was somewhat slower. As the ominous cloud built up beyond the Alps, the magnificent Lorenzo's unlucky successor, Piero de'Medici, sent, in 1493, an envoy to France who may have been intended to remain as resident.[4] A series of special Florentine embassies followed. But official diplomacy proved as ineffective as the intrigues of financiers, and in June 1494 Charles VIII, on his way to join his invading army, abruptly dismissed the Florentines. The collapse of Piero's government prolonged the diplomatic breach. After the Medici had been driven from the city, however, the signory of the restored republic, true to its Guelph tradition, sought, for a time, no European ally except the king of France. At his court Florence was continuously represented, in fact if not by an explicitly designated resident, from the time Charles VIII left Milan on his march towards Naples, on down into the reign of his successor, Louis XII. Meanwhile events had obliged the Florentines to accredit a resident to Spain and, from 1496 on, Florence generally kept up these two embassies outside the peninsula.[5]

Under the pressure of the French invasion, even the papacy abandoned its conservatism. All through the fifteenth century the popes had received resident ambassadors, but sent none. It was the last and most worldly of the fifteenth-century popes who first began to adopt the diplomatic institutions of his secular neighbours. Alexander VI kept one *nuntius* and *orator* at the court of Maximilian for four years after 1495. During most of his reign he had some sort of diplomatic representation in Spain. In 1500 he sent a nuncio to the French court and another to Venice, and kept them at their posts for three years. Each of these moves corresponded to another step along the tortuous road to a consolidated papal (or Borgia?) state in central Italy. Each of them may have been meant to establish a permanent post, but only the one to Venice was actually continuous from Alexander VI's time.

Julius II renewed the resident embassy in Spain in 1506, but the decisive expansion of the papal system came under Leo X and Clement VII. One by one the Italian powers, those which had once been 'the great powers' of Italy, had been swept from the board or reduced to pawns. In 1495 Ludovico Sforza was boasting that his diplomatic skill had sent the king of France scurrying home and saved Italy from the barbarians. Four years later Sforza was in flight from his duchy and Milan was scratched from the list of independent powers. Less than three years later it was the turn of Naples, and seven years after that, in 1509, the greatest of the Italian states, Venice, succumbed in a single campaign to the league formed against her at Cambrai. Another three years and the republic of Florence yielded her independence to Spanish arms and the restored Medici. By 1513 the Florentine-Papal tandem stood for all that was left of Italian diplomacy, and the resident papal nuncios at the courts of the great European powers were as watchful and as absorbed in power politics as ever their secular predecessors had been.[6]

This period of the involvement of Italian diplomacy in the wider European theatre, the real 'age of Machiavelli', has received so much attention from historians that the findings appropriate to it have largely coloured all our views of the diplomacy of the Italian Renaissance. Frederick of Prussia's often applied dictum, 'diplomacy without arms is like a concert without a score', really is, for this period, at least, partly applicable.[7] Fascinated by the new techniques which they had invented, confident of their superior command of the arts of negotiation, and sure that intellectual subtlety must be more than a match for brute force, the Italians went on, year after hopeless year, seeking the right trick to balance all Europe as Italy had once been balanced, seeking to harness the northern titans to serve Italian ends. This doomed effort to make diplomacy do the work of arms, to make the foxes masters of the lions, pitilessly exposed the weakness of the overstrained Italian system. So it became usual, in the sixteenth century and afterwards, to condemn Italian diplomacy as especially shifty, inconstant, and deceitful, blaming either a defect in the Italian national character, or, more kindly, a lack of military strength.

Lack of military strength did give sixteenth-century Italian diplomacy its air of desperate improvisation; the rest is only pseudo-explanation. The major Italian states of the fifteenth century had been no more lacking in calculable military strength relative to one another than the European monarchies were at a later period, or than Italians, as individuals, were, then or later, less reliable than other Europeans. Shiftiness and inconstancy were imposed on the Italian system by the internal political instability of most of the major states, by the delicate balance of peninsular power, and, chiefly, by the continuous struggle of each state against all. The intrusion of the greater powers merely accentuated these weaknesses. To the end of the Italian wars, Italian diplomacy retained its technical superiority and Italian statesmanship its basic aims, but the inconsistency of those aims with political reality became steadily clearer, and Italian diplomacy less and less important.

If, during the first decades after 1495, Italian diplomats retained an apparent importance in negotiations quite out of proportion to the weight behind them, it was because the European powers, other than Spain, were so slow to adopt the new diplomatic machinery. Consequently the experienced, strategically placed and well-informed Italian diplomats really did exert some influence on the decisions of their big neighbours, and seemed, to themselves, to exert even more. This continued until England, France and Austria finally began to be served by networks of permanent embassies like Spain's.

At the time of Charles VIII's invasion of Italy Maximilian of Austria showed every intention of setting up a system of resident ambassadors equal to Ferdinand's. Among the rulers of his time Maximilian had the most alert and widely curious mind. He was always experimenting with new institutions, new military formations, new types of arms and armour, just as he was always eager to pose as a patron of the new learning, the new literature, the new arts. Even if his temperament had not impelled him to have a finger in every European pie, his position would have forced vigilance upon him. From the North Sea to the Adriatic, Maximilian's lands were touched by every threat of French expansion, sensitive to every alteration in the European pattern. And, unlike the French kings, he could not rely on mere military might. He needed every advantage diplomacy could give him, and the promptness with which he followed Ferdinand's lead shows he appreciated the fact. Before the end of 1496 he had dispatched ambassadors to all but one of the main centres of the Holy League, to Rome, to Venice, to Milan and to Spain. Only at the last moment he was persuaded to let Dr. de Puebla handle his interests in England instead of dispatching a resident ambassador there also. The imperial diplomatic network bade fair to rival the Spanish.[8]

The sequel was quite different. Within a few years Maximilian's whole diplomatic network had melted away, because he had quarrelled with his allies, or was unable to pay his ambassadors, or both. The ambassador at Venice was not replaced. Bontius, the humanist, whom Maximilian had accredited to Milan, lingered there as Ludovico Sforza's pensioner, but scarcely functioned as ambassador. The unhappy Lupyan, whose financial arrangements with his Spanish colleague Maximilian had sanctioned but omitted to honour, was finally permitted to escape his shame and come home and his post in Spain was left unfilled. Only Philibert Naturelli, resident ambassador at Rome, stayed on until 1501, and he only because he was accredited as Philip the Handsome's representative as well as Maximilian's, and his salary paid, now and then, from the Netherlands. After Naturelli there seems to have been a four-year gap even in Maximilian's representation at Rome. After Lupyan there was no imperial resident in Spain for nearly a decade.

Maximilian's fickleness and improvidence prevented him from ever establishing a working system of resident embassies. He was always changing allies, always dropping a small but solid advantage to grasp at a dazzling, chimerical one, always elaborating grandiose schemes and then getting bored with them. He had not the temperament for the patient work of permanent diplomacy. But his poverty, or rather (since compared with patronage of war and the arts, diplomacy is relatively inexpensive) his complete irresponsibility about money matters and the hand-to-mouth disorder of his finances were the chief obstacles to his creating a diplomatic service.

He made one more serious try. After the death of Isabella the Catholic, Maximilian was fascinated by the idea of taking over Castile in the name of his son's wife, Joanna, Isabella's heir. In pursuit of that objective he sent resident ambassadors to England, to Rome, and to France, and presently one to Spain also, to levy political blackmail. Frivolity and financial irresponsibility wrecked all four embassies. His ambassador to England found himself unable to negotiate because he was constantly receiving new instructions, and unable to borrow enough to live on because nobody sent him any money. The ambassadors to France, to Spain and to Rome all had an almost equally painful time. One after another they quitted their posts, their patience and their credit exhausted. In his later years Maximilian had no resident ambassador anywhere except at Rome, and might have had none there had not Alberto Pio, prince of Carpi, been willing to accept the protection of imperial credentials as sufficient compensation for his somewhat casual discharge of a resident's duties. Until Maximilian's grandson, Charles of Ghent, inherited the system of his Spanish grandparents, no reliable diplomatic network served the Habsburgs.[9]

The king of France in those days had no minor financial worries. In pensions to Italian exiles about his court and to princelings and cardinals and papal nephews in the peninsula Louis XII disbursed enough to have kept up a dozen embassies without buying a twelfth as much reliable information as one good ambassador could have sent. But, perhaps because he preferred dependents to allies, Louis made almost no use of the new system. He did usually have a proctor-ambassador at Rome, besides a cardinal or two of the French party from whom he expected news, and through whom he could negotiate. He did have ambassadors resident at Venice, perhaps in continuation of the long-established Milanese embassy. But in spite of Milanese precedents, France maintained no other resident ambassadors in Italy, not even with Florence, the ancient ally, or Ferrara, the loyal client, or Savoy, the porter of the Alpine passes. Nor did Louis XII or Francis I in his earlier years have any resident ambassadors outside of Italy, even though both Ferdinand and Maximilian offered the opportunity by sending residents to France, even though Henry VIII in 1514 indicated that he favoured an exchange of residents and in 1518, at the time of the second Anglo-French alliance, such an exchange was provided for by treaty. The French diplomatic service did not begin to develop until, locked in a struggle with the most powerful emperor since Charlemagne, the French began to feel the need of allies.[10]

England was earlier than France in following the Spanish lead. At first, under Henry VII, slowly and cautiously. Henry VII was akin to Ferdinand of Aragon in temperament and methods. He was better furnished with funds than Maximilian, and he had a more flexible foreign policy (and much less military might) than the French. He understood diplomacy and conducted throughout his reign a series of shrewdly planned negotiations for political or commercial advantages. But his ends were strictly limited. Alone among his contemporaries, he coveted no foreign kingdoms, and valued safety (and gold) above glory. He did not feel the pull of Italy or any interest there beyond solicitude for the extension of English commerce. Nor was he the man to undertake avoidable expenses.

Consequently England's diplomatic business was conducted throughout his reign with a minimum of fixed charges. For years there was only one permanent English embassy on the continent, at Rome, the nerve centre of diplomacy and its chief gossip shop. But there the English embassy was strong. There were usually two proctor-ambassadors, similarly accredited, one an Englishman and one an Italian, an uncharacteristic extravagance for Henry, but explicable since both could be paid in ecclesiastical preferment. The double representation seems to have worked. Soncino, Ludovico Sforza's ambassador in London in 1497, wrote that Henry was so well informed from Rome that there was nothing about Italian affairs Soncino could tell him.[11]

Elsewhere Henry VII extended his permanent service slowly. There had been a Spanish resident in London since 1496, but it was not until 1505 that John Stile, on a special mission to Spain, was ordered to remain there as resident. Stile was the first English resident ambassador at a secular court, as odd an ancestor for a distinguished service as was his opposite number, de Puebla. His salary was about the same as de Puebla's; more promptly paid but not enough. Of himself, Stile was without wealth or breeding or courtly graces. He seems to have been neither learned nor intelligent. In all the years of his embassy he never acquired much Spanish, but communicated with Ferdinand's council to the last in what must have been, to judge by his surviving compositions, little better than hog-Latin. Ferdinand thought him an ass, and deceived him again and again outrageously. Yet Henry VIII confirmed him in his embassy, and after he had returned to England in 1511 sent him back for another tour of duty until 1517.

It may be that the English kings were negligent. It may be that they were taken in (or that young Henry VIII was) by Ferdinand's maliciously extravagant praise of Stile. Or it may be, simply, that there was a dearth of men properly equipped and ready to lie long years abroad for their country's good. This may be why the Tudor diplomatic service developed as slowly as it did, and why both Henry VII and, at first, his son, employed so many Italians. At any rate Stile was for years the only resident English ambassador outside of Rome, although Henry VII, towards the end of his reign, sent many special embassies to both Habsburg courts, and kept Thomas Spinelly, a Florentine, in the Netherlands, as a sort of quasi-official agent.[12]

When the young Henry VIII came to the throne, full of vague dreams of glory and determined to cut a great figure in Europe, the tempo of English diplomacy quickened. Stile's salary was promptly raised, and he was advised that he must henceforward make a creditable appearance for the sake of his master's honour. Spinelly was advanced in rank and officially accredited to the Netherlands, while a gentleman of good family, Sir Robert Wingfield, was made resident ambassador to the emperor. Wingfield turned out a somewhat chuckle-headed diplomat, who won from his compatriots the soubriquet of 'old Summer-will-be-green' because of his unshakable confidence in whatever Maximilian told him. But no one denied that Wingfield made a dignified appearance, and he was rumoured to have had the honour of lending the emperor small sums out of his own pocket, as well as to be working hard to get Maximilian a perpetual English subsidy. For Rome, nothing but a cardinal-archbishop would do. The arrival there of Christopher Bainbridge, archbishop of York, in princely splendour, with large, vague plans for upsetting the French, rearranging Italy and generally tidying up Christendom, signalled to all Europe, if not exactly the opening of a new era in diplomacy, at least the arrival of a new, unseasoned player in a game where all the older players, by now, were sore and hard-bitten and wary.[13]

Henry learned, painfully and expensively, but rather quickly. When Thomas Wolsey finally got the reins of foreign policy into his hands, the quality of Henry's diplomacy and of the English diplomatic service improved rapidly. By the early 1520s Wolsey had completed the main outlines of a network of resident embassies by establishing posts in France and Venice, and the king began to be served abroad by diplomats equal in brains, in education, and in skill to the men against whom they were matched. If Henry got little from the game of European politics beyond the satisfaction of a colossal vanity, at least under Wolsey's shrewd guidance, he was able to make his fellow sovereigns feel that he was a player to be reckoned with.

CHAPTER XVII

DYNASTIC POWER POLITICS

'THE wars of Italy and the diplomatic negotiations connected with them rested upon no fixed principles whatever. Neither national interest, nor public morality, nor religious zeal had any place in them. Personal ambition, rivalry, or resentment was their only spring of action.' So David Jayne Hill,[1] sternly summing up the quarter-century between the first French invasion of Italy and the imperial election of Charles V. Even though some of the values Hill assumed seem less certain now than they did fifty years ago, it is still hard to disagree with his judgment.

National interest was still too vague a concept to guide or even to excuse the policies of the monarchies. When the spokesman for the Estates General of 1506 besought Louis XII not to marry his daughter, the heiress of Brittany, to any but the natural heir to France, when an independent member of Parliament grumbled that the last English war across the Channel had cost more than twenty such ungracious dog-holes as its conquest, Thérouanne, would be worth, when the Cortes of Castile besought their king to think less about Milan and Burgundy and more about reducing taxes and clearing the seas of Moorish pirates, perhaps these citizens were fumbling towards what the nineteenth century would have regarded as a valid idea of national interest.[2] But their notions were still unformed. Mostly the third estates just wanted peace and lower taxes, and their infrequent murmurings were dismissed by their betters as the petty and shortsighted views of tradesmen unfit to meddle with the affairs of princes.

The sixteenth-century struggle for power had a dynastic, not a national orientation. The kingdom of Naples and the duchy of Milan were wealthy and famous provinces; the conquest of either would increase the apparent strength of the prince who could effect it, and indubitably increase, for a time, the benefits he would be able to bestow on his captains and counsellors. Whether such conquests would be worth to his people the blood and treasure they would cost was an irrelevant, absurd question. Nobody expected that they would.

Historians have been able to discover one general principle in sixteenth-century diplomacy related to the idea of national interest, the principle of the balance of power. There are, indeed, episodes in the period 1494 to 1559 when it looks as if that principle was really being applied, especially when it was a question of the combination of two or more strong states against a weak one. Here the principle requires such a partition of the victim's territories as not to change decisively the strength of any victor in relation to his partners. In the arrangements for cutting up the Milanese between France and Venice, or Naples between France and Spain, or the Venetian territories among the allies of the League of Cambrai, the principle was more or less consciously observed. But since it really means little more than that the biggest dog gets the meatiest bone, and others help themselves in the order of size, it is hard to be sure that the sixteenth century appreciated the full beauty of a balanced system. It is harder because none of the arrangements lasted, and because each was upset (two of them before they had begun to be carried out) with the full sanction of the chief Italian power, the papacy, which had presided over them in its rôle of special custodian of the idea of balance.

The Holy League of 1495 and the League of Cognac of 1526 illustrate another aspect of what is taken for balance-of-power diplomacy, the combination of a group of powers against an apparent victor. In the sixteenth century, however, what the allies always hoped was not just to balance the strongest power, but to outweigh it. A real balance of power requires at least two groups, so evenly matched that neither can easily defeat the other, with a third holding the balance between them. This classic English conception is usually supposed to have been invented by Cardinal Wolsey, somewhere in the reign of the first two Tudors. But, though Wolsey may have had more in mind than he told his master, on the evidence, what Henry VIII wanted, and what Wolsey persuaded him each time he would get, was not just to preserve the status quo but to be on the winning side so as to share the spoils. None of Henry VIII's fellow sovereigns was any more altruistic than he.

Actually, except for a jealousy of success, nobody had worked out any idea of a European balance of power. All that existed was a rough idea of such a balance in Italy. After the French invasion this tended to take the disastrous form sketched by Alexander VI when he told the Venetian ambassador that for the last eight years the only safety of Italy had lain in the jealousy of Spain and France. So much was true. Yet both men knew that the pope's next word, 'For the love of God, let us lay aside our differences, let us stand together and provide for the common safety,' far from expressing any genuine hope, was merely a pious introduction to a cynical proposal.[3] Little as they trusted each other, Alexander and the Venetians had collaborated two years before in the destruction of the duchy of Milan. Alexander was now inviting them to join him in destroying the kingdom of Naples.

Each of three popes of this period had a separate policy: Alexander VI's scheme of a Borgian kingdom carved out of central Italy; Julius II's equally fantastic drive to make the papacy a first-rate temporal power; Leo X's preoccupation with the fortunes of his Medici wards. Each pope was compelled, in pursuit of his ambitions, to employ the arms of foreigners against Italians, so that each left Italy weaker than he found it. Nevertheless every pope was obliged to work for a strong independent state in central Italy and against the union of Milan and Naples under the same foreign crown. Any foreign power so placed would dominate Italy, and as the sixteenth century read history such an outcome would mean the end of the liberties of the Church. In the phrase then current, should a foreign sovereign come to rule Italy, the pope would inevitably become 'the chaplain' of the victor.

Although successive popes had squandered the moral authority which had once shaken thrones and moved all Christendom like an army, the Renaissance papacy still had resources available for the pursuit of this limited Italian end. If popes could no longer overawe the greater powers, they could often bribe and wheedle them. The papacy could mobilize able and effective diplomatic agents who spoke with authority of Italian matters and appealed to sentiments and interests which no Christian monarch could quite ignore. Moreover, the papacy had natural allies among the higher clergy everywhere. The chief ministers of state were usually ecclesiastics — one thinks of Cisneros, Briçonnet, Georges d'Amboise, Lang, Fox, Wolsey — and so likely, in the conduct of foreign affairs, to feel a divided allegiance. As a result, most apparent manœuvres for a European balance of power turn out, on analysis, to have been directed towards an Italian one. No one in about 1500 thought of a European balance as a vital national interest, if only because the conquest of Europe by any single power was, under existing circumstances, utterly unlikely.

If considerations of national interest had small part in forming the policies of the dynasts, it is easy to believe that regard for public morality or zeal for religion had as little. Of course, such sentiments were frequently invoked. 'For the preservation of peace among Christians', 'for the welfare of the Christian Republic', 'for maintaining the freedom and authority of Holy Church', 'for the defence of Christendom against the infidels', these phrases never fail in the preambles of treaties. Major agreements usually show them all, and elaborate one or more with pious fervour. Ambassadors' formal orations, powers for extraordinary embassies, proclamations of popes and princes were commonly stuffed with them. And, on occasion, there was also big diplomatic talk of 'ending intolerable scandals in the papacy', 'reforming the Church in its head and members', and similar echoes of the militant conciliar movement. But kings generally talked about reforming the Church when they wanted to put pressure on a pope for a political end. When they talked about 'preserving the peace of the Christian Republic' they were seeking a breathing spell after an exhausting war and gathering their forces to begin a fresh one. And when they named the crusade, 'the defence of Christendom against the Turks', they were the most dangerous of all. In the Treaty of Granada, Ferdinand of Aragon and Louis XII of France combined to rob Ferdinand's protégé, the king of Naples, of his kingdom on the pretext that he was plotting 'to call the Turk into Europe'. At Cambrai the emperor, the king of France, the king of Spain and the pope united in a 'most holy league' against the infidel, and under that mask conspired to destroy the Venetian Republic, the chief Mediterranean defender of Christendom against the Turk.

It is not surprising that Machiavelli, after skimming over the treacheries he had seen in his time, concludes a chapter on 'How

Princes ought to keep faith' with the bitter reflection, 'A prince still reigning whom it would not be fitting for me to name [everyone knew he meant Ferdinand of Aragon] never talks of anything but peace and good faith, yet had he ever observed either he would several times have lost his credit and his estates.' And so he leaves his readers with the impression that to keep faith is the last thing a prince should do, since in the ruthless struggle for power there were only the tricksters and the dupes.

And yet, a dismissal of the moral tags in the treaties as always mere hypocrisy may be too easy an attitude. In the days when Frenchmen and Spaniards, Germans and Swiss were fighting over the bleeding body of Italy there was still a European public conscience, just as there were still, in every part of Europe, masses of people — and not just the simple and the humble — to whom religion was more than a mask or a catchword. It is not certain that Erasmus and Contarini, Luis Vives and Thomas More were any less typical of their era than Ferdinand of Aragon or Niccolò Machiavelli. It is not even certain which of the cynical realists of the new politics were as single-minded as we take them to be. The ironies of Machiavelli get their bite from the bitterness of disillusioned idealism, of idealism perhaps not completely disillusioned. Even the real hero-villain of *The Prince* (for surely Machiavelli's praise of the Borgian bungler is no more than satire), even Ferdinand of Aragon himself — do we know how much his pious phrases were meant to deceive others, and how much to appease the uneasiness of his spirit? Perhaps he always did mean (like Henry IV) some day to begin the crusade. Meanwhile he was driven, as other princes and statesmen were driven, by the compulsions of a system organized for power, not for peace.

It is always easier to blame men than institutions when things go wrong, since it is a safe assumption that the heart of man is capable of any amount of evil, and a simple demonstration that if only everybody had behaved with intelligence and goodwill the institutions in question (any set of institutions) would have proved perfectly workable. Yet the heart of man may not have been more prone to evil in the sixteenth century than at other periods, and professions of good intentions may not always have been hollow, even though they were not followed by good results. When we find treaty after treaty full of noble phrases but with consequences squalid or null, the simplest judgment is that the phrases were all hypocritical to begin with. Yet, unless these diplomats and statesmen were capable of completely sustained hypocrisy in their daily behaviour and their most confidential writing, some of them — in fact, ˌa good many of them — did believe in the substance of their professions. One is driven to conclude that some of them at least did actually want peace and the welfare and unity of Christendom, and were at times sickened and bewildered by the elusiveness of ends so simply stated. One sees them again and again roused to an unjust fury of suspicion against those with whom they dealt, each side finding malice and deceit where (sometimes, at least) there were only blunder and bewilderment.

Let us take just one instance, an important one. Wolsey's Treaty of London (October 4th, 1518) was the last of a series after the wars which had followed, one hard upon another, since the League of Cambrai. The Treaty of London was cast in the form of another holy league to preserve peace in Europe and defend Christendom against the Turks. But this time it was, in announced intention, completely inclusive and European-wide, with provisions for arbitration of disputes, and stiff guarantees against aggression. Its drafting embodied the diplomatic experience of a century. Its language sought to avoid the reservations and ambiguities which had flawed previous treaties. It was concluded, to begin with, between only two powers, France and England (as the Treaty of Venice of 1455 was concluded, to begin with, just between Milan and Venice), but it provided for the adherence of all and was, in fact, directed against none. It safeguarded important Habsburg interests, and, if it stymied Leo X's aggressive plans in Italy, it reserved to him the presidency of the league, and aimed at what he declared to be his most important objectives, the liberty of the Church and the peace of Christendom. If it did little directly to advance the crusade, it left the way open for united action. It had no secret provisions.[4]

Historians who cling to the dogma that Renaissance statesmanship was always based on selfish, short-sighted ambition and always proceeded by deceit have variously described Wolsey's treaty as a mask for a new alliance with France, a mere personal coup designed to dazzle the courts of Europe and steal the initiative from Leo X, or a deliberate attempt to stifle Leo's plans for a crusade.[5] It did not seem so to Wolsey's contemporaries. The peace-loving humanists hailed the treaty as a masterpiece of constructive European statesmanship, the realization of an ancient dream by the most modern devices. They may have been sentimentalists and self-deceived. But two of the toughest-minded and most experienced working diplomats in Europe, representing the two powers most likely to be alarmed by an alliance between England and France, de Mesa for Spain and Giustinian for Venice, although at first they entertained the gravest suspicions, ended by assuring their governments that Wolsey's treaty meant exactly what it said, and that the cardinal was sincerely and entirely behind it. At the same time, Lorenzo Campeggio, the papal representative, no child in diplomacy, threw himself enthusiastically into drafting the treaty in spite of Leo X's hesitation, and announced in writing and in action his conviction of Wolsey's complete sincerity. Every surviving document seems to show that these participants were right.[6]

It is true that the Treaty of London kept only an uncertain peace in Europe, and kept it for only some thirty months. It was the prelude to a renewal of the Italian wars, on a wider scale and with stepped-up violence, a new phase of the dynastic power struggle which was to go on, broken by breathing spells, for another thirty years. But it was not conceived as a mere cynical gesture, nor did its chief founder, Thomas Wolsey, surrender the hope it embodied without fighting desperately for it, with all the resources of his diplomatic skill and his formidable character. Peace was defeated, in this case, not by the evil hearts of men, but by the defects of human institutions.

One defect was in the mechanism of the treaty. It was a treaty among equal, independent powers. It sought to bind them to resist aggression by an agreement which each was free to interpret. The language was as clear as Wolsey could make it, and in four centuries his definition of aggression has not been much improved, but no language has ever been adequate to define in advance all possible political emergencies. If it were, there would still have to be someone to judge what the facts are, and when they fit the definition. As things happened, Francis I began the war by supporting rebels in the Habsburg territory, and when those rebels were chased back across the French frontier, Francis claimed that he was the victim of aggression. For this contingency the treaty provided nothing except consultation among its signatories, exhortations to the combatants to submit to arbitration, and then eventual armed sanctions against whichever party refused to cease hostilities. There was no authority competent to declare that an act of aggression had occurred and invoke immediate penalties.

There should have been one such authority, elevated by the respect of Europe above all temporal sovereigns, the pope. But the pope was also a temporal sovereign, the prince of a second-rate Italian state, and the experience of a century had proved that most popes were quite capable of using the moral authority of St. Peter to snatch a bit of land from a neighbour, or install a relative in some petty lordship. As things turned out, Leo X valued a chance to acquire Parma, and perhaps Ferrara, above the peace of Christendom, and devoted himself more wholeheartedly to spreading the war than to stopping it.[7] That left, actually, only Wolsey to act as arbiter of Europe, only the English resident ambassadors with Charles V and Francis I as channels for diplomatic protest. Wolsey could swing the weight of England, and did at last swing it against the chief violator of the Treaty of London. But England had not strength enough nor Wolsey moral authority enough to sway the other powers. Each aligned itself as its interests or prejudices pointed. Nothing was left of the purpose of the league.

A second cause of the failure of Wolsey's league, deeper than any defect of mechanism, lay in the political structure of Europe. Organization around dynastic chieftains had divided European political space among a group of irresponsible, power-eating organizations which jostled each other prematurely, even though their internal tasks were far from complete. At the same time it opened the possibility of the coalescence of these organisms into fantastic political monsters. One such coalescence was about to be consummated. Charles of Ghent, heir to the Burgundies, lord by one title or another of most of the provinces of the Netherlands, had already, in 1518, inherited and assumed the crowns of Ferdinand and Isabella. Within a year he was to inherit also the Austrian lands and to be elected, in succession to his grandfather,

Maximilian, to the imperial dignity. The union under a single ruler of the Burgundian Netherlands, Austria, the Spains and the Holy Roman Empire gave the European power system an unmanageable rigidity.

Had a multiple balance of power been possible, the Treaty of London might conceivably have worked, but the vast extent of the Habsburg domains operated to divide Europe into two opposing camps. It is axiomatic that the more complete any such alignment becomes, the harder it is to keep the peace. As sides are chosen up, each feels more menaced by the other, and feels also an increasing compulsion to strike before the powerful foe becomes more powerful still. Any power system dominated by two competing groups is radically unstable. Even had Wolsey and his master not been drawn by old sentiments, by diplomatic pressures, by personal interests towards the greater mass, the Habsburg empire, they could not have imposed peace on Europe. In June 1522, in conformity with his obligations under the Treaty of London, when the Turks, whom that treaty was supposed to stop, had been for a year in Belgrade and were hammering at the walls of Rhodes, Henry VIII, by his herald, declared war on the king of France.[8]

'So began one of the most purposeless and injurious contests in which England [or Europe] was ever engaged . . . a war of fruitless raids and ravages, framed upon a scheme as disturbing to the balance of power in the west as it was fatal to the interests of Christendom in the east.'[9] And so ended Wolsey's scheme of European peace, the last great public gesture towards the unity of Latin Christendom. Before the guns were silent again the Turks had overrun Hungary, and half the Teutonic north was no longer Catholic.

For the student of diplomatic institutions, the brief history of the Treaty of London has a further somewhat melancholy interest. The origins of resident embassies had been in the Italian power struggle as the liaison agents and spies of competing despots. But with the generalization of the system, after Lodi, there had been some expectation that residents would serve instead the older mission of the ambassador, peace. From time to time in the following forty years they had actually done so, and Wolsey seems to have hoped that the function first suggested in Italy might be realized at last, and resident ambassadors become the watchmen and guardians of peace, the liaison agents of union. For that reason, not because he expected Francis I to be his ally in war, he had sent the first English resident ambassador to France. No one again for a long time would entertain so optimistic a view of the resident's function.

CHAPTER XVIII

FRENCH DIPLOMACY AND THE
BREAKING-UP OF CHRISTENDOM

As the approaching duel between Valois and Habsburg, between Francis I and Charles V, focused the attention of Europe, the normal machinery of diplomatic intercourse yielded to the personal diplomacy of sovereigns. Wolsey's last efforts to save his peace were punctuated by interviews between his master and each of the rival sovereigns. The meeting at the Field of Cloth of Gold of Henry VIII and Francis I was personal diplomacy at its most pompous and spectacular. The two interviews between Henry VIII and Charles V which bracketed and nullified the Anglo-French encounter were personal diplomacy at, perhaps, its most effective. But all three conferences suffered from the drawbacks notoriously incident to personal diplomacy in the Renaissance and perhaps at other periods. It is a fair question which finally did more to embroil and embitter international relations, the Tudor-Valois meeting which was such an immediate and resounding failure, or the Tudor-Habsburg ones which seemed for a while to have been (from the Habsburg point of view, anyway) such a complete success.

Some part of the Habsburg success was due to better diplomatic liaisons, and particularly to the skill and experience of the Spanish resident ambassador in England, Bernardino de Mesa, who handled the English end of Charles V's arrangements with Wolsey. But if anyone suggested as much at the French court there was no response. In that year, 1520, Francis I had only two resident embassies to serve him, those at Rome and Venice. He was slow to establish others and did so only as repeated reverses taught him the folly of neglecting any usable weapon.

French diplomacy outside Italy in 1520 had only one focus of activity, activity which was the result of a victorious battle almost as costly as a defeat. After he had tested their steadiness at Marignano in 1515, Francis I was anxious to have the Swiss infantry on his side next time. By November 1516 his ambassadors had concluded with the Swiss the 'perpetual peace of Freiburg' which laid the basis of all Franco-Swiss relations for a long time, but although the French king offered a handsome price, he did not get the rest of what he wanted without another five full years of haggling. Even by the treaty of December 1521 the Swiss did not become the formal allies of France. But thereafter a Swiss contingent served regularly with the French army, adding to their magnificent heavy cavalry an equally formidable infantry, and denying to their enemies the use of the best mercenaries in Europe.

Such advantages were worth unprecedented efforts to win and continuous vigilance to keep. Between March 1515 and December 1521 nearly fifty embassies went from France to Switzerland, a number of them with three or more accredited ambassadors, so that, although some negotiators were employed practically continuously on Swiss affairs, altogether upwards of forty different persons represented Francis I in Switzerland on at least one embassy. Among these ambassadors there were two who look as if they were meant to be residents. Not long after his first treaty with the Swiss Francis I sent the Seigneur du Savonnières to the league 'to be and reside with them in order to maintain their alliance, friendship and confederation'. Savonnières withdrew in January 1517, and only returned with fresh credentials in August 1518. But the language of his credentials and instructions could not put more clearly the main reason for establishing a resident embassy in this transitional period, and during his total of about thirty-three months in Switzerland he seems to have performed all a resident's normal function. So did Antoine de Lamet during a nearly continuous period from November 1520 to August 1522, though he also had two successive sets of credentials. The first unmistakable resident, however, was the Seigneur de Boisrigaut, sent specifically in that capacity in November 1522. He remained at his post for nearly twenty-two years. After him the series of French resident ambassadors to the Swiss cantons is continuous.

During all this time Francis had been negotiating with the smaller eastern league of the Rhaetian Alps, the Graubunden, or Grisons which, though in uneasy alliance with the western league of the Twelve Cantons, often pursued an independent policy. It underlines the importance which the French attached to the Swiss that, in the anxious months after Pavia, Geoffroy de Grangis, on special mission to the Grisons, was ordered to remain as resident. Thereafter that resident embassy was also continuous.

Both residents, the one at Solothurn to the Twelve Cantons and the one at Chur to the Grisons, had similar missions, simpler and less changing than those of any other diplomats of their century. They had to raise men for the French army, through regular cantonal levies when they could, or, if necessary, by illegal recruitment. They had to transmit the annual payments to the cantons or, increasingly, excuses for non-payment. They were expected to report what they heard of troop movements through the Alpine passes, and to prevent enemies from hiring Switzers. Other diplomatic business the French normally confided to special envoys. The residents were simply the liaison officers of a quasi-alliance. It was a curiously one-sided connection. The cantons maintained that although they permitted the French king to hire their troops, they, themselves, were neutral, a contention which no one cared to contradict since wars with the Swiss did not pay. To emphasize their neutrality, the Swiss displayed an ostentatious lack of interest in French political objectives and sent, for a long time, no resident ambassadors to France.[1]

Events soon proved to Francis I that diplomatic liaisons with Switzerland and Venice were not enough. On February 24th, 1525, he fought at Pavia, and all was lost save honour. In sulky captivity at Madrid he signed a humiliating treaty of peace, and on March 17th, 1526, having pledged his royal word to its observance, he regained French soil, rejoicing that he had so far saved a credit exchangeable against more tangible commodities. Two months later, the League of Cognac was announced, an alliance of France with practically all the Italian states, headed by the pope, for the repudiation of the Treaty of Madrid. The league was buttressed on one side by an alliance with England, on the other by an understanding with the Turk.

The League of Cognac is one of those points in sixteenth-century diplomatic history at which the 'balance of power' is said to have been invented, the point at which 'national interest replaced dynastic interests as the main motive of European politics'. Nobody noticed it at the time. Pope Clement VII, supported, for odd reasons, by Henry VIII, continued to think about a balance in Italy. Francis I, willing to go to any lengths to avenge his defeat and escape its consequences, continued to strive for Milan and Naples and to hang on to every acre of his domain, no matter how acquired. Charles V still clung to Flanders, where he was born, to Navarre and Naples which his grandfather, Ferdinand, had stolen, and to his claim on the duchy of Burgundy which had been in his grandmother Mary's family for four generations. Dynastic politics went on as usual.

Actually the Italian aspect of the League of Cognac, which gave it its specious appearance of modernity, belonged to the irrevocable past. It was only another effort of the Italians to escape one foreign master by calling in another. But the general scheme of 1526 did point to the future. As the scales inclined to-wards the Habsburgs, the Valois were destined to contribute to the breaking-up of Christendom by relying more and more on alliance with heretics and with the Turk.

When Louise of Savoy, queen dowager of France, sent Gian Giacomo Passano to England during her son's captivity, she could have had no notion that she was opening negotiations with future heretics. Wolsey had become impatient with the imperial alliance, and only the news of Pavia had kept him from persuading Henry VIII to change sides. Louise of Savoy probably relied on papal influence with Wolsey, on Henry VIII's exasperation at the emperor, and on a conviction, deep-seated among the French, that the English alliance could be bought whenever it was worth the money. But it was not long before the French diplomats learned, to their delight, that Henry VIII meant to cast off the wife to whom he had been married for eighteen years. Since that wife, Catherine of Aragon, was the emperor's aunt, Charles V's resentment would leave the English no alternative to a French alliance. Within a few years England had broken with Rome also and faced chastisement whenever the emperor and the Most Christian king could be persuaded to unite, so that England was more than ever dependent on France.[2] Francis I paltered with the situation, and even made some half-hearted attempts to reconcile Henry VIII to Rome, but his ambassador knew that the growing Protestant faction in England were the natural allies of French diplomacy. It was only when England swung back towards Catholicism that France was in danger of a renewal of the old Anglo-Burgundian-Spanish alliance.

Whether the breach over Catherine of Aragon seemed a surer

basis of friendship than the Treaty of Westminster, or whether the French had learned more about the uses of the new diplomacy, this time they established a resident embassy in England. On his first mission, Passano necessarily lacked full status. It was possible for Wolsey to assure the Spanish ambassador that this Genoese banker was merely the queen dowager's personal man of business. Nevertheless Passano did reside in England for two years, armed with diplomatic credentials and performing the usual functions of a resident. After him the sequence of French residents is unmistakable. [3]

In the same years events in Germany were preparing another group of French allies. With the suppression of the peasants' revolt, leadership in the religious revolution passed from the preachers to the princes, and the attitude of these latter grew so defiant that the imperial recess of Speyer (July 1526) hastily declared that each prince should so live 'that he might answer to God and the emperor'. The principle of the political and religious fragmentation of Germany, the principle which was to be proclaimed at Augsburg in 1555 and to triumph at Westphalia in 1648, had been announced. Thenceforward there was always a group of German princes determined that, however they might answer to God for their religious beliefs, they would answer to the emperor only sword in hand. With these possible allies Francis I preferred to deal through special emissaries and half-official agents rather than take the grave step of accrediting ambassadors to them; nevertheless French influence waxed among the Protestant princes of the empire. [4]

To win another ally Francis I needed neither religious upheavals nor diplomatic finesse. The Turk was always there. [5] Francis had only to overcome his youthful prejudice against alliance with the infidel. In his first year as king he had assured the pope that he was eager to spend in a crusade his gold, his credit and his life. But since that time, though Suleiman the Lawgiver had taken Belgrade and Rhodes, opening the way into Hungary and the Mediterranean, Francis had not stirred. Then from his prison in Madrid, Francis sent a cry for help to Istanbul. The answer was prompt. 'Be not dismayed in your captivity,' the sultan wrote, '. . . Your appeal has been heard at the steps of our throne . . . Night and day our horse is saddled and our sabre girt. . . .'

With Suleiman action was almost as prompt as words. The Turkish victory at Mohacs was the answer to Pavia.

The year 1526 saw the future of French diplomacy sketched, but the sketch was so smudged and spoiled by the careless artist that most of the work had to be done again. No coalition war was ever worse mishandled, mostly through the slackness of the king of France. His Italian allies melted away in panic, and the one resident ambassador he sent to the last Florentine republic proved an inadequate substitute for the army lost around Naples. The Turks frightened Germany into temporary quiescence, and the Ladies' Peace (1529) which barely included Henry VIII, and was explicitly aimed against Suleiman, left both those sovereigns angry and suspicious. But the heretics and the pope, the Commanders of the Faithful on the Bosporus and the Defender of the Faith on the Thames (who was more and more inclined to think of himself as a new Commander of the Faithful), had no one to turn to for support against the growing power of the emperor except the king of France. It was possible to redraw the lines.

In the process French diplomacy really came of age. Its central organization, long leaving much to be desired, was hardly as efficient as the best fifteenth-century Italian models until it was overhauled by Richelieu. But, after 1529, we hear more often of the *Conseil des affaires* as a regularly functioning body in charge of foreign policy, and of secretaries with competence in special areas. At the same time, one is conscious of a more professional tone in the diplomatic service. In the long (and doubtless incomplete) list of French resident and special ambassadors in the reign of Francis I, some names recur with striking frequency. Of these, a few are always connected with negotiations with a particular power. They are real specialists, as Antonio Rincon was for Turkish, and Boisrigaut was for Swiss affairs. In addition, perhaps a score of persons served for at least a decade on resident or special missions, and about as many more were employed frequently, though less continuously, on diplomatic business. Of this inner group a good many had held some junior post abroad before they were entrusted with larger responsibilities. So, particularly as the diplomatic activity of the reign intensified after 1529, France began to develop an experienced corps of supple negotiators and trained observers who, whatever their social class, legists, clerics, or *noblesse d'épée*, may fairly be called courtiers, if not diplomats, *de carrière*.

The regrouping of diplomatic forces after the Ladies' Peace took seven years. As an immediate consequence of the peace, an ambassador was sent as resident to amuse and observe the emperor with, attached to his staff, aides who could talk confidentially to the German princes, and a secretary who knew Spanish. At the same time another went to reside at the court of Margaret of Austria, regent of the Netherlands, with secret instructions about the princes of the Burgundian circle and the western Rhineland. The ambassadors at these posts helped the residents in Switzerland and at Venice keep track of German affairs, while confidential agents, either from their embassies or straight from France, saw to it that very little happened in Germany in which French intrigue did not have a finger.

In the next decade the liaison with the Lutherans found a more solid base. In 1536 the Lutheran revolution in Denmark was confirmed and the Scandinavian north began to seem a possible make-weight against the Habsburgs. In 1541 Francis sent to Denmark and Sweden, with profuse assurances of friendship, Christophe Richer, the first French ambassador publicly accredited to an avowedly Lutheran sovereign. In the next seven years diplomatic relations between Denmark and France were virtually continuous, and the value of Denmark for contacts with the princes and cities of northern Germany began to be appreciated. After Charles V's triumph at Mühlberg had emphasized this value, Charles de Danzay arrived at Copenhagen in 1548 with credentials as resident. For forty years thereafter, Danzay, a professing Calvinist, served as the representative of the Valois, not only to Denmark but to Sweden and all the Baltic powers, journeying as far as Dresden and Cracow, labouring indefatigably for the great northern coalition which, if it was never achieved, recurrently threatened and harassed the Habsburg power.[6]

In Italy, the French embassies at Venice and Rome were reorganized and greatly strengthened after 1526, and though only one other resident embassy was established and that for only a brief period, the key points were so well manned, and French special envoys and unofficial agents were so active, that French policy makers no longer had to rely, as in the first quarter of the century they had often done, on the estimates provided by Italian diplomats, pensioners and exiles. Meanwhile on the western flank of the emperor's Iberian domains Francis had set up another listening post, a resident embassy at Lisbon.

There remained one major power, the Turk. A disciplined, mobile army, a new, dashing navy made the Ottomans one of the chief factors in any military calculation. The lines of their advance into Europe, south and west from the Gulf of Corinth, north and west from Belgrade or the Iron Gate, made them the natural enemies of the Habsburgs both in the Mediterranean and in the Danubian Plain. And Suleiman the Lawgiver was sufficiently aware of the value of the French diversion on his enemies' flank and rear, and sufficiently eager for a rôle in European politics, to overlook the French king's shabby conduct in 1529. Nevertheless, although the Turks behaved, on the whole, with singular frankness and generosity, repeatedly repelling Habsburg offers, and marking their preference for a French alliance, it was not until 1536, after long, cautious negotiation, that Jean de la Forest signed the vital treaty[7] and remained, in consequence of its provisions, as the first French resident ambassador at the Sublime Porte.

The delay may have been occasioned in part by fear of shocking what was left of the conscience of Christendom, and that fear may have affected the public clauses of the treaty. Francis I wanted a resident ambassador in Constantinople. But in an age when residents were still regarded, at least nominally and popularly, as the agents and symbols of an alliance, only one Western diplomat resided with the Turk, the Venetian *baillo*. His excuse for doing so was the special legal and commercial rights which the Venetian merchant community enjoyed, including the right to be judged by their own laws in a court over which the *baillo* presided. In effect, what the Franco-Turkish treaty of 1536 did was to grant French subjects throughout the domains of the Grand Turk privileges similar to those of the Venetians. Actually they were given greater privileges, exemptions from taxes and dues usually levied on foreigners, and other concessions designed to encourage commerce. But the important clause was the right of French subjects to be judged in French consular courts.

The treaty laid the basis for Franco-Turkish relations for the next three centuries, and for French commercial and cultural preponderance in the Levant. It provided the model for the treaties by which, in the coming era of commercial expansion, European states would wrest from Asiatics the right of exterritoriality for their nationals. But all that lay in the unforeseen future. What Francis wanted and Suleiman was willing to concede was a pretext for maintaining a resident ambassador at the Sublime Porte as the liaison officer of a military alliance. For the next twenty years this was really the chief function of the French residents at Constantinople. It was only as the unbroken series of ambassadors extended into the second half of the sixteenth century and beyond, that what had begun as a pretext became, in fact, the principal business of the embassy. Meanwhile, for a long time, all diplomatic representation at the Sublime Porte was unilateral. The sultans received resident ambassadors but sent none.

French diplomacy never quite achieved the full combination against the Habsburgs at which its network of embassies aimed. England, Denmark, the Lutheran princes, Venice, the minor Italian states, the Pope, the Turk — there were too many opportunities for something to slip. England, for instance, was rescued from its dependence on the French by the timely death of Catherine of Aragon, just before Francis I, his alliance with the Turks secured, began to invade Savoy in 1536. The Italian powers, the pope included, became more and more wary of offending the powerful emperor. But the Turk was generally reliable and once, at least, Francis's heir, Henry II, was able to use the Lutheran princes with brief but deadly effect. Always, however, there was at least a hope of combining most, if not all, of these tricky elements, and French diplomats became adept at the jugglery required of them, sharpening their wits and blunting their consciences as they pried into each widening crack in the structure of medieval Christendom. The decline of the Valois monarchy and the wars of religion interrupted the French diplomatic counter-offensive but did not end it. The policy which Francis I initiated was still, a century later, the policy of Richelieu and Mazarin.

CHAPTER XIX

THE HABSBURG SYSTEM

THE problem of the lesser power caught in the arena of the dynastic duel was to preserve some measures of independence, some effective freedom of action. Among the secular states of Italy, only Venice achieved much success, in part, because of the efficiency of the Venetian resident ambassadors, but in large part, certainly, because, as the shadow of the emperor lengthened over the peninsula, Venice renounced its ambitions and looked simply to its safety. The two other large states of northern Italy both lost their independence, Milan to the emperor and Savoy to the French. In the case of Savoy at least, the backwardness of Savoyard diplomacy, and the consequent lack of political information at a vital moment, must bear part of the blame. Naples, after 1529, was as solidly under Spanish rule as Sicily, and the smaller Italian states tended increasingly to become mere Habsburg satellites, though two of them, Genoa and Florence, tried to maintain diplomatic relations with both sides and so edge back towards a position of neutrality.[1]

Even the papacy found its freedom of diplomatic manœuvre more and more hobbled by the growth of the emperor's power in Italy and the spread of heresy in northern Europe. Five centuries of Guelph tradition dictated opposition to an overweening emperor. But every check to Charles V was a blow to the flagging forces of Catholicism beyond the Alps. Consequently papal diplomacy after 1529 swung between subservience to Charles V and bitter, but usually secret, intrigue against him. For the temporal sovereigns of the papal states, genuine neutrality was as difficult as effective war.

Outside Italy one power used the new diplomacy simply to keep out of Europe's squabbles. Portugal, in the reign of Emmanuel the Fortunate, had reaped the fruit of a century of effort, and found itself lord of the commerce, navigation and discovery of half the globe. By virtue of the wealth of the East piled annually on the quays of Lisbon, Portugal was almost a major power. By the same token, she was involved in diplomatic difficulties pretty much all over western Europe. Foreign interlopers paid as little attention to the papal demarcation line of 1493 as they had paid to previous bulls granting Portugal exclusive rights south of Cape Bojador. Adventurers, mostly French, infested the West African coast, and traded for dye-woods along the bulge of Brazil. Commercial interests at Antwerp raised constant problems with the Netherlands. The exact position of the line of demarcation was a fertile source of wrangles with Spain. Nevertheless Portugal, trying only to avoid European quarrels, got along until 1522, usually without any resident diplomats abroad. At Rome, the king of Portugal maintained a proctor (not always of ambassadorial rank), and at Antwerp the Portuguese royal 'factor' acted as the government agent for the sale of spices on the *bourse*, as the consul of the Portuguese nation in the city, and as the representative of the Portuguese crown whenever it had a communication to make to the ruler of the Netherlands.

Apparently simultaneous action by Francis I and Charles V in 1521, at the beginning of their long duel, brought Portugal into the network of the new diplomacy. Their steps were a tribute, perhaps, to the king of Portugal's reputation for limitless wealth (a much exaggerated reputation), and a testimony to the general belief in the interchangeability of cash and military might. We hear of French and Spanish resident ambassadors at Lisbon first in the early months of John III's reign, and it is a plausible conjecture that both arrived as members of the embassies of ceremony sent at John's accession, and remained as residents to watch each other and compete for the Portuguese alliance.[2] Neither got it. Perhaps it was to emphasize Portuguese neutrality that John III ordered a special ambassador, who had already gone to France early in 1522 with another protest about French poaching in West Africa, to remain there as resident, and about the same time accredited a resident to Charles V. Thereafter both these embassies were continuous until 1580.[3] Besides marking Portuguese neutrality towards the two great rival dynasties, the embassies in France and Spain were useful to keep watch over the two powers that most seriously threatened Portugal's precious commercial monopolies. These two posts and one at Rome were the only resident embassies Portugal established, and their tenants were repeatedly enjoined to demonstrate by their actions the independence and impartiality of their master.

In the long run it was a task beyond the powers of diplomacy. The French were insolently negligent of Portuguese claims in Brazil and West Africa; their interloping was only checked by a combination of force on the high seas, and judicious bribery in France. The Castilians, becoming welded by the Italian wars into a first-rate military power, were aligned along Portugal's untenable land frontier. The emperor was the champion of Catholic orthodoxy in Europe and Portugal was a sincerely Catholic power. Reluctantly, but inevitably, Portugal gravitated into the Habsburg sphere of influence. Even the greatest of the lesser powers found it increasingly difficult not to be drawn into the orbit of one or the other of the dynastic giants. If, in the crucial years of the Henrician reformation, England was able to preserve a certain freedom of action it was only at the price of considerable concessions to French diplomacy, and only because Francis I had no intention of helping destroy a possible ally merely to gratify his rival.

Conscious of dependence, and chafing under it, Henry VIII in the mid 1530s began seeking in Germany some compensation for the influence he had lost by his virtual exclusion from Italian politics. The minister of that policy, perhaps its initiator, was Henry VIII's able secretary, Thomas Cromwell. Because his master could never renounce the hope of spectacular successes, Cromwell's combinations were all too ambitious. He was driven to over-reach himself, like a bold speculator trying to make cleverness and daring do the work of solid resources. His actual intrigues with the Schmalkaldic League, with the Lubeckers, with Cleves all went awry, and the last failure ended his influence and his life. Nevertheless, the general policy sketched by Cromwell was the soundest possible for the England of his day: no serious foreign commitments, and the cultivation of enough nuisance value on the continent to keep the greater powers at a respectful distance. That had been Henry VII's way. And as the politics of the century were developing, the only areas in which England could develop a nuisance value on the continent were the Protestant lands of northern Europe. Elizabeth I was to reach much the same conclusion.

Under Cromwell, English diplomats first began to learn to find their way through the morass of German politics. No permanent embassy with any of the Lutheran powers was established or even projected. But Cromwell's semi-official agent, Christopher Mont, from his base at Strasbourg, began to build up a system of spies, informants and diplomatic contacts which kept the English government admirably abreast of German affairs as late as the regime of the Protector Somerset. Though Mont's work bore no immediate fruit, under Elizabeth he and his friends were again to prove useful.[4]

For the time, however, England followed another and less profitable course. After Cromwell's fall Henry VIII chose to ally himself with the emperor and indulge in a last, unprofitable invasion of France. Under Edward VI and Mary, weakened by religious discord and an uncertain succession to the crown, the realm oscillated between French and imperial influence, eyed greedily by both great powers as a desirable pawn and eventual prey.

In one way or another the major concern of all European diplomacy in the decades after 1525 was the Habsburg empire. Their relations with the emperor, the amount of attraction or repulsion which his sprawling power exerted on each state, really determined their respective position in the European system. And the weight of imperial power in European affairs was only the more impressive because of the relative quiescence of imperial diplomacy.

Unlike his great antagonist Francis I, Charles V, throughout the dynastic duel, scarcely attempted to expand the circle of his diplomatic contacts. He had inherited the admirable Spanish network set up by Ferdinand of Aragon, and except for a resident embassy at Lisbon, an obvious Spanish need, and one or two agents in northern Italy, he established no new posts. In a sense the Spanish network contracted, since the emperor's representatives with his brother Ferdinand, in Austria, and with his aunt Margaret and sister Mary, successively his regents in the Netherlands, were not technically resident ambassadors. Nor did Charles ever try to widen the scope of his diplomatic influence by sending residents to Scotland, Sweden, Poland, or (as was once suggested) Persia.

In part that may have been a realistic judgment that these peripheral powers lay outside the range of effective, continuous diplomatic action. But mainly Charles's failure to imitate Francis I arose from a difference in strategy. French policy was obliged to be dynamic, divisive, disintegrating. The French monarchy could profit from the power struggle only by allying itself with those forces, within and without Charles's dominions, hostile to the medieval world. Imperial policy, on the other hand, was essentially static, defensive, conservative. Its natural allies were the universal church and the feudal spirit, just as those of France were schism and secularism and nascent nationalism. Particularly after 1529 the emperor's greatest asset was the force of inertia, the confidence that, if the status quo could be preserved, the mere mass of the Habsburg possessions would ultimately draw the other powers into satellite orbits, and re-unify Christendom under its traditional overlord.

Neither Charles nor his advisers would have put the case in quite those terms,. What they knew was that the imperial interests lay not in widening, but in limiting and separating the areas of conflict. If the emperor could only put off enough of his difficulties so that he could deal with them one at a time, he might find the strength to master them. The tactical rôle of Charles V's diplomacy was therefore reduced to fighting delaying actions, keeping existing contacts, winning time. Its chief organizational task was to increase the efficiency of a service already as distinguished in European diplomacy as the Spanish infantry was on the battle-field, and to adapt its structure to the more complicated relations of a polyglot empire.[5]

Even in the first years of his reign, when so much was going so badly, the Spanish ambassadors whom he inherited from Ferdinand served Charles well. One of the earliest lessons of his political education must have been the advantages to be derived from accurate political information and from skilful diplomatic pressures applied at crucial points. At Rome and Venice the Spanish ambassadors continued to function as they had functioned under his grandfather, supplying the arguments which kept the Italians from slipping in a body into the French camp. Meanwhile in England, without the skilfully co-ordinated manœuvres of his ambassador Bernardino de Mesa, and his aunt, the queen of England (his unofficial ambassador as she had been Ferdinand's), Charles would have lost the crucial support of Henry VIII.

That was in the days when Charles was still under the tutelage of the provincial-minded Burgundian Chièvres, and his policy was still shapeless. During Charles's long second sòjourn in Spain, when his chief minister was the Piedmontese, Mercurino da Gattinara, who thought like a European and had some experience of the business-like methods of Italian diplomacy, the lesson was applied. Between 1522 and 1529 the emperor's diplomatic service took essentially the form it was to retain throughout his reign. Under Gattinara, the imperial chancellery began to discharge most of the functions of an organized foreign office and, though the emperor often made his own political decisions, all the routine work passed through Gattinara's hands.

After Gattinara's death, Charles V never had another foreign minister of equal authority. Nicholas Perrenot de Granvelle, a native of Franche-Comté, succeeded Gattinara in the main direction of foreign affairs, but Charles, who was beginning to apply the principle he transmitted to his son of dividing his ministers in order to rule over them, gave Granvelle a coadjutor and, in some sense, a rival. The Andalusian, Francisco de los Cobos, became Charles's secretary for Spanish business and chief financial adviser, and the important affairs of Spain, Italy and the Indies channelled through Cobos. After 1530 the emperor had, in effect, two foreign ministers, one for Spain and one for the empire.

In the foreign service the division had been foreshadowed under Gattinara. From first to last all Charles's ambassadors in Italy, not only the minor diplomats in Savoy and Genoa and Milan, but the residents in Venice and the heads of the key embassy at Rome, were Spaniards, in recognition of a preponderant interest. On the other hand, after 1526, the Imperial ambassadors in France were always Burgundians, either Netherlanders like Louis de Praet and Cornelis Schepper, or Franche-Comtois, mostly relatives and clients of Granvelle's, like Bonvalot, St. Mauris and Simon Renard. The common language may be a sufficient explanation for this choice, but it seemed also to reflect (or could the linguistic accident have in part produced?) a fundamental Burgundian bias in Charles's French policy. In French affairs he put the interests of his native Burgundian lands always first, and his rivalry with the Valois had always something of the intimate bitterness of a family quarrel.

Except for Portugal, where, of course, he was represented by a Spaniard, Charles had only one other resident embassy to fill, England, but that was a post of the utmost importance and, as it proved, of the utmost difficulty. Both his Spanish and his Burgundian realms were bound to England by old and strong sentimental and commercial ties. If the principal English trade was with the Netherlands, the main family connection and diplomatic alliance was with Spain. But from the emperor's point of view, the most important point was England's strategic position. Communications between the two chief centres of his power lay at the mercy of the lord of the Channel. In any war with France an alliance with England made an offensive across the Somme relatively easy, while English hostility endangered the Netherlands. An alliance with England was the strongest card the emperor could hold.

In the first years of his reign, the Spanish resident, Bernardino de Mesa, bishop of Elne, an appointee of Ferdinand of Aragon's, had done all that an ambassador could be expected to do in securing an English alliance. After it was signed and sealed, however, Charles replaced de Mesa with Louis de Praet, on the reasonable assumption that a young man, a soldier, a member of the higher Burgundian nobility, would prove more satisfactory than an elderly Spanish bishop as liaison officer for a joint invasion of northern France. The choice proved unfortunate. De Praet had not the patience to wait out a war which went slowly and badly, nor the tact to get on with Wolsey. His embassy ended in something dangerously like a breach of diplomatic relations and, though Wolsey himself engineered the breach by his high-handed seizure of de Praet's dispatches, the cardinal would scarcely have acted as he did without extreme provocation. [6]

De Praet's tardy replacement was a Spanish nobleman, Don Iñigo de Mendoza, the interval having been filled by special envoys from the Netherlands, whose exclusive concern for the economic interests of the Low Countries had done little to advance the emperor's wider dynastic and political schemes. Since Henry and Wolsey had been irritated by Flemish commercial greed and

187

military sluggishness, Charles may have thought that they would receive a Spaniard more favourably than a Burgundian. He may have hoped also that one of her own countrymen would be more likely to stir to action the person who had always been his most potent ally at the English court, his aunt, Catherine of Aragon.[7] But Mendoza had scarcely settled into his embassy before he learned of Henry's plans for a divorce. Not only was Catherine's aid denied Mendoza, but the Spaniard's indignation at the treatment of Isabella's daughter made him worse than useless for a conciliatory mission. Before long he was quite cut off from the English court, and bombarding his master with wild schemes for invasions and rebellions.

A Spaniard and a Burgundian having both failed at the key post, Gattinara found a characteristic solution. Eustache Chapuys, who like Gattinara himself came from outside the emperor's hereditary lands, was sent to England in 1529 as resident and remained there, with two short intervals, for nearly sixteen years. Chapuys was a Savoyard without complicating regional attachments, a tough careerist who could be trusted, Gattinara thought, not to let sentiment interfere with his mission. That mission was to get an English alliance if possible; if not, to ensure English neutrality.

Unless Charles was willing to give way on the question of the queen's divorce, however, Chapuys had an almost impossible task, and Charles would not give way. In consequence, before he had been two years in England, the divorce had come to seem to Chapuys the crucial question, and so completely insoluble by diplomacy alone that he was urging embargoes, feudal rebellions and invasions with all Mendoza's vehemence. Nevertheless Charles did not relieve him and, after Queen Catherine's death, Chapuys justified Gattinara's choice and the emperor's confidence by playing a leading rôle in the negotiation of the renewed Anglo-Imperial alliance, and in the tricky diplomacy which followed.[8] Next to Gattinara himself, Chapuys offers perhaps the best example of the kind of cosmopolitan careerist who made ideal public servants for Charles V's polyglot empire.

Although Spaniards were employed on special missions in England, during Chapuys's embassy and after it, his successors in office until 1556 were all Burgundians. Only one of them, the last, was of more than moderate ability, but the exception, Simon Renard,[9] had one of the keenest and most sensitive minds in the imperial service, and circumstances gave him the opportunity for a triumph even more considerable than Chapuys's. Chapuys had merely contributed to the emperor's normal defensive policy. He had helped provide the diversion which distracted the French while Charles dealt with the Lutherans. But in the static, holding tactics of imperial diplomacy there was one possibility for gaining new ground, a further expansion of the Habsburg domains by marriage.

Europe offered two tempting alternatives, Portugal and England. Forced to choose in 1526, Charles had chosen Portugal, marrying his cousin Isabella, the eldest daughter of Emmanuel the Fortunate. Later he consolidated the position by marrying his son Philip to another Portuguese princess. But Charles had never given up hope of England. By 1553 Philip was a widower, and only the life of a sickly boy stood between Catherine of Aragon's daughter Mary, and the crown. Mary, at thirty-seven, was still unmarried. In the spring of 1553 word reached Brussels that Mary's half-brother, Edward VI, was not expected to survive the summer, and that the Duke of Northumberland was plotting to alter the lawful succession. Like a general ordering up his heaviest artillery at a critical moment, Charles sent Simon Renard to England.

With Renard's help, but mostly by dint of her own stubborn courage and her people's love, Mary broke Northumberland's rebellion with its French backing, and was duly crowned. In another three months, partly by Simon Renard's shrewdness, but mostly by Mary's own infatuation, the queen of England was pledged to marry Philip of Spain. Their eldest son was to inherit England and the Netherlands and, should the widowed Philip's son, Don Carlos, predecease his father, leaving no male heir, all the dominions of Spain as well. Meanwhile, as long as Mary lived, England would surely be drawn back to the imperial alliance. Charles had won a victory which compensated for his defeat at the hands of the French and Lutheran princes in 1551, and, if Charles's dynastic plans worked out, the iron ring would be forged tighter than ever around France.

This time, however, the magic formula, *tu felix Austria, nube,* failed. Mary bore no child. Even if she had done so, one may doubt whether the dynastic union would have succeeded. A new force was at work in Europe stronger than the old diplomacy of family alliance. Little as they approved the Protestantism of Northumberland and his supporters, and sharp as was their temporary defeat, Henry II and his ambassador Noailles, when they backed the Dudley conspiracy were unconsciously backing the future. Religious cleavages, sharpening national differences, were to make such hodge-podge agglomerations as Charles V's empire henceforth impossible. The European politics of the next half-century were to be determined more by religious than by dynastic issues.

CHAPTER XX

THE WARS OF RELIGION

CONSCIOUSNESS of the impending religious crisis may have hastened the Peace of Cateau-Cambrésis which ended the Habsburg-Valois wars in 1559. But peace was overdue anyway. The dynastic duel had ended in exhaustion and apparent stalemate. On the whole Spain had won, but Spain, not the universal Habsburg monarchy which for a time seemed to threaten Europe. Charles V resigned to his son, along with the crowns of the Spains and the vast Spanish dominions overseas, Naples, Milan and the Netherlands, so that Philip II, even without the treasure from the New World, was the most powerful king in Europe. But England had escaped the dynastic net. And Charles had failed to make his son emperor. That ghostly title passed, along with Austria, Bohemia and what was left of Hungary, to the junior branch of the Habsburgs. The empire of Charles V was never to be reunited. Meanwhile, on the surface, France had not come badly out of the long duel. The ancient realm remained intact, augmented even by the conquests of Calais, Metz, Toul and Verdun, acquisitions strategically more sensible than Naples or Milan would have been. France remained the compact centre of Europe and its greatest single state.

To the diplomats threshing out a European settlement at the bishop's château near Cambrai in February and March of 1559 it may have seemed that this time there could be a long peace. The territorial arrangements were sensible, and no large outstanding claims were left unadjudicated. If war was impossible without money (and in the sixteenth century this was accepted as an axiom), there was further hope in the circumstance that the three major combatants, Spain, France and England, were all bankrupt or virtually so. There was hope, too, in the demonstration, proved over and over again for forty years, that France could neither conquer Italy nor be conquered by any coalition that could be brought against her. The independence of Savoy, again a buffer state, of England, clear of entanglements under a new queen, and of the Empire, no longer ruled from Spain, offered the possibility of freer diplomatic manœuvre. A stalemate in the power struggle, and a multiplicity of interests instead of just two grand alliances — under such conditions diplomacy might have its chance.

It may have seemed to increase the hope of peace that the two principal rulers of Europe, Henry II of France and Philip II of Spain, were agreed in detesting the heresies which had grown up during their fathers' quarrels, and that each was determined to put down religious differences in his own dominions, at no matter what cost in his subjects' blood. Unity of belief did not, of course, guarantee peace in Christendom, but it was well known that religious disunity was the first step to revolution and the overthrow of the social order. The feeling of both monarchs that the religious radicals were a common enemy more dangerous than any dynastic antagonist sealed between them the tacit promise that neither would attack the other until the embers of internal revolt were trodden out.

After Cateau-Cambrésis well-informed diplomats probably looked forward not only to an interval of peace but to an eventual restoration of the religious unity of Christendom. History had proved more than once that rigorous and systematic suppression could drive religious protest below the threshold of social consciousness, and therefore below the political danger point. The Spanish and the papal Inquisitions were saving orthodoxy in Spain and Italy. Prompt action might still save it in the Low Countries and France. Temporarily, parts of Germany were lost, but Lutheranism depended on the princes, and once they were deprived of outside support, it seemed likely that a dozen or so petty dynasts would yield to a combination of persuasion and force. Few of the diplomats at Cateau-Cambrésis, or at the last session of Trent three years later, can have imagined that there was any power in Europe strong enough to resist for long the combination of persuasion and compulsion which the re-awakened Church and the reconciled Habsburg and Valois dynasties could bring to bear.

Events proved otherwise. The lines of force were shifting, on the map and in the hearts of men. Already the centre of political gravity was moving from the shores of the Mediterranean to the shores of the North Sea and the English Channel. Already, from its stronghold in a little Alpine city-republic, a new doctrine was spreading which did not need the help of princes to cross frontiers and root itself in disciplined cells from Poland to Navarre, and from Hungary to Scotland. Under the leadership of John Calvin, the militants of the religious revolution were closing their ranks and hardening their ideology. To the orthodox religion of medieval Christendom, the Calvinists opposed the religion of the Book, to the dogmatic certainties of Trent, certainties equally dogmatic, and to the agents of the Catholic counter-offensive an equal readiness for debate or intrigue, conflict or martyrdom.

Like the Church of Rome, the Church of Geneva was international, claiming in the name of religion the ultimate allegiance of its adherents. Wherever the Calvinists were a considerable organized minority (they were a majority in those first decades nowhere), any attempt to enforce conformity to Rome meant civil war. Wherever there were Calvinists at all, the passionate intensity of their convictions and their singleness of purpose made them formidable out of all proportion to their numbers. Against these dedicated revolutionaries no complete victory was possible except by their extermination, just as for them none was possible short of the absolute destruction of the Church of Rome. Longer than the youngest page at Cateau-Cambrésis would live the tension between these opposed ideologies would distort the lines of policy, cut across old allegiances, and multiply the hostilities between states by the implacable hatreds of conflict over absolute, transcendental ideas. What was in prospect at Cateau-Cambrésis was not peace, but a series of religious wars.

Two dynastic accidents determined, if not the nature, certainly the structure and possibly the outcome of these wars. In November 1558, not long after peace negotiations had been begun, Philip of Spain's wife, Mary I of England, died, childless, at the age of forty-two. The following July, Henry II of France, a robust man of forty, died from an injury received in a tournament in honour of the peace, one of those rare casualties which show that the decadent jousting of the sixteenth century was still not quite without risk. Mary was succeeded by her half-sister Elizabeth; Henry by his son, Francis II, a sickly, backward boy of fifteen. Anne Boleyn's daughter could only be a Protestant, so that even before the course of the Church of England was officially determined the exiles came flocking back from Strasbourg and Geneva, Scotland rose against its Catholic regent, and Calvinists everywhere began to look to England as a refuge and a base. Whatever Henry II of France might have done, Catherine de'Medici, who inherited the brunt of his job, had neither the strength nor the fanaticism to stamp out the Huguenots. Embracing Calvinists or murdering them, she betrayed an equal lack of conviction, and all her diplomatic finesse, her tireless activity and her maternal solicitude could barely keep herself and her clutch of incompetent sons balanced precariously above an abyss of anarchy and civil war.

So in the international arena, as the French internal crisis deepened, England and Spain were left facing each other, apparently ill-matched antagonists. Unlike as their rulers were in most respects, they had one thing in common. Neither wanted war. But in spite of their vacillations, evasions and delays, both were swept forward until Elizabeth, champion of a reform whose more violent partisans she heartily detested, faced Philip, the almost equally reluctant champion of orthodoxy, and the revolt in the Netherlands, the troubles in Ireland, the endemic civil wars in France, and the long, underhand Anglo-Spanish naval bickering merged in one general struggle in which the issues of power and ideology were inextricably confused. Or, if they were sometimes distinct in the minds of enlightened statesmen, certainly they were thoroughly merged in the minds of the people, who followed or pushed their leaders into war with an enthusiasm which they could never have felt for merely dynastic quarrels.

Sometimes, as in Spain, and, more slowly, in England, the lines of ideological fission came to correspond with territorial boundaries, and religious loyalties and hatreds hardened and fixed the national temper. Sometimes, as in France and Germany, the cleavage cracked or split old national groups. Sometimes, as in the Netherlands, it helped create new ones. But wherever the lines ran they divided Christendom into two hostile and irrationally suspicious camps. We know now that there was no secret Catholic conspiracy, running back to Trent and the conference of Bayonne, just as there was no organized Protestant plot to overthrow the monarchies of France and Spain and deliver Europe to anarchy and the Turk. But serious statesmen in both camps once believed these things, and serious historians long repeated them. We find it as hard now to imagine that the throne of England could be imperilled by a handful of priests ministering the sacraments in the old way as we do to suppose that the faith of Spain could be shaken by the careless words of a Dutch sailor or the chance importation of a Genevan tract. But death might be the penalty for such acts, and the police of both states were vigilant to track them down. In wars of ideas the sense of proportion, like the knack of compromise, is easily lost. Europe had to wade in blood for nearly a century before it could be persuaded that states with different (not really so very different) ideologies need not necessarily destroy each other. It had to spend a longer time and do itself graver injury before its rulers learned that their subjects could live at peace together in one kingdom, professing different faiths.

The religious wars nearly wrecked the diplomatic institutions with which Europe had been trying to adjust its quarrels. As we have seen, these institutions were weakened from the first by a serious contradiction. According to the medieval rationalization on which they were based, they were supposed to preserve peace among Christians. In fact, they were usually used by the power-eating territorial states for egotistic, often aggressive, ends. The tension between formal and actual purposes, between traditional sentiments and new allegiances inevitably revealed flaws in the system and in the individuals involved.

But making human institutions work usually involves compromises, sometimes compromises between opposites. In time, logically antithetical elements can often be transformed into a relatively coherent or at least cohesive system. As long as European diplomatic institutions served what was, in effect, one society, as long as the European upper classes still shared a common body of standards and sentiments, as long as the dynastic struggles for power were only a kind of family quarrel within a ruling aristocracy, it was possible to hope that the contradictions between theory and practice might be harmonized or resolved. If the European states were to live together in one system, some such development was absolutely necessary.

To any such development, the intensification of religious strife in the 1560s was a catastrophic interruption. Successful diplomatic negotiations require that the parties involved can at least imagine a mutually satisfactory settlement, that neither assumes that the only permanent solution is the total destruction of the other. As long as conflicts between states are about prestige or profit or power, grounds of agreement are always accessible to sane men. But the clash of ideological absolutes drives diplomacy from the field.

After the peace of Cateau-Cambrésis in 1559, Europe saw no general meeting of the greater powers, no serious attempt at the settlement of European questions, until the Congress of Westphalia in 1648. In the interval, diplomats were concerned with espionage and conspiracy, intrigue and bluff, but scarcely ever with their proper business. In that period Europeans almost lost their sense of belonging to a common society. And unless people realize that they have to live together, indefinitely, in spite of their differences, diplomats have no place to stand.

From the first, religious differences narrowed diplomatic contacts. After 1534 England, except for a while in the reign of Mary, maintained no ambassador in Rome. About the same time, diplomatic connections between England and Venice became more irregular; in the last years of Mary's reign her only representative there was the Spanish ambassador.[1] After the accession of Elizabeth, the Venetians, in spite of their commercial connections with England and the hints that they would be favourably received, sent no resident ambassador to England and received none thence. The Counter-Reformation papacy disapproved of diplomatic relations between Catholic and heretic states, and in Italy, at least, its disapproval, reinforced by the papal excommunication of the queen of England, was strong enough to break the last remaining ties. The whole Protestant north remained cut off from regular diplomatic intercourse with Italy until the seventeenth century.

In the rest of Europe, too, diplomatic contacts were decreasing, as each side came to regard the other's embassies as centres of alien and subversive ideas. As early as 1551 a dispute over whether the English embassy with Charles V would be allowed to celebrate an Anglican communion nearly disrupted Anglo-Imperial relations.[2] The issue was never really settled. When it was raised again in 1568 it terminated the English resident embassy in Spain.

Even before that the project of an exchange of resident ambassadors between London and Vienna had been allowed to lapse,
chiefly on account of religious difficulties, even though in those
years the Austrian Habsburgs were more tolerant than the
Spanish.[3] The Spanish embassy in England survived, fitfully and
precariously, for fifteen years or so after the end of the English
embassy in Spain, but on obviously limited sufferance.[4] Among
Catholic sovereigns only the Valois clung to the policy of exchanging residents with Protestant powers, and even in France
the bitter religious passions which raged around the throne and
more and more absorbed the bourgeoisie and the Paris mob made
the position of Protestant residents, particularly the English
ambassadors,[5] often uncomfortable and sometimes actually
dangerous.

CHAPTER XXI

THE AMBASSADORS OF ILL-WILL

MUTUAL suspicion and hatred could isolate the representatives of warring ideologies almost as effectively as a breach of relations. Feria, Philip's first ambassador to Elizabeth, noted the changed climate at once. 'It is impossible for me to find out anything certain at present here', he wrote to Philip only a month after Mary's death. 'Nobody wants to talk to me [he meant nobody in the circle influential with the new queen]; people flee from me as if I were the devil.'[1] That he had described the people in question a paragraph before as boys, heretics and traitors did not keep Feria from being angry at their avoiding him, and, though Cecil and his fellow-Councillors may have guessed Feria's opinion, that was not why they kept away. In ticklish political times, it is not well to be seen talking to the other side.

As soon as he reached Philip II's court at Ghent in July 1559, Elizabeth's ambassador, Sir Thomas Challoner, neither a touchy nor a fanciful man, sensed a similar atmosphere. Even Spaniards whom he knew (he knew a number) were barely civil. Nobody came to call on him or bid him welcome and Feria, just returned from England, on whose good offices Challoner had counted, was pointedly cold and standoffish. Challoner thought the trouble lay in Spanish distrust of recent English innovations in religion, a distrust aggravated by the evil tongues of English Papists lingering in the Low Countries.[2] As for Queen Elizabeth's first ambassador to France, Nicholas Throckmorton, that sensitive and ardent intriguer had hardly reached Paris when he began clamouring for his recall on the grounds that since the Guises 'rule all now' (after Henry II's death) and he was in small grace with them (tied, in their minds, he meant, to the Protestant party) he could not negotiate or collect information in France.[3]

There was an easy, almost an inevitable way out of the isolation incurred by an ambassador whose official faith was suspect in the country of his residence, and that was to make contact with malcontents who held (or pretended) views like his own. Throckmorton found it at once, and soon had plenty of French news to write home. The Guises might avoid him, but the queen of Navarre did not, nor the vidame de Chartres, and sincere Huguenots and discontented politicians filled him with stories of Catholic conspiracies to conquer Scotland and England for Mary Stuart, and put all heretics to the sword. There was just enough truth in the stories to make them plausible, but the agitated tone in which Throckmorton reported them did nothing to ease strained relations, and probably helped persuade Elizabeth to her rash and unprofitable intervention in the first French war of religion.[4]

Sir Thomas Challoner was a cool-headed unenthusiastic diplomat, who could honestly describe himself as one 'that would do the best to please both sides . . . conforming to all tolerable things and reserving his opinion to himself'.[5] A comparison of his dispatches from Spain (1562-64) with the earlier letter he wrote from the Netherlands in 1559-60 shows how hard it was for even such a man to keep his views from being coloured by the excited stories of those who visited him to pour out their fears and hopes and dark imaginings. Relations between Spain and England after '62 were not really better than they had been three years earlier. Reading the dispatches of Bishop Quadra, Challoner's opposite number in England, one would say they were worse. But although Challoner had an occasional brush with the Inquisition and continual vexation over arrested shipping, he was able to see things much more calmly in Spain. There, he was not talking to any native Protestants.

Probably the native opposition party most troublesome to a resident ambassador's clarity of vision was in England. Whether or not the English Catholics made up a large or even a bare majority during the first twelve years of Elizabeth depends on what one means by 'Catholics'. The French and Spanish ambassadors who periodically reported such majorities had no means of estimating the religious opinions of the vast masses of Englishmen, and little interest in doing so. They were concerned with who would support, or at least not oppose, a change in religion. The people they thought worth counting were those who counted politically, mainly the noble families and the gentry. Among these, though one may doubt that there were ever nearly as many Roman Catholics as reported,[6] there were, certainly, a good many, with a considerable activist core of nobles and gentlemen who had lost place and office at the end of Mary's reign, or who resented the rise of new men like the Cecils and the Dudleys, or who were, quite simply, deeply attached to the ancient faith.

At the Spanish embassy, particularly, this 'Catholic party' had ready entrée because Philip as former king-consort of England felt a special obligation to protect and encourage English Catholics, some of whom had been his own servants and most of whom were pro-Habsburg. Later, as Mary Stuart became the chief hope of English Catholicism, members of the opposition party found their way to the French embassy too. In both places they represented the queen's government as a clique of revolutionaries and place-hunters without real support in the country. They told horrendous tales of the virgin queen's private life, of the persecution of devout Catholics and of the constant plotting of the queen's ministers to subvert the religion and government of France and the Netherlands. They declared that if the king of Spain (or the king of France, or the duke of Guise) would only 'give a remedy to these disorders' the millions of English Catholics, all the really solid people in the kingdom, would shower blessings on his head. But if he delayed much longer their affections would naturally turn to the king of France or to the duke of Guise or (if they were at the French embassy) to the king of Spain.

It was difficult for the most level-headed Catholic diplomats in England to ignore such talk or keep it from sometimes distorting their dispatches. For more excitable characters like Bishop Quadra and Don Guerau Despés it was impossible. Their vision became quite clouded by the steamy atmosphere of partisan conspiracy in which they moved, so that they stumbled easily into treasonable plotting. As ideological differences sharpened and hatreds increased, it grew constantly harder for diplomats to stand against the prevailing tides of popular feeling.[7]

The refugees of both parties swelled these tides. In the first months of Elizabeth's reign groups of French and Dutch Calvinists, and soon even some Protestants from Spain, began to arrive in London and the eastern counties with stories of the French king's *chambre ardente* and the Spanish king's Inquisition. At the same time exiled Scottish Catholics appeared in Paris, and the most stubborn English Catholics drifted to the court of their former king at Brussels. Within a decade the flow of Protestant refugees, particularly from the Low Countries to England, had become something like a flood, and that of English and Irish exiles to Spain had increased from a trickle to a steady stream. Each year the stories each group brought became more horrifying and better authenticated. By the 1570s there were enough undeniable or plausible ones to keep partisanship on both sides at white heat.

Just as the ambassadors had to be especially level-headed to avoid being influenced by inhabitants of their own faith, so they had to be constantly on guard against the hostility of their exiled countrymen. Rows with King Philip's disobedient subjects in London bedevilled all the years of Quadra's mission. They incited mobs to stone his residence — or so he reported — and instigated the London authorities to search his embassy for kidnapped Flemings. In Spain both Challoner and Dr. Man suspected with reason that their troubles with the Inquisition were due largely to the denunciations of compatriots. In addition, just as the residents took the news to which they gave most credence, not from official sources, but from a conspiratorial opposition, so, through their counsellors, Philip and Elizabeth listened more and more to refugees, and what they heard tended to increase their distrust of each other, and of each other's ambassadors.

All this mounting suspicion helped paralyse diplomatic communications between Catholic and Protestant countries by converting the residents still exchanged among them into conspirators and spies. Just how far their home governments were responsible for the change it is not easy to say, but, though neither Elizabeth nor Philip was eager to rush into war, both were increasingly alarmed and angry, and neither was willing to abandon any possible advantage that might accrue from the support of conspiratorial groups in the other's realms. In consequence, both tended to pursue a double policy, to hesitate on the brink of adventures in conspiracy and to confuse their ambassadors with contradictory instructions. Add the normal delays of communication at a time when ambassadors often had to make emergency decisions without fresh advice from home. Add the additional delays from which both English and Spanish ambassadors suffered, the English because of Elizabeth's chronic vacillation, the Spanish because all

Philip's industry could never keep him quite abreast of his self-imposed burdens of correspondence. Given all this it is not surprising that diplomats in both services tended to run ahead of the policies of their governments, following the sentiments of their co-religionists.

Among English ambassadors perhaps the outstanding example of the emissary of bad-will was Dr. John Man, dean of Gloucester and Elizabeth's last resident ambassador in Spain. Just why Elizabeth and Cecil thought that a bigoted Protestant divine, without tact or breeding, would prove a successful representative at that ticklish point in Anglo-Spanish relations is a mystery. If they did, his first letters must have undeceived them. 'All the Spanish hate us', he wrote flatly, almost as soon as he got to Madrid, 'for religion's sake.' If Challoner had ever thought the same, he had not said so. In negotiating for the release of English shipping, a matter in which Challoner, ill as he was, had been making progress, Man showed that he expected nothing. He felt that he was in enemy country. When he got into trouble with the Inquisition over his insistence on conducting Anglican services at the embassy, his notion of a diplomatic *riposte* was to make unprintably insulting remarks about Philip, the Inquisition and the Catholic faith to an English Catholic who promptly reported them where they would do the most harm.

Man's punitive detention and expulsion are less surprising than the failure of Elizabeth and her council to blame him more. And this, in turn, is less surprising than that Philip's advisers should have felt that the orthodoxy of Spain was endangered because English embassy servants took communion according to the rite used in their own country, a privilege extended to Spaniards in England and to Englishmen in France. Most surprising of all, neither government proved able to compromise on so minor a point. In consequence, there were no more English resident ambassadors in Spain until the time of James I. No other English diplomat gave quite as effective a demonstration of sturdy prejudice as Dr. Man. But scarcely one in the 1570s and '80s failed to show in action and in writing something like Man's conviction that there could be no truce with the powers of darkness.

Most of Philip's representatives felt exactly the same way. As Spaniards, it was easy for them to confuse the triumph of the

Catholic faith and the triumph of Spanish policy. In England, particularly, where there was a tradition of co-operation between the Spanish-Imperial embassy and the conservative Catholic nobility, a tradition running back to the early days of Catherine of Aragon's divorce, Philip's ambassadors took a line of partisan intrigue far less easy for any government to tolerate than Dr. Man's insolence.

Recognizing that Feria, since he was intimately connected by friendship and marriage with the Marian party, might have trouble in adjusting to the new regime, Philip replaced him by a churchman. Philip thought Bishop Quadra likely to get along with Elizabeth, and inclined by his cloth to peaceful solutions. But the Renaissance maxim that churchmen are the fittest ambassadors for peace as noblemen for war proved false once religious issues entered. Besides, in Bishop Quadra's instructions there was a harmlessly meant but fatal phrase directing him to encourage the English Catholics and assure them of Philip's continued solicitude for their welfare. On the strength of it, before Quadra had been ninety days at his post he was deeper in conspiracy with English, Irish and Scottish malcontents than ever Feria had been. Their incitement and his own enthusiasm led him into a course of intrigue and provocation which had terminated his usefulness in England some time before death terminated his embassy.

His successor, Diego Guzmán de Silva, had instructions no more conciliatory than those given Quadra, but alone among Philip's ambassadors in England he seems to have had the will and the wit to carry them out. He served through a difficult period of Anglo-Spanish relations, a period which saw increasing piracy in the Channel, Shane O'Neill's rising in Ulster, Hawkins's voyage to the West Indies, the crisis of Mary's reign in Scotland, Dr. Man's imbroglio, and the arrival of Alva's army in the Netherlands. Nevertheless he managed to keep the lines of negotiation open, to avoid increasing tensions in his own contacts with the English court, and even to achieve a certain popularity there. He was wary of conspiratorial English Catholics and coolly amused by rumours which Protestant radicals, in England and abroad, spread about his deep-laid plots. But even de Silva's dispatches were no help to the cause of Anglo-Spanish peace.

He, too, really felt that in the long run there could be no peace with heretics.

After de Silva, Spain's diplomats in England all hastened the drift towards war. The next, Don Guerau Despés, like Dr. Man, felt from the first that he was in enemy country, and after taking, on the evidence of his own letters, a leading part in Ridolfi's plot against Elizabeth and perhaps indulging as well in a private scheme to poison Burleigh, ended by being sent ignominiously home. Despés left Spanish affairs in charge of a merchant, Antonio de Guaras, who imitated the ambassador's indiscretions and landed, not unjustly, in the Tower.

The last Spanish ambassador, Bernardino de Mendoza, was specifically charged to try to get matters back on a calmer footing, and was capable, as his first efforts showed, of sensible and conciliatory behaviour. But Mendoza was so certain that the English heretics were Spain's natural enemies that before long he assumed the chief rôle in the Spanish-Guise-Marian conspiracy known as the Throckmorton plot and was, like Despés, expelled from England for conduct which might reasonably have cost him his head.[8] Further diplomatic relations between England and Spain, he wrote to Philip, had become impossible. So it proved. It was more than twenty years before the Spanish embassy in England had another tenant.

Five years later there was no Spanish ambassador at the French court, either. In France, as in England, the Spanish ambassadors had come to play a double rôle, representatives of the Most Catholic at the court of the Most Christian king, but also liaison officers and paymasters for the violent Catholic faction led by the Guises and known as the Most Holy League. Again the decisive agent was that tough cavalry officer whose last message to Queen Elizabeth had been that she would learn that Bernardino de Mendoza was born not to disturb kingdoms but to conquer them. When Mendoza was named ambassador to France in 1584,[9] he was definitely instructed to encourage Guise in the revolution which seemed necessary if Henry of Navarre was to be kept from succeeding to the throne. In the plots which led to the 'Day of the Barricades' Mendoza was deeply involved, and after that insurrection had secured Paris for the league, he was rather Philip's ambassador to Henry of Guise than to Henry of Valois. When

Guise was murdered Mendoza made it his first business to rally the spirits of the Leaguers and reknit their liaison with Spain, so that it is not surprising to find him, after the assassination of Henry III, transferring his embassy to Paris and becoming the best brain of the league's improvised general staff and the soul of its defence of Paris against the heretic king.

In those days when the Huguenot guns could be heard at the Louvre, when, the last of his plate melted up, the last of his horses killed for food, the courtyard of his embassy a public soup-kitchen, and all his able-bodied servants mustered on the walls, the blind old ambassador limped from gate to gate, leaning on the shoulder of a turnspit, gathering the latest reports and telling the captains how towns were held or lost when he had served with Alva, one cannot help feeling that he was better pleased with the part he was playing than he had ever been when he exchanged smooth lies with princes. One cannot help feeling, too, that the veteran ambassador turned partisan leader in the bitterest phase of a civil war was an apt symbol of what the religious wars had done to the Spanish diplomatic service and, indeed, to the diplomatic corps of Europe.

By 1589, then, European diplomatic contacts were interrupted everywhere except between ideological allies. The English network had contracted soonest and most sharply. After 1568, the only English resident ambassador on the continent was the one at the French court, and elsewhere the resident's function as a channel of information and communication was only partially filled by agents whose status shaded down by degrees from the fully official position of the Queen's resident agent in the Netherlands, through the quasi-official agents to the German princes and the tacitly recognized 'pensioners' who served her in Venice, to the unacknowledged but well-known informants who wrote to Walsingham from Florence and Genoa, and so, almost imperceptibly, to the secret spies he kept in Rome and Lisbon and even in Madrid. After 1589, Elizabeth's only official diplomatic residents were with non-Catholic powers, her ambassador with the Huguenot king of France, her agent with the States of the rebellious Netherlands, and her newly established ambassador at Constantinople, sent mainly to try to stir up the Turks against Spain.[10]

The Spanish network had contracted somewhat less. After 1589, Spain still exchanged resident ambassadors with the three major Catholic powers, the pope, the emperor and the republic of St. Mark. The grand duke of Tuscany, the republic of Genoa and, usually, the duke of Savoy, maintained ambassadors at Madrid. None of these states, however, had any permanent embassies with any Protestant power. Meanwhile, the Spanish ambassadors and resident agents in Italy, full of their master's importance as the champion of orthodoxy, often behaved more like viceroys, or like the liaison officers of an anti-Protestant crusade, than like mere diplomats.[11]

Among the three major powers the French had preserved longest the widest range of contacts and greatest freedom of action, and French diplomats had shown the most ability to distinguish between their duties as diplomatic officers and their sympathies in the ideological quarrel, but even the French service had begun to break apart in the 1580s as France itself was torn in two by civil strife and *politiques* were obliged to decide, not so much whether they were Catholics or Protestants, as whether they stood for Guise or Navarre. When Henry IV succeeded, the French service had to be rebuilt from the ground up. For some years, though he would have preferred a wider scope, the French king's only reliable contacts, except for his English and Dutch allies, were with the Austrian Habsburgs and the republic of St. Mark.[12]

After the Peace of Vervins in 1598 between Spain and France, and that of 1604 between Spain and England, diplomatic contacts began to be re-established, but slowly, warily. Resident ambassadors had proved themselves too valuable for sovereigns not to want to use them, once the clash of arms had ceased. But they had also proved themselves too unscrupulous in their religious partisanship and too dangerous for most states to be anxious to receive them. More important, the fears and hostilities of the religious wars were still unabated, and their political problems still unsolved. Spain could not believe that its effort to restore Christian unity by force would have to be abandoned. The Protestants, particularly the English and Dutch, could not believe that they were yet safe from the thumbscrews and the stake. And after so long a conflict in which no faith was kept and no mercy shown, in which conspiracy, insurrection and assassination were weapons as normal as fleets and armies, in which no diplomatic conferences were entered except to assist a military ruse, and no ambassadors sent between opposing sides except for espionage and subversion, nobody was quite able to believe in compromise and common sense, in common interests and a common code.

Therefore peace in the first decades of the seventeenth century was never much better than an uneasy truce. Its diplomatic arrangements, like most of its political arrangements, were merely provisional, pending the resumption of the religious wars. Only one major sovereign of the period really believed in peaceful diplomacy, and James I's stubborn conviction that kingdoms could live at peace with one another though embracing different creeds earned him nothing except the title of 'the wisest fool in Europe', the mocking scorn of his contemporaries, and the lofty reprobation of subsequent historians. Nothing, that is, except almost twenty years of the peace he sought. Continental Europe had to endure that series of paroxysms which we call the Thirty Years War, and the two principal contestants had to slog it out in slow motion for another eleven years, like pugilists too dazed to leave the ring, before most European statesmen began to come to anything like James I's conclusions.

By that time, if the old dream of European unity in a common faith had altogether faded, so had its ugly reverse image, the mirage of a unity to be achieved by force. From time to time, visions of one or the other continued to tempt a despot or a philosopher, but after 1648 most men were content to accept a society broken up into a congeries of autonomous individual states, states which balanced their forces, conducted their wary intercourse, fought their limited, selfish wars and made their limited, selfish treaties of peace according to rules which diplomats worked out for them.

After the Treaties of Westphalia and the Pyrenees the period of modern diplomacy really begins. After more than a century of travail, the European state system had reached the stage of heterogeneous organization, of precarious equilibrium, which the Italian system had achieved after Lodi. In the interval the Europeans had adapted Italian diplomatic institutions to the more complicated needs of their greater and more complex system, and though these institutions were continuously elaborated, basically they remained about as the diplomats of the mid-seventeenth century received them from the sixteenth. They served the European system until it, too, was disrupted by the pressures from a larger area of political space.

PART FOUR

EARLY MODERN DIPLOMACY

CHAPTER XXII

THE PERFECT AMBASSADOR

IN 1620 there was published at Seville a small, elegant pair of quartos entitled *El Embajador*. The author, Don Juan Antonio De Vera, was a young man of distinguished lineage, and already, at thirty-two, of considerable achievements. A scholar, soldier, courtier and minor poet, he had served honourably in Flanders, and represented Spain on embassies to Savoy and Venice. He was to go on to greater honours, to be Spanish ambassador at Rome, Councillor of State and first count of La Rosa, to match wits with Olivares, and to write a long epic poem on the reconquest of Seville for which his countrymen styled him, perhaps too generously, the Spanish Tasso. But Europe always remembered him chiefly for his first book. He had called it simply *The Ambassador*. But as it was translated into French and Italian it picked up, inevitably, an adjective in its title. Most aspiring diplomats read it throughout the next hundred years. In one edition or another, probably most often in the fat, ugly, little Parisian duodecimo of 1642, it may have travelled in the saddlebags of more ambassadors than any other treatise of its kind. By then its title was *Le parfait ambassadeur*, 'The Perfect Ambassador'.

It seems surprising that no earlier work had usurped the title. The perfect prince, the perfect courtier, the ideal magistrate, the perfect knight were subjects dear to the sixteenth century, and ambassadors had proved themselves useful to the new monarchies as captains or councillors. Diplomatic service had become a recognized step in the courtier's career. The ambassador's lonely task of upholding his master's honour at a foreign court, aided by no more than his own wit, courage and eloquence, was calculated to excite the imagination of the baroque world, its taste for magnificence, its interest in extraordinary individuals, its appreciation of complicated intrigue. But although Tasso had attempted the portrait of the perfect ambassador forty years before De Vera, and a number of less distinguished writers had handled the same theme with more solidity, before Tasso and after him, all these, in popular esteem, were De Vera's precursors rather than his rivals. When the seventeenth century spoke of 'The Perfect Ambassador' it meant De Vera's book.

Looking back over all this literature on which De Vera drew, one is struck by how tardy it was. By 1540 the Italian system of diplomacy was thoroughly established among the greater European states. The northern humanists had long been urging, as one of the principal reasons for teaching Latin to gentlemen's sons, the necessity of that tongue for diplomacy, so that the king need not rely for his envoys on base-born clerks; and gentlemen, called on to parley in the king's name, 'shall not be constrained to speak words sudden and disordered, but shall bestow them aptly and in their places'.[1] Yet for the first forty years of the sixteenth century scholarship can list no printed works under the heading 'Various treatises about ambassadors and embassies' except three brief tractates on the canon law applying to papal legates.

In the 1540s appeared two books from which, at last, royal servants might learn something of the qualifications, duties and privileges of ambassadors: a humanistic little essay by Etienne Dolet[2] based on his experience as a junior in the French embassy at Venice, and a ponderous, legalistic, rather backward-looking treatise by a German scholar, Conrad Braun.[3] Thereafter nothing worth noticing for nearly twenty years. In 1566, a Venetian, Ottaviano Maggi, published a graceful pamphlet, *De legato libri duo*, the first sixteenth century book about diplomacy by an Italian, drawing on Ermolao Barbaro, and on Italian, particularly Venetian, experience. Maggi was both a working diplomat and a humanist with juristic training. His treatise seems easier, more modern and discriminating than Braun's, more self-assured and systematic than Dolet's. It balances classical references with contemporary illustrations and provides at least some suggestion of historical background other than the Renaissance pseudo-antique. It was republished in 1596, but was always more plundered than cited.

After Maggi nothing for more than a decade; then four important contributors within six years of each other, two French jurists, Ayrault[4] and La Mothe Le Vayer,[5] one at least with diplomatic experience, and two Italians, Torquato Tasso[6] and Alberico Gentili,[7] one a poet, the other an Anglicized exile who was regius professor of the civil law at Oxford. With these four we

212

begin to have something like a coherent literary tradition. Le Vayer had read Ayrault and perhaps Dolet, Tasso echoes Maggi and may have read Barbaro, Gentili knew at least Tasso. Le Vayer and Gentili were both republished in the 1590s, Gentili three times. Ayrault on Roman law went through many editions well into the seventeenth century. Tasso's *Il Messagiero* was included in all editions of his prose dialogues. So that all these writers remained available, and were influential on the subsequent literature.

Towards the end of the sixteenth century, as Europe grew weary of its wars, interest in diplomacy increased. All the important earlier books except Dolet's and Braun's were reprinted at least once in the 1590s and there were two new major contributions. One, the work of a learned Pole, Christopher Warsewicki, may have been meant chiefly to summarize the western theorists for eastern Europe, though it was cited respectfully as far west as Salamanca and Oxford.[8] The other by Carlo Pasquale (*aliter* Paschal or Pascalius), an Italian jurist naturalized in France, has the distinction of being the longest book about ambassadors written in the sixteenth century, the most pompous and dogmatic, the fullest of classical illustrations of startling irrelevance and dubious authenticity, and in about the dimmest and most lifeless Latin prose.[9] It was also, judging by frequency of citation, one of the most respected books about diplomacy for several decades, though perhaps not the most often read.

After the Peace of Vervins, and the revival of hope that diplomacy might find a substitute for the tiresome alternation of open war and underhand conspiracy, there was a spate of books about ambassadors. For the hundred years 1498-1598 one can find only sixteen separate titles. For the twenty-one years 1598-1620, between Paschalius and De Vera, there are twenty new ones besides numerous reprints, and of the new ones at least three attained a European reputation. One was by a Huguenot diplomat, Jean Hotman de Villiers,[10] one by a German jurist, Herman Kirchner,[11] and one by a stodgy, methodical Belgian, Frederick van Marselaer.[12] In the same decades the art of diplomacy, the problems of sovereignty, and the management of international affairs were being commented on and critically re-examined by minds as different as Francis Bacon's and the Duke of Sully's, Fra Paolo

213

Sarpi's and Father Juan de Mariana's. The great Spanish school of international jurisprudence which stems from Francisco de Vittoria was then culminating in Suarez's *De legibus ac Deo legislatore*, and John Selden and Hugo Grotius were writing their earliest pamphlets.

If De Vera was not fully abreast of all this literature, the range of his citations shows that he had read widely in it and had most of the more important writers on diplomacy either in memory or at hand. In spite of the aristocratic nonchalance with which he wears his scholarship, he thoroughly shared the serious and thoughtful temper with which his age was approaching international questions. And though he cast his book in the form of a dialogue, in imitation of his favourite poet's attempt at the same subject, he meant it to be, unlike Tasso's, a useful and comprehensive treatment of all the topics which his predecessors had found relevant. He undertook to deal, then, with the legal status of ambassadors, their privileges and immunities, with diplomatic practice and procedures, with advice about the practical conduct of an embassy, both in general and with reference to particular courts, and with the physical, intellectual and moral attributes desirable for a diplomatic career — in other words with the portrait of the perfect ambassador.

Not all De Vera's predecessors tried to deal with all the headings he tackled. Some, like Gentili, wisely omitted the practical advice, being themselves without practical experience. Some, like Tasso, soared above the legal entanglements with airy generalizations. But none, not even those unpublished drafts of model instructions preserved in most European chanceries, ignored the question of the qualities which the perfect ambassador should possess.[13] The portrait of the perfect ambassador was more than just the occasion for the kind of literary exercise De Vera's generation loved. It contained, like the portrait of the perfect magistrate or of the perfect prince, the kernel of a serious problem.

Fortunately, for a composite portrait of the perfect Renaissance ambassador we do not have to dissect each writer in detail. One of them, Jean Hotman, cheerfully announced 'I am so far from blushing at having borrowed from ancient and modern authors whatever I found to my purpose that I vow that most [of my book], except perhaps for some thirty examples from my own experience, comes from my reading or from my friends . . . To anyone who reads as I have the modern writers on this subject, Brunus, Magius, Gentili, Le Vayer and the rest, it will seem that they have all borrowed from one another though they have all wrought learnedly.'[14] Whether they all wrought learnedly or not, they certainly all borrowed, so that while most authors' 'perfect ambassadors' have each a few distinctive traits, they have all a strong family likeness.

Everybody agrees, for instance, that an ambassador should be rich, well born and handsome, though emphasis varies. As to wealth, one or two writers are impractical enough to say that if the ambassador has the other requisite qualities, his sovereign should make up any deficiency in his fortune.[15] But De Vera expresses the general opinion: without a large personal income no one can be expected to keep up the proper state of a major embassy.[16] The increasing ostentation of court life and the grim experiences of resident ambassadors who had tried to avoid bankruptcy while waiting for overdue salaries made the judgment unarguable. Only Dolet says that birth is of small account. Himself a humbly born humanist he is sure that true nobility is conferred only by virtue. All the others agree that the perfect ambassador should have a 'well sounding name', and some pretentions to ancient lineage. But even the writers one would expect to be strongest for blue blood, Marselaer and De Vera, regard it as merely advantageous, not indispensable. All think a good appearance important. Little, grizzled, battle-scarred Jean Hotman would settle for a freedom from absurd or crippling deformities, but most writers want more. Gentili quotes Aristotle to the effect that beauty is the best letter of introduction, and De Vera puts a handsome appearance high on his list.[17]

From all these lists, there is an odd omission: health. It is agreed that an ambassador should not be deformed or crippled, but only because such defects provoke ridicule. If one or two writers add that an ambassador must be physically able to carry out his duties, nobody thinks the point important. Perhaps it was not. One remembers De Puebla's limp, Chapuys's crippling gout, Mendoza's blindness, Gondomar's fistula, and suspects that, in that tough period, diplomacy was regarded as one of the more sedentary and valetudinarian occupations. Today the physical strains Renaissance diplomacy imposed would seem almost its most trying requirement.

About the proper age for an ambassador there was divergence of opinion. Braun, himself elderly when he wrote, thought highly of experience and venerable aspect; a vigorous sixty would be about right, one gathers. De Vera, who had successfully completed two embassies before he was thirty, thought twenty-five not too young. Only Dolet, also young, would have agreed. Most of the other authors, middle-aged men, voted for middle age as the Renaissance calculated that imprecise term; older than thirty, they said, citing the Romans, and younger than fifty.

About one qualification time brought a shift of opinion. Before 1560, ecclesiastics had been rather commoner as ambassadors than laymen, and earlier theorists only discussed which missions were more appropriate for men of the gown and which for men of the sword. But as the century drew towards its close it began to be asked whether churchmen ought to be ambassadors at all, and though no one, not even Hotman, a Protestant, said an unqualified 'No', the hesitations about saying 'Yes' without many qualifications grew more and more pronounced. Among the later writers, the instances, modern and classical, which came most readily to hand, all seemed to indicate that priests sometimes served another master than their natural sovereign. The oblique glance was, of course, at the Counter-Reformation papacy. That an ambassador who was a priest might be embarrassed by his allegiance to a Master even more exacting than the pope seems not to have occurred to anybody. Whatever else it may have retained from the later Middle Ages, by 1620 diplomatic theory had lost any overtones of religiosity.

In the way of education the theorists demanded a good deal, nor were their expectations always moderated by experience. Ottaviano Maggi had served on embassies, and must have known the usual level of culture among his colleagues, but, perhaps since he was describing an ideal, he scarcely omitted anything from what an ambassador should know: First of all, theology and sacred letters. Then all branches of secular knowledge: mathematics, including architecture and mechanical drawing, music, geometry, astronomy. The whole of philosophy, natural and moral, including, of course, a special mastery of the civil and the canon law, as well as of the municipal law and statutes both of his own country and of that to which he was assigned. Everyone insisted that the perfect ambassador had to be deeply read in literature and eloquent in the Latin tongue, for to be an orator was the ambassador's office. Maggi thought Greek as necessary as Latin, and would have added all the principal modern languages, Italian, French, Spanish, German, even Turkish.[18] Not English, however. Nobody in the sixteenth century except an Englishman was expected to speak English, not even the perfect ambassador.

Few expectations were quite as high as Maggi's. Gentili does not list the languages other than Latin which the ambassador should know, but thinks he should know at least three, and one or two more if he can manage it, including if possible that of the people with whom he is negotiating. In addition, Gentili most insists on history as a practical guide to conduct, and with it a certain amount of philosophy, moral and political, such philosophy 'being, in a sense, the soul of history'. But not too much philosophy. It is unnecessary, says Gentili, for men of action to be able to speculate about the eclipses of the moon and the ebb and flow of the tides. Even in the law it would be foolish to try to master the details of private law, forensic practice and municipal regulations. All diplomats need is the general philosophy of law, though 'I would not tolerate as an ambassador a philosopher without a sound knowledge of history.' Literary studies, though not entirely necessary and, if pursued to excessive bookishness possibly injurious, yet, indulged in with restraint, may be an ornament to character, and win desirable fame. Here Gentili adds a list of ambassadors, ancient and modern, who were successful literary men.[19] Perhaps he knew that the rising young diplomat and courtier to whom he dedicated his book also had literary aspirations. The name in the dedication is Philip Sidney's.

On the whole, subsequent writers were more inclined to agree with Gentili than with Maggi, and the two most influential and experienced, Hotman and De Vera, asked the least of the ambassador's education. De Vera, in particular, though he makes some parade of his own learning, says very much less about the perfect ambassador's intellectual accomplishments than about his moral virtues, and though De Vera was almost as much at ease in French, Italian and Latin as in Spanish, he insists that the ambassador should use, wherever possible, his native language. 'No one can ever be as eloquent in a stranger's as in his mother's tongue,' and besides, 'it is an honour to a prince that his language should be heard in every land'.[20] Here speaks the seventeenth century.

The part of the portrait of the perfect ambassador on which the theorists all lavished their chief space and pains, their most elegant rhetoric and their choicest store of classical anecdotes was the delineation of his moral virtues. Across the centuries their voices seem thin and remote to us now, their anecdotes irrelevant, their saws almost flippantly banal. But we may take it on faith or learn it by study: there was nothing perfunctory or flippant in these writers' attitudes, and to them nothing remote or banal in their subject. Their age took with deadly seriousness the importance of the standard moral virtues in a career of public service.

It is therefore permissible to note two things. In the first place, the discussion of the moral qualities an ambassador should possess occurs in these late sixteenth- and seventeenth-century writers in a kind of vacuum. It is not related to the duties they perform except in so far as those duties afford an opportunity for the display of the virtues in question, that is to say, it is not related at all to the ends a diplomat should seek. And it is altogether divorced from the discussion of the ambassador's legal status, of the privileges he may expect and the limits he may not overstep. This divorce would have puzzled even the driest of the late medieval jurists.

In the second place, the moral qualities recommended fall into a distinct category. Alberico Gentili found the appropriate headings, and subsequent writers, whether or not they observed Gentili's rather formal and scholastic organization, substantially followed him. The ambassador should be loyal, brave, temperate and prudent. Some, remembering Aristotle, add a fifth virtue, 'magnificence' or 'magnanimity', which for an ambassador takes the double form of liberality and a due assertion of his master's importance, but usually this is treated as a principle of tactics rather than a virtue.

It is easy enough to recognize in this conventional tetrad one Renaissance form of the four pagan virtues possible to man by the aid of natural reason. The Middle Ages knew them too, and Bishop Bernard du Rosier did not omit them from his catalogue of the qualities desirable in an ambassador. But he included others, which suggest an omitted triad. He thought that an ambassador ought also to be humble, patient, pious, charitable, beneficent, a man of good will, sweet to his fellow men in word and deed. In this part of the list the passage of nearly two centuries had wrought some change. By De Vera's time, though the theorists were in general agreement that an ambassador ought to appear to be a good Christian, and some even went so far as to assert that he ought to be one, they had little else to say about Christian virtues. Indeed the erosion of experience had set in long before. Even Bishop Bernard had hesitated to assert that diplomacy was a business in which one could recommend the unstinted exercise of faith, hope and charity.

One moral problem experience had thrust well into the foreground of attention in De Vera's age. It was a complex problem, sharpened by the bitterness of ideological conflict but unavoidable ever since the beginning of the new diplomacy, and most acute in the case of resident ambassadors. It involved the exercise of fidelity, that observance of truth and loyalty which was the form of justice appropriate to the work of an ambassador. Most simply stated the problem was, 'What faith does the ambassador owe to the prince or republic he serves and what to the principal to whom he is sent? And what must he do when the two duties conflict? Or when the wishes or orders of his own government seem to him contrary to the true interests of his country? Or to his own honour? Or to the law of nations under which he lives and by which he is protected? Or to the interests of peace which he is supposed to serve?'

Ermolao Barbaro, it may be remembered, had cut clean across the argument. The ambassador's business is the preservation and aggrandizement of his own state, Barbaro said; he owes no other faith and has no other mission. He may and should argue for whatever course seems most likely to serve that end (he must envisage no other), but once the decision of the state has been communicated to him, he must close his mind to doubts of its wisdom or morality and obey. Later Italian writers from Maggi to Bragaccia were none of them so succinct and decisive as Barbaro, if only because the growing interest of their age in nice points of moral casuistry invited them to expand and qualify and distinguish. But most of them, however reluctantly, and by whatever devious windings, ended in a position not unlike Barbaro's.[21] They all fell back on some form of the axiom, 'Salus populi, suprema lex', and meant by 'populi' no more than the prince or government the ambassador happened to be serving. Only Alberico Gentili, a Protestant exile living in a northern climate, roundly dissented. The ambassador, he agreed, must carry out his instructions no matter how unwise he thinks them. But he is not bound to obedience if the prince's orders contravene the moral law. To substitute the will of the prince for the will of God, and the safety of the state for the safety of one's soul is sinful folly. That being so, not only will the perfect ambassador refuse to abet conspiracy and murder, even at the command of his prince, but he will refuse to lie or to break his word. 'I know very well,' Gentili adds apologetically, 'how much I depart from the current code, but I paint ambassadors not as they are, but as they ought to be.'[22]

None of the non-Italian theorists were quite as forthright as Gentili, but none of them was without qualms and pangs. Born in more complex and organic, in some respects more backward, societies, accustomed to balancing loyalties, to accepting the new without abandoning the old, to seeing in the soft northern light that blurs the sharp edges of facts, they were equally reluctant to admit that the will of the sovereign could override the moral law; or that a loyal subject would disobey his king. Most of them followed Conrad Braun in increasingly elaborate distinctions and qualifications. Most of them followed Braun, too, in dodging the toughest questions and taking refuge in examples from Homer and the Bible.

Jean Hotman, devout, Bible-reading Calvinist was as familiar as anybody with Old Testament stories of diplomatic deception practised with every evidence of divine approval. But one gathers that he drew little comfort from the chicaneries of the patriarchs, feeling perhaps, that, whatever the closeness of their relations to the Deity, they were not quite gentlemen. If he had been sometimes obliged to imitate them himself, he had done so reluctantly. 'It goes against the grain for a man of honour', he wrote, 'to lie and cheat . . . like a low-born and low-hearted rogue . . . I know of some who would willingly have passed on this service to cleverer liars [Hotman had been ambassador to the Swiss at the time of St. Bartholomew's] . . . but one must conceal the follies of the *patrie* as one would those of a foolish mother . . . sometimes in the service of the king there is no choice.'[22]

That is what most of the northern writers seem to be saying, 'There is no choice.' Some of them say it bitterly or savagely. Some of them, like Marselaer and Paschalius, for example, bring the deterioration in diplomatic morals home to the new Italian institution of the resident. A special ambassador can be an honourable Christian gentleman, seeking peace, and behaving with dignity and probity, but a resident is at best a kind of licensed spy, and is lucky when he does not have to play the conspirator as well. The best thing would be to have no more of this recent and doubtful institution and go back to the simpler customs of the past. No state is obliged to receive resident ambassadors, and if their use could be abandoned altogether no state would be the worse. Even writers who do not go so far seem to agree that, by the nature of his functions, no resident can be a perfect ambassador.

De Vera took no such unrealistic view. The first Spaniard to write about ambassadors, he was a member of a service which had made use of residents for a hundred and twenty-five years. Spain, by 1620, maintained residents even with Turks and heretics, and found them, in the slow decay of its financial strength and military might, the strongest prop of its empire. But De Vera saw very well that it was, indeed, the position of the resident, alone and far away, and for that very reason unable to disregard instructions or even to resign without grave danger to his country, which made the moral problem of diplomacy so acute. His ethical sensitivity was aroused, and he sprang upon the problem and turned it about with all the eagerness of one of his contemporaries among the dramatists giving a new twist to the point of honour.[24]

In the course of his casuistry De Vera says some sensible, some witty, and some rather subtle things, and manages to hit on a number of entertaining illustrations. He shows himself a sincere Christian, a courtly gentleman and a man of delicate feelings. He repeats that the ambassador must never forget that his object is peace. (This is only a little weakened by an ingenious presentation of the conventional argument that the object of war is peace.) He rejects lying and espionage and conspiracy as unworthy alike of the ambassador's functions and of any gentleman. He insists that the ambassador's first duty is always to tell his master bluntly the whole truth, no matter how unpalatable he knows it will be, or how dangerous to his career. He adds, however, that, for the sake of peace and to avoid dishonour and disaster, the ambassador may sometimes deceive a foolish or ill-advised master for his own good, even as Tasso had suggested.

But as De Vera spins the web of his distinctions, the possibility of an ultimate conflict between the honour of the ambassador and the good of the state, between the welfare of the state and the welfare of Christendom only becomes the clearer. To dodge out between the horns of the dilemma, De Vera resorts to some slippery dialectic. Deception, he argues, is permissible in war, and the first thing the reader knows diplomacy has become a kind of continuous warfare, in which it is permissible to do the enemy any sort of injury as long as the object is not to hurt him but to help one's country. Even if the act in question seems morally wrong, the ambassador may clear his conscience by considering that the king and his council are probably better informed than he, and that theirs is the responsibility. Nevertheless De Vera can not avoid recognizing that one must bear the burden of one's own acts, and that an unjust order from the king places the recipient in danger of sin either way, since he must either knowingly do evil or sin by disobeying his king. The only consolation De Vera can offer his readers is that a truly Catholic king will never command his subjects anything to the danger of their souls. Tasso had put the matter more succinctly forty years before. 'To have the perfect ambassador,' he wrote, 'you must first have the perfect prince.'[26]

CHAPTER XXIII

THE IMPERFECT PRINCES

THOSE who said that the perfect ambassador could only be found in the service of the perfect prince were thinking, of course, of that shadowy figure cast by medieval idealism on the vapours of humanistic rhetoric, the shadow of a prince brave, wise, clement, but above all, just, a prince who never sought anything not rightfully his, never acted out of pride or anger or greed, and never preferred his own profit to the general good. In the service of such a prince, an ambassador could take the longest and hardest step towards perfection. He could reconcile his duty to such a prince with what was still held to be equally his duty, service to the Christian republic's quest for peace. In the Europe of the early 1600s, probably only the most sheltered scholars could have hoped that any ambassador would find such a prince.

The men who struggled with the tasks of diplomacy in the uneasy lull before the final tempest of the religious wars were more immediately distressed by more practical imperfections in the beings they served. Ambassadors could hardly expect to function as the just and disinterested officials of the Christian republic, since the connection between that ideal figment and European realities had long ceased to be perceptible. But they could not function, either, as the efficient agents of power-politics because the entities of which their princes were the symbols, the greater territorial states, had not yet come of age. It would be some time still before the European monarchies matured enough to be able to supply the requisites of a first-rate diplomatic service: adequate funds, trained public servants, foreign offices with reliable archives and permanent staffs, with definite policies and the means of co-ordinating activities abroad. Throughout the sixteenth century the energy and prestige of able princes had at least partially masked the defects in the ramshackle political mechanisms over which they presided. But a constellation of European monarchs like Philip III and Philip IV of Spain, Rudolph and Matthias in Austria, Marie de Medici and Louis XIII in France, a constellation among whom James I was the most impressive luminary, was scarcely bright enough to blind anyone to the structural weakness of the new states.

That weakness was most conspicuous at the top. It was the day of the *privados*, the favourites. And what favourites! Only such incompetents as Somerset, Lerma and Concino Concini could have made their successors, Buckingham, Luynes and Olivares look like major statesmen. The simultaneous appearance in the three great European monarchies of these powerful and inept favourites signifies more, however, than just the laziness and bad judgment of their princes. As the crown rose higher above the ancient estates, some sort of first minister, some subject who could execute the king's decisions or make them for him, argue policy with counsellors and ambassadors, and, at need, assume the burden of the king's mistakes became increasingly necessary. At the same time, ministers with Atlantean shoulders fit to bear such burdens became harder to find, not merely because the actual business of government had become more complex, but also because the increase of royal power had left the crown isolated and irresponsible. Barons and clergy had lost their medieval functions and degenerated into courtiers. At the same time the disciplined corps of bureaucrats who were to provide the mystical idea of the state with its physical body had scarcely begun to form. Everywhere outside of Italy political relationships, like most relationships in a feudal society, were still personal and, in some of its most important aspects government was, in 1600 as in 1500, still just the king's household and his retinue. Thus the widening of royal power actually narrowed the king's choice of servants. As the pinnacle of majesty rose, all subjects were diminished, and the arts which distinguished one man from another in that perspective, the arts of a courtier, combined too rarely with the abilities of an administrator or the vision of a statesman.

In foreign policy the regimes of the favourites too often pursued unreal and shifting ends. They aimed at prestige rather than at solid advantage. Their firmest plans were diverted by court intrigues or changed abruptly to satisfy the vanity of a prince or the pique of a minister. Diplomats suffered. Some really able residents were so hamstrung by contradictory instructions and general uncertainty that they were reduced to almost total in-

activity. Others, bolder-minded, developed practically independent foreign policies of their own, risking, as in the case of
Bedmar at Venice, results even more harmful to themselves and
their governments. In the decade after 1610, French, Spanish and
English diplomats abroad had one thing in common. None of
them could be certain that their objectives harmonized with those
of their fellows at other courts or with the real views of their
government, or whether, if this were so today, it would remain so
tomorrow.

It may be doubted, however, whether the diplomatic services
of the three major powers suffered as much from these dramatic
uncertainties as from weaknesses in routine administration. Although war and diplomacy had been the major preoccupations of
the great monarchies since the 1490s, none of them had developed
a foreign office as really businesslike as that of the papal curia or
the Venetian signory of their time, any more than any of them had
developed a standing army as disciplined and well-organized as
they could see among the Turks. For both failures the institutional
habits of their medieval past and the feudal-aristocratic tone of
their society are at least a partial explanation. The difficulty in
diplomacy as in war was a dependence on a nexus of personal
relationships, and the accompanying patterns of behaviour surviving from an age when government and war were alike functions
of interlocking groups of households. In justice and finance,
feudal habits had begun to yield relatively early to the need for
trained personnel. But in the employments more fit for gentlemen
old ways persisted.

Some advance towards an organized foreign office was made by
each of the three major powers in the middle decade of the
sixteenth century, through the increasing activities of the royal
secretaries. Essentially only confidential clerks in charge of the
king's correspondence, these officials became the principal
channels of royal communication with councils and with foreign
governments. The routine conduct of foreign affairs fell, therefore, largely under their charge. The kings' secretaries drafted
letters to foreign courts and drew up instructions of ambassadors.
They held the ciphers and kept registers of diplomatic papers. To
them their masters' envoys addressed explanations or requests too
trivial or too informal for inclusion in regular dispatches. They

often acted also as intermediaries in discussions with foreign ambassadors at their masters' courts. The more diligent among them were the recipients of a considerable volume of secret intelligence. Really active and able secretaries, like Cecil or Villeroy or Antonio Perez discharged most of the duties and assumed most of the responsibilities of ministers of foreign affairs.[1]

Nevertheless, the secretariats failed to develop anywhere into regularly organized foreign offices. If the ablest secretaries behaved almost like foreign ministers, most others functioned merely as glorified chief clerks. And none of them was without a distracting mass of other responsibilities. An English manuscript 'Treatise of the Office of a Principal Secretary to Her Majesty' from the last decade of the sixteenth century lists a bewildering variety. Besides all the duties of a foreign minister, and those of a chief of security police and counter-intelligence, the secretary was supposed to concern himself with aspects of the Church, the armed forces, finance, justice, the administration of Wales, the Scottish Border, Ireland, the Channel, the royal household — in short with any matter which the privy council might discuss or any document which the queen might have to sign. No wonder an Elizabethan wrote, 'Amongst all ... offices ... in this state there is none ... more subject to cumber and variableness than is the office of the principal secretary, by reason of the variety and uncertainty of his employment.'[2]

In England, whether it was the 'cumber and variableness' of the duties, or simply the jealousy with which sixteenth-century monarchs so often regarded their more important officers, after the fall of the first great Principal Secretary, Thomas Cromwell, in 1540, two secretaries were appointed, although the office itself was left undivided. That is to say, both individuals were 'to have, enjoy, and use the place of the Principal Secretary' with the consequent right to open all correspondence and intervene at any time in any of the business of the office. This odd arrangement persisted for more than a century except for two intervals, and in spite of the opportunities it offered for muddle and bickering, usually worked fairly well. But not even such vigorous secretaries as Francis Walsingham and the two Cecils were always able to keep all the threads of foreign policy in their hands, and after 1612 the office of Principal Secretary degenerated again into a routine clerkship without having taken the next step towards specialized organization which it had so nearly approached.

In France, a greater kingdom with an even more bewildering variety of duties for the royal secretary, the multiplication of officers had begun earlier and reached, before long, a kind of specialization. Francis I had generally at least two *secrétaires d'État*, and in the last years of his reign, four. This number was fixed in 1547, and special duties were assigned to each. But instead of a logical separation of foreign and domestic affairs each of the four supervised both certain French provinces and the relations with certain neighbouring states. Thus the secretary for Normandy, Picardy and Flanders handled the correspondence with England and Scotland; the one for the south-western provinces of France dealt with Spain and Portugal; the one for the south-eastern with Rome, Venice and the Levant, while the secretary for Champagne and Burgundy managed business with Germany and the Swiss.

Whatever excuse there may have been for this arrangement probably lay in the feeling that the secretaries' duties should be kept clerical and administrative, and that it was more important for them to be acquainted with courier routes and frontier intelligence than with the over-all picture of foreign relations. In practice the ablest of the four secretaries generally intervened in a good many affairs outside his own division, and the arrangement, although it continued for more than forty years, proved even more inconvenient than the English one. In 1589 a single secretary, Villeroy, was for the first time entrusted with all the correspondence with foreign governments, and under Henry IV that minister began to build something like the nucleus of a *Ministère des Affaires Étrangères*. But even during Villeroy's tenure this specialization was not always observed, and, after Henry IV's assassination, foreign affairs, like the rest of the royal government, fell again into confusion.

Spain, under Philip II, probably moved farthest towards the development of an organized foreign office. The very complexity of the Spanish realms, the separate crowns and separate legal systems even within the peninsula, obliged the development of a group of parallel councils, and inhibited the growth of a single, undifferentiated royal secretariat. Internal justice and administration were necessarily divided among the councils of

Castile, of Aragon, and so forth, to each of which a separate royal secretary was attached. War and foreign affairs were left to the Council of State, with whom the king communicated through his Secretary of State. On his accession Philip II terminated the anomaly of a dual administration of foreign affairs which had developed under Charles V, and his first Secretary of State, Gonzalo Perez, had the entire supervision of foreign correspondence, much as Cecil had at the same time under Elizabeth, without being distracted by as many other responsibilities.

Gonzalo Perez never exercised anything like Cecil's influence on policy, was never really a minister at all, but he had a gift for administration and, assisted by his king's growing passion for bureaucratic routine, he gave the Spanish diplomatic service an orderly and relatively efficient central office. After Gonzalo Perez's death, two Secretaries of State were appointed. Perez's brilliant son Antonio was charged with northern affairs, France, England, Flanders and the empire, and a colleague, Gabriel de Zayas, with Italy and the Mediterranean. Antonio, however, more minister than secretary, soon intervened in Italian negotiations, while before long the situation was further complicated by the rise of the king's 'arch-secretary', Mateo Vasquez, who handled mostly domestic affairs but through whom Philip sometimes communicated with foreign sovereigns or with his own envoys without notice to either of his Secretaries of State.

More than most of his royal contemporaries Philip II believed in dividing his own servants to rule them. He allowed no man but himself to know all the moves on the board, and in the latter part of his reign, his jealous secrecy and fatal industry, his passion for seeing and handling, annotating and eventually answering all important correspondence himself, lay like a dead weight on the conduct of his foreign policy. As a result, responsibility among his Secretaries of State remained dispersed and uncertain, and, though they were abler and more independent men than their successors under Philip III, they shrank in stature and initiative after 1580. Instead of growing into a real ministry, the office of Spanish Secretary of State was already dwindling to the routine clerical status which was all its holders could pretend to in the seventeenth century.

The importance attached by their society to personal status and a personal nexus of relationships was certainly one obstacle impeding the development of the secretary's office. Unless he was a person of great force of character, and very confident of his master's support, the secretary found it difficult to deal with the magnates of the royal council. He was likely to be snubbed and by-passed and kept in ignorance of things it behoved him to know. On the other hand, each secretary tended to make himself as much like a great lord as he could by performing the tasks of his office as far as possible with members of his own household, loyal to him, responsible to him, and dependent upon him as an individual rather than as a royal officer. No impersonally loyal bureaucracy such as served the Venetian signory developed, and this failure contributed alike to the intrigue and cross-purposes between competing secretaries, and to royal suspicion of the office, and consequent willingness to keep it divided.

When the secretary's office was weak, naturally ambassadors suffered. The lack of an orderly hierarchy of administration made it impossible for an ambassador to be sure he was receiving the information and advice he needed, or that the secretary to whom he was addressing his requests and explanations any longer had the ear of the king or even, perhaps, any place in the negotiations in hand. A prudent ambassador, therefore, did not rely on official channels, but cultivated some private friend at court who could keep him posted, a precaution which, before long, the theorists were recommending as standard.[3] Private connections were more reliable than official ones, as long as social rank and individual prestige counted for more than official status.

The tendency of the age to convert public offices into personal domains, wherever possible into bureaucratic fiefs, retarded the development of another function of the secretary's office, the keeping of proper records. Exactly because the conduct of diplomacy becomes enormously more difficult without adequate files, royal secretaries and their underlings were even more likely to monopolize and sometimes to plunder the king's papers than negligence and jackdaw covetousness would have made them anyway. In consequence, until almost the middle of the seventeenth century, none of the three great western powers possessed diplomatic archives as orderly and usable as those of the Florentines or Venetians two hundred years before.

Spain, under Philip II, took the longest step forward. Philip's first Secretary of State, Gonzalo Perez, began the concentration at Simancas of Castilian royal archives, founding the great collection which historians have since found indispensable. But the grim castle of Simancas can hardly have been a convenient place to consult current records, even when the court was, as often in the first years of Philip II, at Valladolid. When Madrid became the usual seat of government, papers could be stored at Simancas, but scarcely used there. In consequence, we hear of a great collection of state papers of all kinds which the secretary, Gonzalo Perez, kept in his own house in Madrid. This practice was continued by his son Antonio, who was able to control a mass of government documents long after his fall from power, and to make off with a damaging selection of them at the time of his break for freedom. For a long time, the inconvenient location of the older records and the private hoarding of the current ones were another drag on the leaden pace of Spanish diplomacy.

England and France were even farther than Spain from main-taining usable foreign office archives. In England in 1592, Robert Beale complained: 'Heretofore towards the latter end of King Henry VIII, there was a chamber in Westminster where such things [dispatches, instructions and other documents] were kept and they were not in the Secretary's private custody. But, since that, order hath been neglected, and those things which were public have been culled out and gathered into private books, whereby no means are left to see what was done before, or to give any light of service to young beginners, which is not well: And therefore I would wish a secretary to keep such things apart in a chest or place and not to confound them with his own. And the want of so doing was the cause that, on the death of Mr. Secretary Walsingham, all his papers and books, both public and private, were seized on and carried away, perhaps by those who would be loath to be used so themselves.'[4] In spite of Beale's wise sugges-tion, things were very little better ordered decades later in the last years of James.

In France, they were worse ordered still. The migratory habits of the Valois court and the confusion of the Civil Wars would have inhibited any attempt to set up a central depository of documents, even if each of the four Secretaries of State had not been jealous of his control of the papers of his own department. Villeroy's unified administration brought only a temporary improvement. When Richelieu took over the direction of foreign affairs, he was obliged to write to the French ambassadors serving abroad and ask them for copies of their most recent instructions. None were available at his master's court.

If, for want of an adequate basis for comparison, diplomats were not quite aware how much the work of the resident embassies was hampered by the failure of the new monarchies to develop efficient foreign offices, they were acutely conscious of how much they suffered by the parallel failure in the field of public finance. Upon none of the royal servants did the disorder of the sixteenth-century fiscal administration bear harder. Of course there was no dependable separate budget for foreign affairs — none of the services of state in the three great monarchies had anything of the kind. But the domestic services usually had each its access to some reasonably regular source of revenue. Counsellors and household officials were likely to be assigned pensions on particular tax and rent rolls. Officers of justice and finance could pay themselves out of the monies they handled. Moreover, in the pyramid of place-holders who jostled each other on the steps of the throne, all, from ushers and gate-keepers to the highest judges and ministers of state, were accustomed to presents and commissions, the 'sweeteners' which were normal lubricants of official business. Finally, an official at home could hang about the proper ante-rooms until by sheer persistence he collected at least a part of what was due to him. But ambassadors, like the army, served abroad. They were dependent, like the army, on what ministers could and would spare from the general treasury, without the army's recourse of mutiny or desertion or plunder if no money came. In an age when revenues were rarely adequate to expenditures, an age of rising prices, extravagant courts, obsolete fiscal methods and haphazard emergency financing, there was never enough public money to go round. Hence constant complaints of tardy payment and mounting debt throughout the diplomatic correspondence of a century, and De Vera's realistic judgment that a solid private fortune and a fat rent roll were among the most important qualifications for a major foreign embassy.

It is a tribute to the kind of loyalty which the new monarchies were able to command that this most crying imperfection of the princes, their inability to pay their most important servants abroad as regularly and faithfully as they paid their grooms and ushers, did not occasion more frequent derelictions of duty. The general standard of honesty among public officials was, to say the best of it, lax and uncertain. Ambassadors often possessed secrets worth a fortune. Yet very few ambassadors proved corruptible. The imperfect princes were better served than their treatment of their servants seemed to merit.

CHAPTER XXIV

MEN SENT TO LIE ABROAD

GIVEN the difficulties which obsolescent, inefficient adminis-tration and chaotic methods of finance created for dip-lomats serving abroad, it is less remarkable that the age saw few perfect ambassadors than that the average quality in the three chief European foreign services remained as high as it was. For any ambassador the chance of financial embarrassment was almost a certainty, that of failure and frustration through no fault of his own very high indeed. Nor can the rewards have seemed at all commensurate with the risks, especially for those men who bore the brunt of the service, the resident ambassadors.

Certainly the immediate pecuniary rewards were not very tempting. Throughout the sixteenth and early seventeenth centuries some offices under the new monarchies proved extra-ordinarily lucrative, but the normal compensation of resident ambassadors, though it rose fairly steadily between 1560 and 1610, barely kept pace with the necessary increase in their ex-penditures. To begin with, both Ferdinand of Aragon and Henry VII tried paying their earliest residents far less than Italian ex-perience had proved necessary. Rodrigo de Puebla in England was paid, or rather promised, about twenty-five ducats a month, and John Stile in Spain about thirty, at a time when their Vene-tian colleagues were drawing four times that, plus travelling expenses and the services of a paid secretary. But by 1510 England and Spain were both meeting or slightly bettering the Venetian rate, and it would be fair to say that the average maintenance allowance of a resident ambassador of that date was between three and four ducats a day. Fifty years later, 1550-60, the allow-ance had about doubled; six to eight ducats was usual. In another fifty years the rate had about doubled again; around 1610 a resident ambassador at a major post might be allowed no more than twelve to fourteen ducats a day or as much as twenty. If the extra allowances around 1610 were more generous than they had been a hundred, or even fifty years before, the extra expenses were definitely greater so that the result was about the same.[1]

233

Necessarily all this is very imprecise. Each government, of course, stated the pay of its envoys in one of its own monetary units, not always the same one, and the values of these units and their exchange rates against one another varied, though the fluctuations were not as violent as those the twentieth century has become used to. There was a difference between services. Around 1510 the Venetians were probably the best paid diplomats in Europe, by 1560 they were dropping behind, by 1610 they could not afford the display which custom imposed on the representatives of the great powers. There were differences between posts in the same service. Charles de Danzay, for instance, serving France in Denmark around 1560, was allowed less than half the sum granted the French ambassadors at Madrid and Rome. And there were fluctuations, down as well as up, in the pay of the same service for the same post. But it would be safe to say that there was an average normal allowance for the resident ambassadors of major powers at major posts, based on the kind of establishment the ambassador was expected to maintain, and that this allowance just about quadrupled during a century in which Europe experienced something like a fourfold rise in prices.

There is no use trying to restate an ambassador's income in 1510 or in 1610 in terms of present day purchasing power; there are too many incommensurables in the problem. But we can say about what a normal stipend meant in terms of contemporary status and standards of living. In the first years of Henry VIII, the Spanish Ambassador in England drew a maintenance allowance which would work out at a little more than £300 a year in the money of the time; fifty years later, in the first years of Elizabeth, twice that, or rather more than £600; fifty years later again, in the reign of James I, nearly £1300. Now three hundred odd pounds a year around 1515 was not the income of a wealthy bishop or a great nobleman, but it was quite that of a prosperous merchant or well-to-do country gentleman. It would run to a household of twenty or so, a certain amount of entertaining, and a good appearance at court, though without lavish ostentation. In 1615, four times the money would do about as well. This, or a little better than this, was the scale at which a resident ambassador was expected to live. He could just about manage to do so, if he had some income of his own to fill in the chinks, and if his stipend was paid promptly.

It rarely was. The first and the last Spanish ambassador in London during the period we are speaking of were both unusually unlucky. Out of Rodrigo de Puebla's meagre stipend of three hundred and fifty crowns a year — say seventy pounds — the Spanish treasury managed to hold back, between 1495 and 1508, some three thousand crowns or about two-thirds of his whole salary. It still owed him that amount when he died. De Puebla had but little property in Spain. Naturally he was driven to mean shifts and only escaped a debtor's prison by the king's grace. Don Diego Sarmiento de Acuna, later count of Gondomar, was a wealthy man when he went to England in 1613. His allowance was five hundred crowns a month, about sixteen times de Puebla's. In one year, 1617, he received from Spain more actual money than de Puebla saw throughout his entire embassy. But Gondomar's expenses were proportionally heavier, and at need he was ready to meet out of his own pocket, not only his own expenses but the king of Spain's other obligations in England. If all the money promised Gondomar had been paid promptly he might just barely have managed. But by 1621 the Spanish treasury owed Gondomar 33,000 crowns for unpaid maintenance allowance and other authorized expenses. One by one he had mortgaged his estates in Spain until on his death-bed he could write, like de Puebla a century before, that his embassy in England had reduced him to beggary. Beggary for a nobleman like Gondomar would have been the height of affluence for Dr. de Puebla, but given the difference in their circumstances, their sacrifices were not dissimilar.

De Puebla's and Gondomar's stories can be balanced by a few instances on the other side. There was, for example, that shrewd, hard-fisted Savoyard, Eustache Chapuys, who represented Charles V in England from 1529 to 1544. Chapuys's allowance was rather below the average for his period, yet he did not stint in the emperor's service. His household and staff in the 1530s were at least as large as Gondomar's eighty years later and he, too, knew the value of magnificence on occasion, although he had no private means with which to support it. He found the emperor's treasury as slow as royal treasuries usually were, and he, too, ran into debt. But at last his services were recognized by the gift of a handsome sinecure. In the final years of his embassy, by skilful investment of his surplus income on the Antwerp bourse, he made enough to retire in affluence, restore the fortunes of his family, and found two colleges, one at Louvain and one in his native town of Annecy. A few other diplomats, like Walsingham, made a resident embassy a stepping-stone to a lucrative career at court, but I know of no one except Chapuys who got rich at diplomacy itself.

Most ambassadors finished their missions poorer than when they took them up, and most of them found that long absence from the king's court and long association with foreigners were the wrong road to advancement. Nevertheless, diplomatic service throughout the Renaissance continued to attract its share, or better than its share, of able, even brilliant men. If they were not the paragons demanded by Ottaviano Maggi, they were certainly a high average of the classes that served the crowns of Europe in their day, both in education and in natural talent, and this in spite of the fact that their selection was capricious, and their training for diplomacy only began with their actual service.

The only language one could be sure that most diplomats would have studied, for instance, was Latin. Few ambassadors were completely without Latin, and most of them were capable of composing and delivering a passable formal oration in that tongue, or of using it to inspect the clauses of a treaty. A few were notable classicists, more apparently in the first half of the century than in the second; a few could converse in Latin, fluently and elegantly. But such a command of conversational Latin as endeared Gondomar to James I was beginning to be rare among diplomats by 1600, and its use in actual negotiations except in eastern Europe had been declining for some time. Fewer ecclesiastics sat in royal councils, and it may be that the higher standards of grammatical purity imposed by the humanists somewhat embarrassed easy conversation. About 1500 Louis XII's council, Maximilian's and Henry VII's all spoke Latin with ambassadors; so, though none of them were exactly elegant Latinists, did those monarchs themselves. But of their successors only Henry VIII was a better Latinist; Francis I rarely attempted Latin impromptu and Charles V could never converse freely in anything but French. At about the same time, negotiations through interpreters became common for all three royal councils. After 1550 the language barrier widened further. Among their royal contemporaries only

Elizabeth of England and James I were sound classicists, and in the Latin of the ambassadors who addressed them both usually found more to smile at than to admire. Their councils in dealing with foreign diplomats used Latin only as a last resort.

Meanwhile, no other common language of diplomacy had arisen. In the first half of the century, the accident that the great rival of the king of France, Charles V, was also French-speaking, made that tongue widely accepted, but even in Charles V's lifetime most of his Spanish nobles seem not to have bothered to learn French, while its currency among the English was declining. Among Edward VI's ambassadors to French-speaking courts, Heynes, Bonner, Paget, Morison and Thirlby were all too deficient in French to use it for negotiation, and after making heavy weather in Latin both Paget and Thirlby were fain to try Italian.[2]

Italian was, indeed, probably the commonest modern language in Europe in the second half of the sixteenth century. Far more of Philip II's courtiers spoke it than could or would speak French. It was the only modern language other than their own which most educated Frenchmen attempted to master. It seems to have been almost as current at the Austrian Habsburg court as Spanish, and more Elizabethans learned it than learned French. Yet, though it frequently provided the medium of social intercourse, it never became the accepted language of diplomacy, and some ambassadors were either sadly deficient in it or lacked it altogether.

Except in Italy, French diplomats usually spoke French, Spaniards Spanish. At Madrid regularly, and at Brussels frequently, representatives of the Austrian Habsburgs also used Spanish. The Italians could usually get along in their own tongue, with Latin for formal occasions. The English, who did not expect foreigners to speak English in England or understand it abroad, made shift with whatever continental languages they happened to know. The occasional envoys of the German princes usually leaned on Latin, but the fact that after 1550 a number of French diplomats deliberately learned German as an aid to their careers shows that Latin was no longer thoroughly reliable as a medium for informal negotiation in the Germanies.[3] Roger Ascham had noticed this as early as 1546.

It was with the other subjects demanded by the theorists as it was with languages. Ambassadors were more likely to know classical than recent history, and as late as 1600, after a century of brilliant scientific progress in geography, to take their notions of the world outside of western Europe from absurdly obsolete texts. As the graces of the courtier began to be considered the most important requisite for an ambassador, fewer trained legists, as well as fewer churchmen, served on missions abroad, and even a knowledge of the civil and canon law, normal among diplomats around 1500, was uncommon a century later.

In compensation for this, in most of the subjects which the Renaissance considered appropriate for a gentleman's education, the diplomats of the three major powers would seem to have been better grounded than the average of their class. There were not a few poets and scholars among them, a number of discriminating patrons of letters and arts, and some earnest students of political philosophy. Several ambassadors, like De Vera, were distinguished in all of these pursuits. In spite of its doubtful rewards and in spite of the haphazard manner in which its members were selected, a diplomatic career seems to have had a peculiar attraction for alert and inquiring minds.

It can only have been the fascination of the game of high politics for its own sake which led men of talent and principle to accept and even seek posts as resident ambassadors and to spend on them, out of their own fortunes, far more than they could expect in return. For there was another drawback to the position which, in an age avid of fame and reputation, and sensitive to points of honour, must have been felt with special acuteness. Although resident embassies had been established in Europe for more than a century there were still grave doubts about the propriety of a resident's functions.

The embarrassment with which Alberico Gentili speaks of them is revealing. All diplomatic missions, he says, are either for business, or for ceremony, or for a period of time.[4] He was reluctant even to use the term 'resident', though it had long been in common use, and puzzled how to say what a resident was supposed to do. According to the accepted tradition, both missions of ceremony and missions of negotiations were properly entrusted to special ambassadors. But what duties did that leave for the resident?

Little more than transmitting the views of his government and reporting to it news from abroad. In the beginning when residents were liaison officers between allies, such functions were valid enough. But what Gentili saw in his day were residents exchanged between all but open enemies. Under such circumstances, what could a resident be but an official liar or a licensed spy, unless, as in the case of Bernardino de Mendoza, which had set Gentili thinking, he was the instigator of a treasonable conspiracy? On such assumptions, it was broad-minded of Gentili to argue that residents really were genuine diplomats, and resident embassies not necessarily and inherently an evil. [5]

To Gentili's fellow-emigré, Carlo Pasquale, resident embassies were clearly an evil, and not clearly a necessary one. In these latter days, he says, ambassadors come not to negotiate peace and friendship, but to spy, corrupt and betray. Most of the other theorists, from Dolet to Marselaer, are inclined to agree with Pasquale's condemnation of 'this new unhappy birth of this unhappy time'. [6] If residents must be received at all, everyone concurred they should be received with caution. If they must be sent, they should be carefully selected for the kind of work they have to do. It is not until De Vera that, in any writing outside of Italy, we find resident embassies accepted as a matter of course, or much recognition of the possibility that a resident might have other things to do besides lying about his employer and spying upon his hosts. Most of Sir Henry Wotton's contemporaries would have accepted the literal Latin of his epigram as readily as its punning English. 'A resident ambassador is a man sent to tell lies abroad for his country's good.' [7]

CHAPTER XXV

THE EMBASSY ROUTINE

JUST as the notions of the 1590s about residents would have seemed old-fashioned to Ermolao Barbaro in 1490, so, in that century, the procedures of diplomacy changed but little and its ceremonial patterns still less. By the early 1600s, the ambassador's solemn entry and public reception had lost something of the popular pageantry of the waning Middle Ages, and taken on more of the formality of a court masque, but its main outlines, like those of other diplomatic ceremonies, would have been familiar to Machiavelli or Commynes, or even to Bernard du Rosier. So would the documents with which diplomats dealt, and the legal framework within which they negotiated. And Machiavelli and Barbaro, at least, would have recognized in the organization and routine operations of a resident embassy around 1600 much they had known.

In some respects, indeed, European resident embassies in about 1600, like the foreign offices of the European monarchies, remained less business-like than their Italian prototypes. As the staffs of the royal secretariats tended to get confused with the households of the royal secretaries, so embassy staffs with the households of ambassadors. The resident's confidential secretary, who had charge of the cyphers, kept the files and took down from dictation the dispatches — this important official who, in Italy, would have been a state appointee with separate credentials, was in French and Spanish and English embassies as much the resident's personal servant as his maître d'hôtel, his cook or his groom. The ambassador selected his whole staff and paid them. Except for under-servants engaged on the spot, they accompanied him to his post and, when he left it, left with him.

As early as the reign of Charles V the Spaniards had found more than once how gravely this might interrupt the operations of an embassy. If the previous ambassador happened to leave, as Louis de Praet did in 1525, before his successor arrived, there was no one to explain the state of current negotiations, or the attitudes of influential counsellors, or to point out reliable informants.

Weeks might be wasted in picking up threads which should never have been dropped. If business, not covered by the new ambassador's instructions, was still pending, it had to remain in suspense. If delayed dispatches in the old ambassador's cipher arrived, nobody was able to read them.

For it was with embassy papers as with embassy staffs. During his mission, each ambassador was expected to preserve the originals of all papers received (transcripts of all documents transmitted, and copies of all dispatches originating in the embassy, these last normally in letter-books), so that the entire correspondence of any embassy was represented by two complete files, the ambassador's and the royal secretary's. But throughout the sixteenth and seventeenth centuries the embassy files were the ambassador's personal property. Sometimes he took them home with him. Many books and bundles of embassy papers now in national archives were long in the muniment rooms of private families. Sometimes a departing ambassador destroyed most of his papers before he left. Once or twice he just abandoned them in the vacant embassy to be snapped up by the agents of his recent host. In any case the embassy files were usually left bare. The next resident could not count on finding even the texts of major treaties; whatever documents he needed he had to get before he left, from a royal secretary.

Before the end of the fifteenth century, the Venetians had found a better way of managing things. Not the ambassador but his official secretary was, in their service, the custodian of the embassy files, and the secretary was expected to remain at his post for some time after the departure of his chief. But the greater powers were slow in arriving at so sensible a solution. As late as 1650 the only means they had found for ensuring continuity in the operations of their embassies was to try to see that the old ambassador stood by long enough to settle his successor into his job. This would have worked better had not the replacements often been so tardy in arriving and the incumbents usually so anxious to depart.

The jobs into which the residents had to settle were more varied and exacting than such writers as Gentili and Marselaer represented, but, though residents were expected to be far more than just liaison officers and intelligence agents, intelligence agents they remained. The collection and processing of information to be relayed to their home government was still, in the Europe of 1620, as it had been in the Italy of 1490, their steadiest and most unremitting task.

It was a task still subject to all the difficulties that beset it in Barbaro's time. It had to satisfy a thirst for information which grew with each intensification of the struggle for power. It had to collect this information without the aid of any of those commercial satisfiers of curiosity, like news services, which are such a help in these days to organized espionage. And it had to contend with the addiction of Renaissance statecraft to an elaborate, fantastic secretiveness, often about matters which there was no real hope of keeping secret. In addition, ambassadors at the major European courts had difficulties unknown to their Italian precursors. The larger areas to be reported on, the large and growing differences in language and customs and culture, were serious obstacles to accurate reporting. Religious disunity was a graver one still. As the schism in Christendom widened, inevitably ambitious and energetic ambassadors adopted intelligence methods which the theorists were obliged to condemn.

Developments in the Spanish embassy in London afford an illustration.[1] When Rodrigo de Puebla took up his post there, he found normal Italian intelligence techniques adequate for his notion of his duties. He had no money to buy information, but among his many wants he never noted that one. He did find ways of trading for news, gathering all he could from his letters from Spain, from his colleagues in London, from the Spanish resident ambassadors in the Netherlands and Germany, and even from Spanish and Italian merchants, and making himself so well-informed and so readily informative about affairs in Europe that when such matters were on the table he often functioned practically as a member of Henry VII's council. But mostly, as Ermolao Barbaro had advised, he just listened. He cultivated the confidence, or at least the tolerance of the king and of important counsellors, and reported what they told him, circumstantially and at length, adding shrewd comments. As his long embassy wore on, he picked up some English and apparently one or two of his servants spoke it, but this made little difference in his methods. The kind of news he reported was all his masters wanted; he did not try to widen his range.

During the next twenty years, subsequent Spanish ambassadors did not improve much on de Puebla's range and methods. One of his immediate successors spent a little money, rather fruitlessly, on court gossip. Several of them, like de Puebla himself, culled occasional scraps of information from the Spanish merchants in London. And after 1520, the pensions which Charles V agreed to pay, not only to Wolsey but to a number of magnates supposed to be important on the royal council, should have secured for his ambassadors a group of friendly informants; might, indeed, have done so had they been promptly paid. But the chief reliance of the Spanish ambassadors during all these years was Henry VIII's queen, Catherine of Aragon. Even after Wolsey had shouldered her out of her former intimate contact with every aspect of foreign affairs, Catherine still knew more of what was going on in court circles, and in the royal council and in the king's mind, than any ambassador could hope to know. And even when imperial pensions went unpaid and relations between England and Spain were officially cool, she could still be counted on for friendly counsel and for really vital news.

The crisis of the queen's divorce forced a change in the intelligence methods of the Spanish-imperial embassy. When Eustache Chapuys reached London in 1529 he found Queen Catherine isolated and spied upon, rarely able to manage an unsupervised interview with her nephew's ambassador, or even an uncensored message to him, and more rarely still able to tell him much even about her own affairs. Nor could Chapuys rely on any of the other chief sources of his predecessors. The imperial pensions in England were left unpaid, and Henry VIII's counsellors were wary of being thought on too good terms with the emperor's ambassador. Even petty gossip was difficult to get at because, as Catherine's avowed champion, Chapuys preferred not to be seen too often at court, and, when he did go there, was conscious that he was never unwatched. At the same time, Chapuys felt that full and accurate information about affairs in England was more important than ever to his master. Henry VIII's suit for divorce had not only altered the currents of European policy, it had reached into every corner of English political life. Chapuys, a veteran of the political battles of pre-reformation Geneva, appreciated that parliamentary manœuvres, theological disputes and the trends of middle-class opinion might be as important to imperial policy as court and foreign intrigues, or military and naval preparations.

Therefore, in the deadlock of Anglo-Imperial negotiations, Chapuys made his intelligence system his chief concern. In the first place he enlarged the embassy staff, getting into debt to do so. He took into his service several of Catherine's former servants, English, Welsh and Spanish, including her gentleman usher, Montoya, a Spaniard who had served more than twenty years in England, and whom Chapuys made one of his principal secretaries. He recruited young gentlemen from Flanders and Burgundy, insisted on their learning English and, although he did not go frequently to court himself, encouraged them to do so, expecting, probably, that half a dozen adroit, agreeable, unobtrusive young men could overhear more than one dignified and conspicuous one. Besides Montoya, he usually had two secretaries who spoke good English, and provided each of them with particular English contacts. In addition, he engaged as his personal valet a taciturn Fleming who went with him everywhere, on the excuse that the ambassador's gout made it difficult for him to walk unaided. This servant's linguistic talents would certainly have surprised the counsellors who, counting on Chapuys's ignorance of English, sometimes talked among themselves too freely in his presence.

Chapuys also spent a good deal on outright espionage. After 1533, he must have hired five or six full-time agents who, in turn, were always glad to pay modest sums for miscellaneous items of information, such as any details that innkeepers could supply about interesting foreigners who passed through London, what an underservant knew of who visited Thomas Cromwell, even what a stable-boy might notice of the state of a courier's horse. Now and then there were big coups, like the corruption of Marillac's principal secretary which provided a set of French ciphers and transcripts of correspondence for eighteen months, or of one of Anne Boleyn's maids who reported regularly to someone at the imperial embassy for more than a year. Mostly the items gathered were petty and miscellaneous, many of them, we can be sure, never included in dispatches at all, but enough of them fitted into their proper places and guardedly but (a historian may be grateful) adequately identified as to source, so that from Chapuys's dispatches one can get a representative picture of Renaissance espionage in action.

Chapuys also cultivated the Spanish merchant community in London, many of whom were by now residents of long standing. Unlike his predecessors, he was equally attentive to the merchants from the Netherlands, went out of his way to do them small favours, and received in return invaluable news of the movements of money, arms, and English agents in and out of Antwerp, besides help in transmitting his dispatches and handling his funds. In addition, perhaps because he was not himself a native of any of Charles's hereditary domains, perhaps only because he foresaw the possible profit, Chapuys took the widest view of his duties to imperial subjects. He voluntarily intervened on the side of the German merchants of the Steelyard, made their problems his affair as no previous imperial ambassador had done, and won them over as cordial allies. Presently they were telling him a good deal about the movements of their Lutheran compatriots in London, and of Henry's agents in the Germanies. Italian bankers were equally grateful for his attitude that the emperor's general overlordship of Italy authorized an imperial ambassador to act in behalf of any Italians without diplomatic representatives of their own. In return, they helped keep track of the movements of English funds abroad, and of French and English agents (often Italians) on the continent. Merchants found Chapuys, who was, himself, of middle-class burgher background, easy to get on with. They came to the embassy to dine, to air their grievances, to take advice, to exchange items of news and gossip. 'The merchants who visit me daily' is a recurrent phrase in his dispatches. He valued their news of the English hinterland, and their sidelights on English opinion, and the English friends they brought to the embassy. Probably Chapuys got more important information from merchants than from his hired spies.

Naturally, he did not neglect the normal diplomatic sources: what he could learn from Henry and his ministers, what he was told by courtiers and counsellors, some of them bound by old ties of imperial friendship, some timid or self-seeking, some merely indiscreet, some trying to mislead him. And he was the first to develop systematically another source: the friends of the queen, the intransigent devotees of the old religion, the feudal reactionaries, all the elements that were to constitute the ultra-Catholic party. Chapuys had enough information, and was shrewd enough to evaluate what that group told him better than some of his successors did. But he began the practice of linking the Spanish embassy with partisans having special political aims, and of dabbling, not merely in internal politics, but in something like treason.

Chapuys's intelligence apparatus represents about the most diversified development of the sixteenth century. He left at least its skeleton, as he left his embassy files, to his successor, but one good example was not enough to break a bad custom. Vanderdelft and Scheyve failed to cultivate Chapuys's sources, and even Simon Renard, until he became practically Queen Mary's privy councillor, was less well informed about English affairs. As for Philip II's ambassadors, they were increasingly trapped by their own and their king's orthodoxy into dependence on the ultra-Catholics who gave information to Spain because they put their faith above their country, and who were believed and quoted by one Spanish ambassador after another more because of the purity of their motives than because of the accuracy of their facts. That is probably why what Spanish ambassadors said about English public opinion drifted farther and farther away from reality as Elizabeth's reign wore on, and why, although some of them, Bernardino de Mendoza for example, had a great deal more secret service money to spend than Chapuys, they got, by and large, a great deal less for it.

By the early 1600s, the collection of information by resident ambassadors had become a more complicated business than it had been in Italy a century before. If it probably took less of the ambassador's own time, it was a much heavier burden on his staff, official and unofficial. In the order of their increasing novelty (and decreasing respectability) the methods may be listed as follows: Gathering the views and receiving the communications of the prince and his counsellors for transmission home. (This was the resident ambassador's primary original function.) Trading for items of political information by offering items useful to one's hosts. Gathering items for political background by ordinary observation. Cultivating informants, a method which might range from ordinary social courtesy, through the doing of special favours for probably useful persons to the payment of 'pensions' to highly placed officials and the plain bribery of understrappers. This method shaded into espionage and the employment of undercover agents often not officially connected with the embassy. By 1600 most embassies used such agents. And this, in turn, might be supplemented by conspiracy with political malcontents, usually the ambassador's co-religionists, whenever opportunity offered. At London and Paris, at least, in the later sixteenth century, this, too, was standard procedure.

Evaluating the intelligence from all these sources, and casting the sifted information into the form of dispatches, primary ones, addressed to the king (even when he was not expected to read them) and supplementary ones addressed to a royal minister or private secretary was the ambassador's own task. Then the dispatch had to be transmitted, and at this point not only the perennial difficulty of slow and expensive communications entered but the additional difficulty of keeping the contents of the dispatch secret.

Almost as soon as residents began their intelligence functions, royal ministers began to take counter-measures. In the 1520s Cardinal Wolsey and Charles V's minister, Gattinara, operated with forthright simplicity. When they suspected that an ambassador was up to something they disapproved of, they stopped his couriers and opened his dispatches. By Thomas Cromwell's day things were somewhat more subtly done; dispatches were delayed by accident and opened by mistake, but they got opened just the same. Later still, ministers like Walsingham, Bellièvre, and Antonio Perez exercised considerable ingenuity in getting copies of suspect embassy dispatches without the ambassador's ever learning that his pouches had been tampered with. Finally there was always the chance that some enemy might intercept dispatches. In the 1580s, for instance, bands of Huguenots were a constant nuisance to Spanish couriers, particularly in the western Pyrennees; at the same time English communications between Paris and the Channel were endangered by prowling Leaguer cavalry and French royal governors with Guisard sympathies.[2]

Against these risks the ambassador could take only two kinds of precautions. He could choose what seemed under the circumstances the safest method of transmission. And he could put his message in cipher. There were several ways dispatches might be sent. The one an ambassador was expected to use was one of his own government's couriers, either a royal servant on a return journey or a man on his own staff. The advantages were speed and whatever security a sealed embassy pouch afforded. The disadvantages were publicity (embassy couriers were marked men) and, generally, shortage of man-power. Ambassadors rarely had as many couriers as they needed. They could compensate for this by using the pouches of the government to which they were accredited, a courtesy always extended to them, but prudent ambassadors sent only the most harmless messages by such means. They could also avail themselves of some service for merchants, like the Merchant Strangers' Post which carried letters for a fee between London and Antwerp, a means perhaps a little safer than the royal pouches of their host, but also somewhat slower. Or they could prevail upon a merchant returning to their country to carry a dispatch. If it remained unsuspected, this was perhaps the safest arrangement of all. But no method could make a dispatch absolutely safe from interception.

As a further precaution it had been standard procedure since the last quarter of the fifteenth century, to put compromising dispatches in cipher.[3] By the 1620s, a number of ingenious methods of enciphering had already been worked out, but in practice they were too cumbersome or easy to get hopelessly scrambled, so that the method everyone used was so old that in the 1470s the Milanese chancellor Cecco Simonetta is supposed to have formulated the rules for breaking it. Substantially it was the simple substitutional cipher, that is, letting a numeral or arbitrary symbol stand for each letter of the alphabet. This kind of cipher is very easily broken, like the one in Poe's *Gold Bug*, by the method of frequencies, provided the message is long enough so that the letters and combinations of letters oftenest used in the language employed can be identified.

From the first, chanceries were aware of the vulnerability of this method. They sought to protect it by a partial suppression of frequencies, by including nulls (that is, meaningless signs thrown in at random), and using three or four signs for each vowel and two or three for frequent consonants. Often doubled letters got a special notation, and usually a dozen or more of the commonest combinations, the 'the's' and 'and's' and 'who's' and 'that's' in

English, for instance, a separate single sign. For further protection the Spanish, after about 1560, liked to code proper names which occurred frequently; thus Bernardino de Mendoza called the duke of Guise 'Mucio', and Gondomar gave the personages of James I's court names from romances of chivalry and classical mythology. The French, rather more sensibly, preferred arbitrary signs. All this may yield as many as a hundred separate symbols, though the usual number is between sixty and eighty, and written without breaks between the words can look dismayingly enigmatic.[4] Actually even the toughest of these ciphers will yield fairly quickly to persistent attack, especially if the decipherer knows, as he would, what language he is attacking, and suspects, as would be likely, at least a part of the content of the message.

Haste and carelessness made breaking these ciphers easier. Eighty signs is a good many, and sometimes a secretary forgot for a dozen lines or more to use another symbol for 'e' or signalled the presence of an important word by putting down precisely the same sequence of letters half a dozen times on the same page. Sometimes cipher was mixed with plain language so that the sense of the ciphered passage is ludicrously plain. And generally, although the risks of doing so were known, ambassadors used the same cipher for years on end. Thomas Spinelly, representing first Henry VII and then Henry VIII in the Netherlands and Spain, used the same one for upwards of fourteen years. In 1522 Wolsey gave his replacement in Spain a fresh one, because 'Spinelly's had come into too many hands.'[5] From 1529 to 1541 Eustache Chapuys always corresponded with the emperor in the same cipher; Thomas Cromwell's experts had broken it by 1535. In 1590 the French ambassador in Madrid wrote to Henry IV in the cipher he had used in letters to Henry III four years before, although in the meantime some of the staff of Henry III's secretariat had taken service with the pro-Spanish League and although, even supposing Henry IV may not have known that the Spanish had broken Longlée's cipher in 1587, he must have known that his own partisans in Bearn had succeeded in doing so from the first batch they captured. The Spanish ambassador at Prague from 1581 to 1608 held several ciphers, but employed only one in most of his important correspondence throughout his embassy, though for years Heidelberg, Dresden, Paris and Venice all held keys.

In fact embassies and foreign offices were not so naïve about their ciphers as might appear. All secretaries of state employed expert decipherers, and all knew that no cipher simple enough to be written rapidly and deciphered accurately could remain unbreakable when present in the bulk usual in long dispatches. But they knew, too, that a relatively simple cipher had many real uses. It protected the message from hasty perusal by dishonest embassy servants or officious frontier captains. Unless there was time to make a copy, there would be no use in some spy's opening a dispatch and then resealing it. And if any indiscreet passages were in cipher, an ambassador might, as a proof of his perfect frankness, pass his latest instructions across the council table, and be sure that the minister who glanced at them would not be able to grasp the sense of the enciphered passage, even though his clerks might have long been in possession of the key. One ambassador wrote, 'When the packet arrived, feeling sure that it would contain nothing offensive *in plain writing*, I opened it at once in the king's presence.' A really cautious ambassador phrased nineteen-twentieths of his correspondence so that even if it should fall into the hands of his hosts and be deciphered no serious harm would result. About the transmission of the twentieth dispatch he took elaborate precautions.

From the moment the ambassador began to listen to the reply to his first oration to the final enciphering and transmission of the intelligence collected by official and unofficial means, the embassy staff was performing what the theorists regarded, with whatever reluctance, as the proper work of a resident mission. In fact, however, the work of resident ambassadors had always been larger than that, and by the early 1600s it had to do with most matters which the theorists persisted in ascribing to special embassies. Not only did residents frequently undertake those courtesies once assigned to embassies of ceremony, but the ceremonial significance of the resident's office itself had become of great importance. And not only were resident ambassadors often charged with particular negotiations such as were formerly entrusted to special embassies, but the resident had come to play a rôle in the execution and sometimes in the shaping of high policy beyond the reach of any special mission.

In the later Middle Ages, it was in embassies of ceremony that ambassadors acted most clearly as the symbolic representatives of their principals. The whole point of the embassy of ceremony lay in the convention that in the gesture of obedience or condolence or congratulation which the ambassador performed, he acted as if in the person of his prince. Even though the capitals of the Italian states lay relatively near one another, the convenience of using residents for these symbolic courtesies began to be appreciated there by the 1470s, and not long after 1500 the earliest residents north of the Alps began to serve also as the representatives of their masters on occasion of ceremony. It may have been this function which led to an increasing emphasis on the representative character of the ambassador's office. Ermolao Barbaro had appreciated the point, but it was one thing to represent in Milan the special seriousness and integrity of the Venetian character, and quite another to represent at the court of one European sovereign the power and dignity of another crown, with all that implied in the assertion of national prestige.

For one thing, it meant an increasing care for the interests and safety of one's fellow-countrymen resident abroad, since they were under the protection of the crown one represented. None of the earliest ambassadors seem to have taken this point of view. If Rodrigo de Puebla was useful to Spanish merchants in London, it was because they could be useful to him. Ferdinand of Aragon's ambassadors in the Netherlands once reproved the Spaniards of Bruges for disturbing the dignified progress of state negotiations with tradesmen's quarrels. But gradually ambassadors began to behave as if an injury to their master's subjects was an insult to his crown, and to intervene to protect their fellow-countrymen without waiting for specific instructions to do so. By the early 1600s, although general instructions were still vague, and the theorists were silent on the point, this had become the customary attitude of most resident ambassadors.

The chief burden which his representative function imposed on the resident, however, was in maintaining the dignity of his master's crown in the eternal wrangle over precedence. In the fifteenth century the conjunction of a number of special embassies at a given court occasionally raised the question of precedence, especially at Rome where papal masters of ceremonies kept tables (rather variable tables) of the relative dignity of the powers of

Christendom, but resident ambassadors were not much affected, until after about 1530, perhaps because of remaining doubts about their genuinely representative character. Except at Venice and Rome, where local rules prevailed, residents, before about 1530, seem to have had no special place in protocol and, consequently, no right to expect any particular position at court ceremonies. Here and there peppery individuals raised momentary difficulties, but the prevailing attitude seems to have been that of old Dr. de Puebla who told his successor, Fuensalida, in 1508 that it was his custom to attend court ceremonies when he was invited and to sit or stand wherever he was placed, since his business was to maintain friendship between his master and the king of England, and he thought it would be ill-served by making a fuss over trifles.

In the rules of the Roman curia, which provided guidance elsewhere, the emperor always came first, and the king of France second, so that among the three major powers there was no ground for serious dispute as long as the crowns of Spain were united to that of the empire.[6] But after Philip II succeeded to most of his father's realms, but not to the imperial dignity, real difficulties arose. Everywhere thereafter, the representatives of His Most Catholic challenged those of His Most Christian Majesty. Philip II regarded the emperor as representing only the junior branch of the Habsburgs, and could not admit that the king of Spain was second to any monarch in the world. At Trent his ambassador won a victory which, in spite of an apparent element of compromise, proved decisive for Vienna and significant for Rome. He was given a special place, really more dignified than that assigned the French, and Spain signed directly after the empire. Thereafter, Spain took first place at the emperor's court, and the French, in order not to acquiesce in the slight, ceased to maintain there a resident of ambassadorial rank. At Rome Philip II began to press at once for a position of at least equal dignity with that of France, and at Venice he urged the emperor Ferdinand to accredit the Spanish ambassador as his own 'in order to avoid quarrels about protocol'.[7]

For the next century and more, whenever they came together, French and Spanish ambassadors disputed precedence, sometimes with bitter words and dangerous diplomatic gestures, sometimes with the undignified jostling of coaches, sometimes with drawn swords. Naturally the smaller powers followed suit, and the whole story of diplomacy in the seventeenth century is filled with this pointless squabbling. At least it seems pointless now, but people at the time took it seriously enough.[8] To otherwise sensible statesmen it seemed to involve a vital point of national honour. A deadlock over precedence helped prolong the war between France and Spain for eleven years after the treaties of Westphalia. And to skilful diplomats, victories over precedence sometimes gave the keys to positions of real value.

To any resident ambassador worth his salt, positions of real value meant those from which he could advance his sovereign's policies. For although the theorists might be slow to recognize the fact, negotiation, in one form or another, was the chief function of the resident. Increasingly governments were relying on the man on the spot, rather than on special embassies and personal interviews, for the bulk of diplomatic business.

Personal diplomacy declined after the 1530s, in part at least, certainly, because the results of those spectacular interviews between sovereigns which had studded the first phase of the dynastic wars had proved again that the fruits of this method of negotiation were not worth its risks. Major treaties of peace still called for conferences of special commissioners, and other really important pacts generally entailed at least one special embassy, but minor agreements became more and more the business of residents, and even in major negotiations residents were called on to do most of the spade-work. When residents failed to find firm grounds for agreement beforehand, special ambassadors usually made their journeys in vain.

Much of the business of the resident, however, was of a sort not pointed towards any immediate treaty, and not contemplated at all in the older theory of diplomacy. He was the man counted on to influence the policies, or perhaps simply the attitudes, of the government to which he was sent in a sense favourable to his own; to minimize frictions, to win concessions, to achieve co-operation (or, what was sometimes just as valuable, the appearance of co-operation), and if worst came to worst, to sound the first warning that the situation was getting out of hand, and that other pressures were required. In this game, the gathering and use of information, the winning and exploitation of prestige, the negotiation of specific agreements and conciliation of particular disputes, were all sub-ordinated to the patient stalking of objectives of high policy in a series of moves planned far ahead, yet kept flexible enough to meet any possible check or opportunity. The resident ambassadors who succeeded at it were more than mere pieces on the diplomatic chess-board. They were players; not just the executants, but to some extent the shapers of high policy.

CHAPTER XXVI

THE GAME AT CHESS

No group of resident ambassadors within the whole period of this study were such virtuosos of diplomacy or moved on the board of European politics with such formidable, independent life as those who served Spain in the second half of the reign of Philip III. That particular moment in history, the dozen years between the Twelve Years Truce of 1609 and the fatal spreading of the Thirty Years War, offered Spanish diplomats a unique opportunity. Between 1598 and 1609 some sort of peace was patched up, first with France, then with England, and finally with the rebellious provinces of the Netherlands so that, although many problems were left unsolved, there was again something like a community of nations in which diplomats had room to manœuvre. At the same time, though Spanish power was little more than a husk, Spanish prestige was scarcely diminished.

In fact, the decadence had set in. The same year that peace was made with the Dutch, the Moriscos were driven from Valencia in the most disastrous of Spain's many purges. Just then, the inflow of bullion from America turned notably downwards. Every year thereafter the revenues dwindled while the court spent more, and the already overgrown bureaucracy proliferated further. After its mauling by the Dutch at Gibraltar, the Spanish fleet existed largely on paper. The *tercios* which had been the admiration and terror of Europe were reduced to handfuls of ragged starvelings who robbed neighbourhood hen-roosts and begged at the gates of their garrison forts. But the king of Spain was still lord of the Americas and of the navigation and commerce of Africa and Asia where, so far, the Dutch and the English had no more than a toe-hold. In Europe, he still ruled Belgium and Franche-Comté, Milan, Naples, Sicily, all the islands of the western Mediterranean and the whole Iberian peninsula, and was still, not just in the eyes of James I but of most European statesmen, the most powerful of kings. It was the chance for diplomacy to regain the initiative, and reassert the domination which arms had lost since the defeat of the Invincible Armada.

A whole corps of diplomats worked manfully at the task, seniors in the service in which Juan Antonio de Vera was a brilliant junior, but four were particularly notable: Balthasar Zuñiga and Iñigo Vélez de Guevara, successively resident ambassadors at the court of the Austrian Habsburgs,[1] Alfonso de la Cueva, marquis of Bedmar,[2] resident at Venice, and their contemporary, Diego Sarmiento de Acuña, after 1617 count of Gondomar,[3] who represented Philip III in England from 1613 to 1618 and again from 1620 to 1622. Different as they were in temperaments and methods, there is a strong family likeness among these four who were the most striking figures of a decade in which the Spanish genius for diplomacy came to its fullest flowering. They were all aristocrats, and in this typical of the Spanish service. They were all men of considerable culture, tact in negotiation and personal charm; all sincere, devout Catholics and intensely patriotic Spaniards. Again, these qualities were not rare in their service. But in addition, they were all men of keen intellects, strong passions and powerful wills, determined, all of them, to win fresh glories and triumphs for Spain, even if they had to do so in spite of a do-nothing king and incompetent ministers. It was this shared determination which, because of the laxness with which Spanish policy was conducted at Madrid, led all four to write their names large in the history of their time.

One did so by a sensational failure. The marquis of Bedmar with the support of the Spanish viceroy at Naples and the Spanish governor at Milan, but without the slightest encouragement from Madrid, came within an ace of overthrowing, by a remarkably engineered conspiracy, the republic of St. Mark, and completing the Spanish domination of northern Italy. Bedmar's plot was so daring, and its disavowal was so prompt (and on the part of Madrid so clearly candid), that it used to be believed that the journalistic accounts of it, such as the one on which Otway based his *Venice Preserved* had little relation to serious history. But, except as to his personal danger, Bedmar took fewer risks and a less appalling responsibility than Zuñiga and Guevara. In a last desperate throw to re-establish Catholic domination and Spanish-backed Habsburg preponderance in the decaying Holy Roman Empire, those two, with little encouragement from Madrid, prepared the catastrophe of the Thirty Years War and ensured its spread from Bohemia throughout Germany.

Bedmar, Zuñiga and Guevara were all three remarkable diplomats, and a sketch of the methods of any one of them would serve
to illustrate the variety of a resident ambassador's activities in the
early seventeenth century, and the scope for individual initiative
which the office offered a gifted individual. But perhaps none of
them was as typical as their colleague Gondomar. Zuñiga and
Guevara were, after all, the liaison agents of a family partnership
in which the Habsburg emperors were distinctly junior to their
Spanish cousins, and Bedmar represented the menacing greatness
of Spain in Venice when that republic was fast slipping from the
rank of even second-class states. But Gondomar came as ambassador to a power which only ten years before had emerged victorious
from a war with Spain, a power, too, which was as naturally the
head of any Protestant coalition as Spain was of any Catholic one,
and the most vocal part of whose people regarded Spain and
Spaniards with invincible hostility. Any success which Gondomar
won in England (and perhaps no ambassador so handicapped was
ever so successful) he had to win by the arts of diplomacy, without
a threatening army at his back, or family purse-strings to unloosen,
or even any feeling of common faith and common interests to
which he could make confident appeal. His successes aroused a
storm of furious comment in the England of his time. Now the
publication of his correspondence makes it possible to study in
detail the way the various functions of a resident ambassador, as
intelligence officer, as symbolic representative, and as negotiator
could be combined in skilful hands to carry out and to shape the
designs of high policy.

In the London of the 1620s, popular opinion, sharing the
prejudices of the theorists, regarded Gondomar's function as
primarily that of a super-spy. Shortly after the end of his embassy,
Thomas Middleton made Gondomar the hero-villain of a patriotic
satire on Spanish diplomacy, *A Game at Chess*[4] in which the Black
Knight (Gondomar) thus recounts his own activities:

'I have sold the groom of the stool six times . . .
. . . I have taught our friends, too
To convey White House [English], gold to our Black King-
dom [Spain]
In cold baked pastries and so cozen searchers . . .

Letters conveyed in rolls, tobacco-balls . . .
, . . Pray, what use
Put I my summer recreation to,
But more to inform my knowledge in the state
And strength of the White Kingdom? No fortification
Haven, creek, landing place about the White Coast,
But I got draft and platform; learned the depth
Of all their channels, knowledge of all sands,
Shelves, rocks and rivers for invasion properest;
A catalogue of all the navy royal,
The burden of the ships, the brassy murderers,
The number of the men, to what cape bound:
Again for the discovery of the islands,
Never a shire but the state better known
To me than to her best inhabitants;
What power of men and horses, gentry's revenues,
Who well affected to our side, who ill,
Who neither well nor ill, all the neutrality:
Thirty-eight thousand souls have been seduced, Pawn,
Since the jails vomited with the pill I gave 'em.'

(IV, ii, 41-75)

Middleton was only repeating the charges of a widely circulated pamphlet,[5] and giving more seemly form to sentiments which for years the London mob had expressed with hoots, and sometimes with stones and rotten vegetables, at sight of Gondomar's sedan chair.

Of course, conspiracy in Middleton's sense was the last thing Gondomar had time for, nor did a Spanish invasion of England figure in any of his plans. But equally of course he did collect intelligence, of military affairs as well as of other matters, though he gave military information, as a rule, rather a low priority among his wants, and it never bulked very large in his dispatches. Even the youngest aides on his staff had better things to do with their holidays than wander along the coast taking the soundings of creeks and inlets.

Gondomar did employ several young gentlemen who spoke English, but he rarely used them for anything beyond carrying messages and maintaining social contacts. He did spend a little (but not very much, probably less than Chapuys eighty years before) on professional espionage agents and part-time informers, but he seldom reported anything from either of these sources. After he began to find his way around in England, he bought some specific kinds of information, scrupulously setting down the items in his accounts: 'M. La Forest and other persons in the French embassy, for valuable news, 4533 reals; to a servant of Mr. Secretary Lake's, for summaries of important dispatches, 3000 reals; to the person who gave me copies of the treaties of Gravelines from the English archives, 1200 reals'; besides gifts to porters and other palace servants, 4844 reals, which may have bought no more than good will.⁶ But expenditures like these were to plug minor holes in his intelligence net. Its main strands he inherited from his predecessor, who left him two kinds of informants, sincere English Catholics who looked to the king of Spain as the champion of their faith, and highly-placed persons at court who were receiving Spanish pensions. The two categories were not mutually exclusive; the earl of Northampton, for instance, and James I's queen, Anne of Denmark, were in both.

From this basis, Gondomar developed his intelligence network primarily as an operation on the highest levels. Sometimes, as when he wanted background for a report on the East India Company, or on the Virginia colony, or on the long and tiresome dispute about whaling rights off Greenland, he supplemented what he could learn from secretaries and royal counsellors by what his diligent young men and their humbler Catholic friends could pick up in the city or along the docks.⁷ And he did listen, although with an increasingly sceptical ear, to the reports of the priests who slipped in and out of London and whom he periodically delivered from English jails. But he mainly relied on a restricted circle of court and official informants. If he wanted the latest strength of the English navy or the movements of Dutch and English ships in the narrow seas, Sir William Monson, since 1604 commander of the Channel fleet and since 1604 also recipient of a handsome Spanish pension, was glad to oblige. George Calvert, another pensioner and probably for years before his avowed conversion a secret Catholic, brought news of the deliberations of the council, particularly about foreign affairs. Lady Suffolk was an inexhaustible source of court gossip. And if Sir Francis Bacon did no more to earn his modest stipend than discourse about politics, about James's need of money and his troubles with the Puritans, these, nevertheless, were items which Gondomar knew how to turn to account. From higher still there was a stream of messages from the Queen, whose pro-Spanish partisanship outran anything that her complimentary pension or her Catholic faith required, to say nothing of the indiscretions, more frequent and revelatory as the years went on, of an even more exalted pensioner of Spain.[8]

At Madrid or Venice or Brussels or even at Vienna or slack, careless Paris, and certainly in London at an earlier day, an ambassador would have probably had more difficulty in collecting and transmitting as much information as Gondomar did, and all but the most highly placed of his informants would have got into trouble. Under Francis Walsingham, no power in Europe, not even the secretive Venetians, had a more efficient system of security and counter-espionage, such that 'not a mouse could creep out of any ambassador's chamber but Mr. Secretary would have one of his whiskers'. But counter-espionage, in spite of alarms like the Gunpowder Plot, had declined under Robert Cecil (who, a secret pensioner of Spain himself, may not have been too eager to catch his fellow culprits), and it almost collapsed at his death.

Somerset and later Buckingham used what secret agents they had to spy on their rivals at court rather than on foreign envoys. Sir Ralph Winwood, during his short tenure as secretary (March 1614-October 1617) was as suspicious of all Spaniards as Walsingham had ever been; he was also honest, zealous, and moderately intelligent. But Winwood had no time to rebuild his organization. He was hampered at every turn, and proved rather a nuisance to Gondomar than a menace. In most European courts the newly created official, 'the Conductor of Ambassadors', was expected, besides arranging for the lodging and reception of residents, to keep a sharp eye on all their doings.[9] In England, however, Sir Lewis Lewkenor limited himself to ceremony and protocol without prying into the less public activities of his charges.

Nevertheless, the information suborned in London was promptly identified in Madrid. There Sir John Digby, James's ambassador, somehow got hold of all Gondomar's most secret and important dispatches, unriddled their veiled language, and sent copies back to his master, with appropriate comments. This went on for years, to the helpless exasperation and cynical amusement of all concerned. For in London somebody, usually Calvert, regularly notified Gondomar that his recent dispatch had come back, deciphered, straight to the king. In vain, Gondomar changed his ciphers and his couriers, and begged the authorities to make sure that his papers passed only through selected hands. In vain Don André Velasquez de Velasco, Conductor of Ambassadors and 'Espia Mayor', head, that is, of the Spanish counter-espionage and intelligence service, was alerted to set new, trustworthy spies on the English embassy. In vain the duke of Lerma himself laid traps for the members of the Council of State and their clerks. The source of the leak was never discovered. Gondomar, having tried every precaution he could think of, finally convinced himself that some very highly-placed counsellor must be implicated, but years later Digby told him that no more had been involved than the simple interception and copying of the original dispatches, while his courier rested at the last stage before Madrid. As for the ciphers, Digby had broken them all without difficulty.

By that time, Gondomar could accept the check philosophically. It had not spoiled his game, after all. James had repeatedly received lists of the secret Spanish pensioners at his court (one wonders whether Digby had been tactful enough to leave James's own designator in its flimsy code) and no action had ever been taken. For nearly five years James had read the most damaging selections from Gondomar's secret correspondence, and the king's affection for and confidence in the Spanish ambassador had only increased.

Gondomar had never liked the under-cover side of his mission, anyway. In the first months of his embassy he had written to the duke of Lerma, 'It's a nasty job being an ambassador since one has to be mixed up in business like this', and before two years were out, he was telling Lerma that it would be better to lop the English pensions and apply the money to the decaying Spanish fleet, advice which he repeated with greater emphasis at intervals as long as Lerma remained first minister.[10] He was confident that he could get all the information in England he needed without Lerma's grandiosely conceived and tardily paid subsidies. The image he had built up in England of the power and magnificence of the king of Spain and of the Spanish ambassador's intimacy with and influence on the king of England drew sincere Catholic and self-seeking courtiers alike to bring him all the news they could. No corruption had been needed, probably none would have availed, to effect his most spectacular coup, obtaining the copy of Walter Raleigh's secret map showing the goal of his Guiana voyage. That fateful document passed into the ambassador's hands from the hand of the king of England himself.[11]

The real key to Gondomar's success in England lay in his relation to James I. It was not a simple one; certainly it was not, as it has sometimes been represented, just the dominance of a weak character by a strong one; much less, the gulling of a fool by a knave. James was a complex character in whom elements of weakness were surprisingly mixed with traits of real strength; Gondomar, at least, never made the mistake of under-rating him. Nor did he achieve his influence at a stroke, or storm the King's favour with a mixture of bullying and flattery. It was the work of years. In part it was because Gondomar was able to make James like him. The Spaniard was a brilliant conversationalist and a good listener, a sound Latin scholar and an experienced politician, courtly without servility and easy without undue familiarity. As he studied James's character, and came to appreciate that, in the last analysis, it was the king, not his ministers, who shaped English policy, Gondomar found just the right tone to put James at his ease.

Nor was this all acting on the ambassador's part. The two men, unlike as they were in some respects, had enough in common for the basis of a genuine sympathy, and, if James came to adopt some of Gondomar's views, Gondomar also adopted some of James's. But besides gradually winning James's confidence and liking, from the first Gondomar compelled his respect. He never disavowed an opinion which he sincerely held, nor retreated from a position because of the king's displeasure. And if he always accorded James the deference due to a king, he always insisted on being treated as the representative of the greatest king in Christendom. No ambassador ever appreciated better the advantages to be won from prestige and protocol, or exploited them more thoroughly.

The first incident of his embassy, before he had seen James or estimated what his own position might be, showed how he was determined to play that part of his game. When the two galleons which brought him to England made Portsmouth harbour, they found there the flagship of the Channel fleet and exchanged with her equal courtesies. It was not until Gondomar had gone ashore to be welcomed by the city fathers that the English captain (the vice-admiral was not aboard) sent word that he was sure the Spaniards would now pay the customary honours which they must have omitted through inadvertence. In any harbour of the Narrow Seas, all ships were required to strike their flags and keep them lowered as long as one of His Majesty's ships was in port, just as, at sea, they must dip their flags three times, strike their topsails, and pass to leeward in token of the king of England's sovereignty of the seas. The Spanish commander forwarded the demand to Gondomar, and Gondomar, speaking as the direct representative of the king of Spain, ordered him not to strike his colours.

Now, no point of naval etiquette was dearer to the English than this. There was a firm tradition (perhaps a truthful one) that Philip II on his way to marry Mary had been obliged to strike to the English admiral. Certainly the king of Denmark's ship had done so recently; so had the Spanish squadron which brought the duke of Frias as special ambassador in 1604. And in the presence of the duke of Sully, special ambassador of Henry IV, the vice-admiral of England had fired into the flagship of the vice-admiral of France and compelled him to lower his flag in Calais harbour itself. No wonder that on Gondomar's refusal the English captain threatened to blow the Spaniards out of the water. Gondomar replied that he hoped the impending battle could be delayed until he had time to send a message. To James he wrote a bald narrative of the imbroglio, merely adding that he begged, if circumstances were to prevent his fulfilling his mission in England, to be allowed to return aboard the Spanish flagship, since if it were sunk, he was determined to go down with it.

Probably James fumed and fretted; of course he knuckled under. James's weakness (though Gondomar could not have known it) was that he was too civilized a man to risk killing an ambassador and starting a war over an empty salute. The result was a notable victory for Spanish prestige. It may have been also the first step towards the ascendancy which the ambassador established over the spirit of the king.[12]

Though the first-fruits of his assertion of Spanish prestige were sweet, Gondomar was too skilful a player to force his game. In the crucial matter of diplomatic precedence he moved slowly, snubbing his minor colleagues no more than he thought necessary to his position, and waiting to find the ground firm beneath his feet before he tried his next move. Then he began to refuse to attend any functions at which the Dutch ambassador was present, until that worthy found himself, as Gondomar's favour grew, practically cut off from court society. But the Spaniard avoided an outright challenge to the long-established precedence of France until he felt confident of his position and saw an immediate advantage worth the risk. Not until Twelfth Night, 1617-18, did he refuse to attend the festivities unless his place were higher than the French ambassador's.

There was much coming and going of agitated officials, but Gondomar got his way. Desmaretz, the French resident, was taken completely off balance. He had delicate and complicated negotiations in hand, but he was so outraged that he could talk about nothing but the slight put upon him. He was unwise enough to demand an unqualified assurance of precedence over his Spanish rival and, when James refused, Desmaretz wrote to the queen regent that the honour of France required his recall from England, to be followed by an ultimatum and, if necessary, war. The French government did not go so far as that, but in a year of European crisis France was cut off for months from her most potent possible ally by Gondomar's exploitation of a question of protocol.[13] Throughout the rest of his embassy, in spite of furious French protests, the Spanish ambassador kept the precedence he had gained.

Precedence, to an able diplomat like Gondomar, was no more an end in itself than the collection of information, or the personal favour of the king. Nor did he allow himself to be distracted by the minor business with which his embassy was charged: the support and protection of English Catholics, the prevention of buccaneering, the surveillance of the new colonies of Virginia and Bermuda, and the frustration of petty anti-Spanish diplomatic moves in London. He made his pursuit of these ends, each minor victory, even each minor defeat, serve his main objective: the achievement of a position which would enable him, when the time came, to keep England neutral in the impending continental war.

Everybody knew that the coming war, though it might announce itself as between Catholics and Protestants, threatened, in spite of the best efforts of Spanish diplomacy, to turn into a coalition of most of Europe against the Habsburgs. With the Dutch, Spain had no more than an uneasy twelve years' truce. Germany was like a dry forest, full of the deadfalls of religious schism, the tangled undergrowth of old princely claims, where any spark of conflict might start a devastating blaze. Religion and ambition alike would involve the Scandinavian monarchies. And every other independent state in Europe chafed at the Habsburg preponderance. France was always jealous; only an assassin's dagger had prevented Henry IV from starting war in 1610. The duke of Savoy was a constant trouble-maker. Venice was hostile and uneasy. But the worst threat to Spain was England. A combined Anglo-Dutch fleet could sweep the Spanish from the seas. English money and the prestige of the greatest Protestant monarchy could weld the north into a formidable coalition, and the assurance of English hostility to Spain would be an almost irresistible temptation to France and Savoy and perhaps Venice, as well, to fall upon the stricken giant. The southern Netherlands would certainly be lost and how much more besides no man could tell. In London, Gondomar talked big about the power of his master, but he had no illusions about the inner rottenness of the Spanish monarchy.[14] A coalition war could mean the end of Spanish greatness.

In England there were powerful forces eager for such a war: Puritans, moved by fanatical conviction that true religion could not be safe anywhere until all men believed like themselves; merchants and seamen who remembered the profits of the war of Elizabeth and had forgotten the losses; adventurers like Raleigh and other unemployed captains, and the young men who longed to imitate them. To oppose all this, Gondomar had nothing except the hollow prestige and dwindling wealth of Spain, the feeble support of the persecuted English Catholics, and his own diplomatic skill. Nothing, unless we count King James's own real preference for peace. But James was scarcely a reliable character. The firmness and finesse had to be Gondomar's, and the victory was his.

How he won it, one may read in his own dispatches. To increase his influence with James, to estrange the King from his Parliament, to increase James's regard for the power, wealth and magnanimity of Spain, these were the lesser objectives patiently pursued which gave Gondomar positions from which he could move to the desired stalemate. His timing was masterly. Just at the moment that James's son-in-law, Frederick of the Palatinate, was summoned to Bohemia, James took the bait which Gondomar had been dangling: the marriage of Prince Charles to a Spanish princess.

In the critical opening years of the Thirty Years War, England was immobilized by these vain negotiations. The mere threat of English intervention might have kept Spinola out of the Palatinate and gone far to restore the pre-war balance in Germany, but James allowed only a token force of English volunteers to defend his son-in-law's hereditary lands. With Gondomar at his elbow to remind him that he was no king if he suffered the impertinence of the Commons, James dissolved Parliament (the best stroke for the Catholic faith since Luther's time, Gondomar wrote) and jailed the preachers and politicians who clamoured for war with Spain.

That year, 1621, the ambassador who had begun his embassy by his defiance in Portsmouth 'harbour was at once the dictator of England's foreign policy, the chosen companion of the king's leisure hours, and his closest friend. It would be hard to name an ambassador before or since who had attained such a position, or exerted by sheer personal force such influence upon the affairs of Europe. Only years of daily contacts, of careful study and preparation could have achieved so much. Gondomar's success illustrates the potential of the resident ambassador at its highest.

It illustrates, too, the irony of the diplomat's career, the irony of which the theorists were uneasily conscious, of serving ends always double and often contradictory. Whatever may have been his mood when he first opened the marriage negotiations in which James was ensnared, before 1618 Gondomar had persuaded himself that his own mission had escaped this contradiction. He really believed that the ends sought were good for England and good for Christendom as well as good for Spain, and the intense fervour of his conviction must have added enormously to his effectiveness.

By the device of an Anglo-Spanish marriage, the revival of the old policy of Ferdinand and Charles V, Gondomar hoped to win

266

toleration for the Catholics in England and peace and security for Spain. Simply from the point of view of an ardent Catholic and a patriotic Spaniard, it seemed to him that the value of these ends must persuade the court at Madrid to make the necessary concessions in return. Gondomar was no apostle of universal toleration, but he believed that if the free exercise of the Roman Catholic faith in England were once granted, it would reconquer the realm as Poland was being reconquered, and he was willing to risk the popular abuse which his manœuvres brought upon him and his co-religionists for the sake of that ultimate triumph.

Gondomar was no pacifist, but he knew, few men better, that Spain could not stand the strain of another long war, and he hoped, even after Spinola had invaded the Palatinate, that in payment for the English marriage Spain might intervene to restore James's son-in-law to his hereditary estates. Then the fire of straw in Bohemia might burn itself out, the war in Germany be ended by a return to the status of 1618, the French be awed into peace by an Anglo-Spanish alliance, and Spain be free to deal with the Dutch, or better still to defer the day of reckoning until internal reforms had given the kingdom the strength for that task. And in all this, Gondomar was able to tell himself, there was no treachery to the best interests of his friend, the king of England, and true service to the best interests of the Christian republic.

Before he died, Gondomar must have seen how far he had let himself drift from reality. Madrid had never intended to let Prince Charles have a princess on any terms which the English could possibly grant, and the return of Charles and Buckingham from Spain, disappointed by the failure of their experiment in reviving personal diplomacy, had set off the fiercest wave of anti-Catholic and anti-Spanish sentiment which England had seen since Armada days. Inevitably, when Spinola had mopped up in the Palatinate, the automatic reflex of Spanish policy was to press the war against the Dutch, encourage Ferdinand in Germany, and laugh at any talk of compromise or concession. States, like individuals, retain their appetites after their capacities have waned; the decadent Spanish monarchy was still hungry for power. And almost equally inevitably, the humiliation which Charles and Buckingham had endured threw them into the arms of France and into a war of retaliation which fanned the embers in Germany and, except for their fickleness and incompetence, might have been even more disastrous for the Catholic cause.

The result of Gondomar's skill, therefore, was not to save his country from war, but to help entangle it in a continuous series of wars which sapped its energies for the next forty years and removed it thereafter from the ranks of the major powers. Gondomar could not see so far ahead, but he may have seen that, had he not succeeded in diverting James, Spinola might not have marched, the war in the Germanies might have ended in compromise, and Spain might have avoided the unpredictable dangers of the smouldering ground-fire spreading across northern Europe. Gondomar's success as a diplomat meant the ruin of his aims as a statesman. Perhaps he and his friend De Vera discussed the paradox as one more instance of the difficulty of reconciling the two chief duties of the ambassador, to serve one's prince and to serve peace. They recorded no solution.

CHAPTER XXVII

THE NEW IMMUNITIES

THE gravest ethical problem raised for theory by the new diplomacy, the possibility of conflict between the ambassador's duty to his prince and his duty to peace, also underlay, though unrecognized, the most vexing legal question concerning diplomats, the question of ambassadorial immunity.[1] On the fundamental assumption that ambassadors were public officers of the general community owing to its highest interest, peace, their primary allegiance, the late medieval civilians had worked out a pretty consistent theory of diplomatic immunity. While an ambassador was on mission his person was inviolable, and he, his suite and his goods enjoyed a wide immunity from any form of civil or criminal action, either in the country where he was accredited or in any through which he might pass.[2]

This immunity was precisely limited, however. It was meant to guarantee everything necessary to the discharge of a proper mission and therefore forbade any molestation of the envoy and his suite, or any distraint of his goods or person on account of old claims or charges. But it was not intended to shield diplomats from punishment for current misbehaviour. If an ambassador indulged in conduct unbecoming his office, he lost his immunity. He could not safely indulge in treasonable conspiracy or other activities harmful to the cause of peace, any more than in private crimes. For espionage, homicide, rape, theft, and so on down to petty fraud and the non-payment of debts incurred during his embassy the ambassador could be haled before the proper court and tried according to law.

The proper court was the prince's court. The ambassador was free from the jurisdiction of any lower one while he held his office. The appropriate law, no matter what that of his own land or that where he was tried, was Roman civil law, which, as the common law of Christendom, every prince's court was expected to administer when occasion arose. About all this, by 1450, there was no serious doubt or disagreement whatever.

The doubts arose as European political space filled up, and the

269

greater powers began to employ permanent diplomacy as a weapon. Medieval theory had regarded diplomacy as an out-stretched hand, not a sword. Of course it had been used aggressively always, and with increasing frequency since the thirteenth century, but sporadically rather than continuously, so that it was possible to treat such use as an anomaly, to be deprecated and discouraged rather than as a practice which had to be assimilated. As the dynastic wars increased in intensity, however, the warnings of the jurists that diplomats should not aid or countenance aggression faded into uneasy silence. Practical statesmen saw that a blow struck at an opponent's diplomatic liaisons might be as effective as one at his troops or his purse, and began to act accordingly.

They found one vulnerable spot in the immunity guaranteed ambassadors in transit to their posts. Fifteenth-century writers had been specific. In travelling the ambassador was entitled everywhere not only to all immunities, including exemption from tolls and taxes, but to every courtesy and assistance which would facilitate his journey. His one obligation was to notify governments whose boundaries he crossed of his route and status; though passing through states at war, he was expected to ask for and receive a safe-conduct. But all sorts of marginal cases were possible. What if war should break out while the ambassador was on his way? What if some state on his route did not recognize one of the powers named in his credentials? What if he proceeded without a safe-conduct, or failed to notify the proper authorities, or attempted to conceal the character of his mission? These turned out to be useful pretexts for arresting or delaying dangerous embassies when they ventured into risky territory.

The most famous violation of diplomatic immunity in transit occurred near Pavia in July 1541. Antonio Rincon, French envoy to the Sublime Porte, and Cesare Fregoso, accredited to Venice, were ambushed and murdered by Imperialist soldiers at a time when France and the empire were nominally at peace. Almost certainly the imperial governor of Milan ordered the deed, perhaps with the knowledge of the Emperor Charles V himself. France made the incident a cause of war, and for the next hundred years theorists argued the case, the French hot in condemnation, the Spanish less warm in defence. Nevertheless the emperor's apologists had a distinct point. Not because Rincon's mission was to include an alliance with the Turks against the emperor, nor even because he was a Spanish renegade whom Charles had promised to hang and Fregoso a Genoese exile with a price on his head. But because the two ambassadors, aware that neither of them would be granted a safe-conduct, had tried to cut across the emperor's territory, concealing their missions and their identities. The circumstance scarcely justified assassination, but it weakened any claim to diplomatic immunity.[3]

Fifteen years before, the French had been guilty of a similar violation which, though it never became so notorious, was in some respects more flagrant. Don Iñigo de Mendoza, Charles V's ambassador to England, was sent to his post overland through France just after the Treaty of Madrid. In spite of the treaty, a resumption of the war was in the air, and Mendoza decided that he needed a safe-conduct. He went all the way to Lyons to get one, and the French court was delighted to see him. Here was their chance to stymie the opposition to their new understanding with England. Francis I's counsellors said they were astonished that an ambassador should seek a safe-conduct in time of perfect peace. They delayed and delayed, handing Mendoza from one person to another, and finally told him that his suspicions were insulting to French honour. He could have his safe-conduct and an escort if he chose to wait; if not, he was free to go. Mendoza left, and was scarcely out of Lyons before he noticed a clump of lances shadowing his march. They let him get almost to the Flemish frontier before they bore him off to prison in the castle of Arques where he spent four dismal months writing protests. At last, with profoundest apologies for the mistaken zeal of underlings, the French let him go.[4]

The real point of this episode, and of the Rincon and Fregoso affair, and of all similar incidents during the sixteenth century, is not that dynasts, when the stakes were great enough, violated ambassadorial immunity, but that they always disavowed responsibility and offered apologies and excuses. Francis I declared that frontier guards had mistaken Mendoza for a spy; Charles V, that Rincon and Fregoso had been killed by lawless soldiery who took them for merchants trying to evade the Milanese customs. And for every other incident there turns out to have been some official explanation, pleading special circumstances. No sixteenth-century government ever justified itself by asserting that embassies in transit were not protected by the law of nations, and in fact, even in the religious wars most embassies, all but a very few, travelled in safety. But the publicists by this time had begun to abandon the sweeping claim for immunity of ambassadors in transit. They did so less because of occasional violations, than because theory had lost touch with the basis for such a claim.[5]

It was the spread of resident embassies which imposed the critical strain on the old legal structure. The theorists had always been uneasy about residents, not only because the standard texts did not apply to them, but because the mission and function of a resident made nonsense of the usual juristic assumptions. In the end, the increasing importance of permanent embassies so emphasized the contradictions between medieval theory and modern practice that the relevant legal doctrines had to be completely re-worded, and ambassadorial immunity based on the curious fiction of exterritoriality. Theory was obliged to assume or pretend that the ambassador and the precincts of his embassy stood as if on the soil of his homeland, subject only to its laws. But this was a doctrine of slow growth. For more than a century the councils of European princes wrestled with the legal difficulties presented by resident embassies without much help from the theorists.

The simplest example of these difficulties, and historically the first to arise, concerned a resident ambassador's debts. Late medieval doctrine was clear. The ambassador enjoyed complete immunity for debts contracted before his embassy, but for subsequent debts he could be sued like anyone else and, in theory, his goods and person distrained to compel payment. The reference was to the *Corpus Juris*, but the doctrine made perfectly good sense in terms of medieval practice. The entertainment of a special embassy was at the charge of its host. Therefore any debts which an ambassador or a member of his household might contract during the course of his embassy would normally be only for purposes unconnected with official business. No suit for such debts was at all likely to arise during a special embassy, but if an ambassador who had bought goods to take home with him looked like leaving without paying up, it was reasonable to allow his creditors legal remedy.

The resident was in a quite different position. He had to live for years at his post, and as soon as the first non-Italian embassies were established, it turned out that some residents had to live for long stretches on practically nothing. These early embassies were usually not reciprocal, and it was as absurd to expect Henry VII to dip into his own purse to support a foreign ambassador as it was to expect his royal contemporaries to pay their servants promptly. As a result the king of England had to intervene in the early 1500s to keep both Dr. de Puebla, the Spanish ambassador, and Sigismund Frauenberg, the emperor's, from being arrested at the suit of their impatient creditors. Similar civil action against embarrassed residents similarly halted by princely intervention are commonplace in the sixteenth century. If residents generally escaped the worst consequence of unpaid debts, it was by the prince's favour, not by law.[6]

Most jurists were as cloudy about the legal question involved as Sir Edward Coke, who wrote that ambassadors must answer to local jurisdiction in contracts good 'by the law of nations' (*jure gentium*), but failed to say whether he meant thereby to distinguish between debts contracted for subsistence and the kind of debts for which under the older law of nations an ambassador would have been liable. In practice the distinction might have proved difficult, but the publicists dodged the point about an ambassador's right to public entertainment, just as the princes and the law courts did. They would only say that any distraint of an ambassador's goods which would interfere with the exercise of his functions was not in the public interest, and ought to be avoided.

Grotius went further.[7] Since the ambassador must have security of goods as well as of person to carry out his mission, Grotius said the creditor's only recourse, if courteous application to the ambassador and to his sovereign failed, was to use those means of recovery available against debtors living abroad. In other words, Grotius could only rationalize the civil immunity which residents needed by the fiction of exterritoriality. He proposed that their position in civil suits should be the same as if they had never left their homelands. In fact, local courts, reinforced by tradition and conservative opinion, refused to admit so much, and princes did not always intervene. In the conflicts of opinions and uncertainties of practice there was some discomfort both for insolvent ambassadors and for their creditors.

The acute question, however, was immunity not from civil but from criminal jurisdiction. About crimes generally disapproved by Western standards and therefore assumed to be contrary to the laws of God, of nature and of nations, there was little difficulty. Ambassadors were not, as a class, much given to homicide, robbery with violence, or the more spectacular forms of rape. Almost without exception, publicists well down into the seventeenth century agreed with the legists of the fourteenth and fifteenth that diplomats who indulged such impulses could be tried and sentenced where the infraction occurred. That might actually have been done had occasion arisen. When embassy servants committed such crimes, ambassadors were generally quick to hand them over to the local authorities and, if they sought any mitigation of the punishment, to seek it simply by favour.

But the crimes resident ambassadors were likely to be charged with were political, and here medieval theory was difficult to apply. The simplest and most usual older statement of the limits of diplomatic immunity was that ambassadors might not exceed their missions without loss of status. The limits of a given mission, in turn, were to be determined by the text of credentials and public instructions, supplemented by the general theory of diplomatic functions.[8] Three instances may serve to illustrate the difficulty of applying such rules to sixteenth-century cases.

In 1511, Girolamo Bonvisi, whom Julius II had been indiscreet enough to send as special nuncio to England, wormed out of the Spanish ambassador the secret of England's alliance with Spain against France, and promptly notified the French, probably not without being paid for his news. Thomas Wolsey, who had been watching Bonvisi, swooped down on him, had him flung in the Tower, and by threat of torture extracted from him all he knew of the manœuvres of the pro-French party in England and in Rome. The violation of ambassadorial immunity was flagrant, but Bonvisi had certainly betrayed his master, Julius II, who was heart and soul for war with France, and the English reported the whole affair with full confidence in the pope's approval.[9]

Now nothing in Bonvisi's credentials or public instructions spoke of war with France. They were full of the usual phrases about peace and the security of Christendom. As an ambassador, and especially as the ambassador of the Sovereign Pontiff, the maintenance of peace among Christians was the nuncio's first duty. Bonvisi could have argued that to warn the French of the danger of war was one way of trying to avert it. Naturally, neither Henry VIII nor Julius II would have paid any attention to such an excuse, and we may doubt whether Bonvisi himself relied on it. Anyway, he was treated as if, by departing from his master's real intentions, he had derogated from his office. An earlier period might have decided differently.

In 1524, Wolsey tried a similar trick. Louis de Praet, the emperor's resident in England, guessed that Wolsey aimed to detach his master from his alliance with Charles V and persuade him to join the French, with whom the allies were at war. De Praet began to write that Wolsey and Henry were untrustworthy, and to advise making a separate peace with France before they did. He even suggested an alliance with France against England. But de Praet had sent too many of his dispatches by the English post, and Wolsey had not let them go unread. Wolsey was expecting envoys from France, and was irked by suspicious observation. Therefore he arranged to have one of de Praet's couriers arrested, as if by accident, at the city gates, used the letters secured as an excuse for seizing others, and on this evidence confronted the ambassador before the royal council and accused him of having derogated from his office. The charge was that instead of maintaining peace and friendship between the allies, as his instructions prescribed, he was stirring up discord. His slanders against Henry made him guilty of *lèse-majesté*, and his deception of his master probably constituted treason. Clearly he was no longer an ambassador. He was ordered to remain in England under arrest, to be punished at the king's pleasure.

Wolsey's brazen use of intercepted embassy dispatches to ensure the impotence of a hostile observer while he worked his delicate change of sides, the prompt indignation of the Habsburgs, and de Praet's release and departure with full ambassadorial honours, have all obscured the legal points of Wolsey's operation. Technically it did not involve the inviolability of ambassadorial dispatches. For opening the first set Wolsey had, and offered, no legal justification. That, he pretended, was due to a misunderstanding between the ambassador's courier and the city watch, a farce which the Under-Sheriff, Sir Thomas More, carried out in the pure spirit of Dogberry, in spite of finding that, contrary to expectations, de Praet's courier was an Englishman and spoke just as good English as his captors. Nor did Wolsey pretend to the right to imprison an ambassador. He first brought his accusation before the king's council, and only when that court, the proper court to try an ambassador, had found that de Praet had forfeited his immunity, did Wolsey order his arrest.[10]

However absurd Wolsey's charge may have been, given the political facts of 1524, it was not absurd according to the laws under which diplomacy was still, nominally, being practised. Whatever de Praet was doing, he was not cementing peace and friendship. Nothing in his credentials and instructions authorized the line he was taking. Indeed, his alarmist tone and the hostility and suspicion he displayed towards England were most unwelcome in Spain. In the traditional sense de Praet had indubitably exceeded the limit of his mission. There was far less legal excuse for his conduct than there was for Bonvisi's.

Had de Praet been the kind of ambassador for whom the old rules were framed, he would certainly have deserved recall, and perhaps punishment. But he was not. He was a resident ambassador, and therefore 'an honourable spy'. He was a servant of the new diplomacy, and so the first tacit clause of his instructions was to do nothing except for the preservation and aggrandizement of his state. These new axioms had not yet achieved public respectability, but de Praet and most of his colleagues already acted on them, and Charles V's approval showed he accepted them. The conflict between these assumptions and the old one that the business of an ambassador is peace was corrosive to the ancient legal framework.

In the next hundred years a good many other ambassadors exceeded their mission through zeal for a dynasty, a country or a cause. But the legal and political questions they raised were less difficult than those in a third group of cases, cases in which ambassadors undertook actual crimes, with the approval or even by the orders of their governments. In such cases the actual purpose of the mission included, either from the outset or from some determinable point, a deliberate violation of the law of nations upon which the immunity of the ambassador and the whole system of diplomatic communication depended.

Sir Thomas Wyatt, the poet, for instance, when English resident in Spain, undertook as a part of his diplomatic duties to have Reginald Pole murdered while the cardinal legate was visiting the emperor. Antoine de Noailles conspired to overthrow Queen Mary, not merely with the knowledge but apparently at the orders of the king of France. If Philip II did not instigate or wholeheartedly support the Ridolfi plot to murder or kidnap Queen Elizabeth and place Mary of Scotland on the throne, he watched it with benevolent interest, and showed no disposition to punish or even scold his ambassador in England for his share in it. And though much still remains obscure about the similar enterprise twelve years later, the Throckmorton plot, there is no doubt that another of Philip's ambassadors, Bernardino de Mendoza, was at the heart and centre of it, acting this time in full accordance with his master's wishes. By the 1580s treason and murder had become the normal weapons of ideological warfare.[11]

In the end, diplomatic immunity was stretched to cover even this third variety of misconduct. Perhaps it would not have been had ambassadorial plots been more successful. Had Wyatt's cutthroats succeeded in waylaying Cardinal Pole, had the Dudley plot, or the Ridolfi, or the Throckmorton come to anything serious, some ambassador might have illustrated on the scaffold the rule that such crimes forfeited immunity. As it happened, though guilty ambassadors were occasionally arrested, the worst that befell any of them was to be sent home 'to be punished'. And although, as one publicist dryly remarked, it was optimistic to expect a prince to punish an attempt which he himself had instigated, gradually the doctrine began to prevail that dismissal was the most that could be done.

Grotius, characteristically, argued that although justice and equity required equal penalties for equal crimes, the law of nations made an exception of ambassadors because their security as a class was more important to the public welfare than their punishment as individuals. Their security would rest on a slippery foundation if they were accountable to anyone but their own sovereigns, he observed resignedly, since the interests of powers sending and those receiving embassies were usually different and often opposite.[12] So, the only solution was to regard ambassadors as not bound by the laws of the country where they resided. In the world of the 1620s, Grotius thought it idle to ask whether any magistrate could be trusted to enforce a higher and more general law.

Whether Grotius's modern view was a stroke of legal genius or merely an evidence of the anarchy into which Western society was falling, his arguments, with their implication of complete diplomatic exterritoriality, did finally prevail. But slowly. Down to the end of the seventeenth century, jurists and philosophers could be found to defend the older doctrine, and delinquent diplomats escaped the penalties of the law rather by clemency than by right. For a long time, how ambassadors were treated was more 'according to the rules of precedence and mutual concerns and temperaments among princes . . . than according to the strict rules of reason and justice'.[13]

The immunity of the ambassador's suite and the freedom of his residence from invasion by local officers developed also according to prudence and the temperament of princes rather than to legal logic. About these matters, as about the ambassador's personal immunity, the rules which had served the Middle Ages and the sentiments which upheld them were overstrained by the effort to make them cover situations alien to their spirit.

Throughout the later Renaissance conflicts between ambassador's households and local authorities were numerous. Sovereigns were usually anxious to preserve diplomatic contacts, and consequently tolerant of the incidental frictions which such contacts entailed. At the same time the growing embassy staffs, groups of specially privileged foreigners resident among populations quick to suspect them of misbehaviour and evil intentions, multiplied the opportunities for friction. Embassy staffs ranged from grave secretaries and young aristocrats through tough couriers and lackeys down to horse-boys and turnspits. They were not always carefully selected. Usually they included nationals of the country of residence. As such groups began to realize that their immunity from local prosecution could be extended by the insistence of the ambassador they served, it is not surprising that municipal authorities and city mobs responded to their provocations with violence. Embassy servants were attacked in the streets. Embassy precincts were forcibly invaded by local officers. Now and then some ambassador's residence stood for days what almost amounted to a siege. Violence was by no means one-sided. Embassy servants with drawn swords swarmed into the streets to rescue comrades. Peace officers were mauled and maltreated. More than one ambassador resisted what he thought illegal encroachment with barricaded doors and marksmen posted at his windows.

In the end most of these imbroglios were settled by the intervention of the prince, who took less account of the principles of international law than of the truculence of the ambassador involved and the importance of the power he represented. In consequence, by De Vera's time, the customary immunities of embassies varied in almost every European capital, and these differences increased throughout most of the seventeenth century. As the Spanish Habsburg power decayed, for instance, the embassies in Madrid, which under Philip II had been the most strictly controlled in Europe, came to share with those in impotent Rome the notorious *franchise du quartier* which made each embassy and its adjacent area a privileged sanctuary for debtors, smugglers, and all sorts of notorious criminals.

About so confused and changeable a situation only loose generalization is possible. On the whole, no government willingly conceded privileges as extensive as its envoys claimed abroad. Theory, still restricted by the notions of an earlier age, did not warrant as wide immunities as all governments conceded in practice. Concessions were won, primarily, by the ambassadors themselves, each of whom thought it due to his sovereign's dignity to achieve the widest possible privileges, and not to be put off with less than had been granted to his predecessor or to some rival. Governments yielded just to the extent that rulers thought it better to suffer probably illegal encroachments than risk a diplomatic breach. But it was hard to deny to one embassy what had been granted to another, and acts of special favour tended to harden into customs. Such customs prevailed the more easily since it was increasingly unclear what the applicable law was, or whether there was any alternative to subjecting the ambassador and his household to local law, except pretending that he, his staff, and his residence were legally still in his homeland. The embassies became islands of exterritorial sovereignty.

Probably the largest single factor in preparing men's minds to accept this extraordinary fiction was the embassy chapel question. What kind of services could be celebrated in an ambassador's chapel and who might attend had to be asked sooner or later, but until about 1550, in spite of Lutherans in Germany and Henry VIII's defiance of the pope, no resident ambassador needed to carry a chaplain in his train. Chapuys could take communion at the hand of Bishop Bonner, and Sir Thomas Wyatt bow before the elevated host at Valladolid, maintaining among the major powers, at least formal observance of that ancient worship which had been the chief visible sign of European unity. The insistence of Edward VI's ambassadors on following the new English prayer book marked the break, and Charles V's refusal to countenance heresy at his court proved only another of his vain medieval gestures. In a few years the divisive principle *cuius regio eius religio* was legally confirmed at Augsburg, and in another fifty it became an axiom universally accepted. The religion of the prince was the appropriate religion for all his subjects. The sentiments which had bound Christendom together were diverted to reinforce the separate nationalisms of the sovereign states.

It followed that, as a mark of loyalty, ambassadors and their staffs insisted on worshipping according to the rights of their homeland, however dangerous and scandalous such worship might seem to their hosts. Moreover, every ambassador was obliged, as a point of honour and an evidence of his faith, to try to secure for nearby compatriots and co-religionists the privilege of attending his chapel. At first embassy chapels were permitted only in England and France, and there only for political reason. In Spain, though the issue was confused by Dr. Man's bad manners, the chapel question closed the English embassy. In Italy, papal alarm at the prospect of seeing heretical worship on Italian soil excluded all Protestant resident ambassadors from the peninsula throughout the sixteenth century. Meanwhile the Dutch republic and the Scandinavian kingdoms were slow to exchange permanent embassies with Catholic powers.

Spanish and Italian rigidity was more in accordance with prevailing sentiment than English and French tolerance, as protests by bishops and magistrates and hostile demonstrations by mobs in London and Paris made abundantly clear. The attitude shared by the bishops and the mobs was perfectly natural. When the ancient faith of Christendom broke into fragments, heresy did not cease to be treason; it only became a more dangerous form of treason. Everywhere the official religion, whatever it might be, was regarded as a basic part of the constitution. To challenge it was to challenge the structure of society. Among Catholics and Protestants alike, genuinely religious persons were prone to feel that tolerance of a false religion was dangerous to men's souls and a defiance of God which might bring down His incalculable wrath. Meanwhile the least fanatical of statesmen could see the disadvantages of nourishing under the shelter of diplomatic immunity the active cells of an alien and hostile ideology.

Nevertheless, in the uneasy years before the Thirty Years War, the exchange of residents between Catholic and Protestant powers became general, and the embassy chapel question was tacitly solved. After the accession of James I, English residents went again to Spain and Venice, and those powers re-established their embassies in London. France and Spain both sent residents to the Scandinavian kingdoms. The Dutch received Catholic resident ambassadors and sent Calvinists to Venice and to Paris. And in all these embassies in all these capitals the right of the ambassador's chaplain to conduct within the embassy divine service according to his country's use was not seriously challenged.

But the relative silence in which the issue was settled, the lack of discussion by the theorists or of rulings by the courts or of stipulations in treaties, should not mislead us as to the portentous nature of this departure. Open defiance by an ambassador of the state's fundamental law went so far beyond anything the medieval system of diplomatic immunities had contemplated that the immunities implied in the growing doctrine of exterritoriality could seem like necessary corollaries. If embassies were licensed to flout the most sacred laws of the realm, it was easier to think of them as not being within the realm at all. And if all the nations were not to live under the same laws of God, who could think of them (St. Thomas More had made the point clearly) as subject to any common law? By arrogating to themselves supreme power over men's consciences, the new states had achieved absolute sovereignty. Having done so, they found that they could only communicate with one another by tolerating within themselves little islands of alien sovereignty. It was that, or fall apart into as many isolated societies as there were dominant faiths.

CHAPTER XXVIII

LAW AMONG NATIONS

THE Renaissance publicists who found it hard to explain and justify the way governments dealt with ambassadors were no less embarrassed when they tried to rationalize other aspects of the changing relations between states. Besides books on what we now call 'the international law of diplomacy', the century before the Treaties of Westphalia saw serious writing about other urgent problems: about the rights and obligations of Europeans in their new colonies, about freedom of trade and of the seas, and about how to bring under some sort of rule of law the wars which racked a divided Europe.

Even in theory none of these problems has ever proved easy. In practice, none of them has ever been solved, except temporarily and provisionally. But Renaissance publicists, though not lacking in sincerity or intellectual power, seem to have found a special difficulty in stating these questions or discussing them with any logical consistency and practical relevance. Their confusion about diplomatic immunity — where the task was less to impose a set of ideal standards than to formulate the theory of what actually was being done — illustrates their central difficulty.

It is usual to say that these harassed theorists were engaged in founding the science of international law.[1] Once this achievement was credited without contention to Hugo Grotius alone. It was neat and convenient to put Grotius into a list of originators of the modern sciences along with Descartes and Galileo, Harvey and possibly Francis Bacon, his great contemporaries. Few people talk so any more. But in the history of international law, at least, the quest for some founder continues. For years now, the most popular candidate has been that high-minded Dominican friar, Francisco de Vittoria who, in the 1530s, lectured his students at Salamanca on their right, or lack of right, as Spaniards, to dominate and exploit the Indians of the new-found world.

It is true that a good many of what were once hailed as Grotius's 'inspired intuitions' and 'divinations of broad moral principles' are to be found, substantially unchanged, either in Vittoria himself or in one of the great Spanish ethical jurists, Soto, Covarruvias, Suarez, who were in some sense Vittoria's followers. In consequence Grotius has even been described as 'the last genius of the Spanish school'. If this is less than just to the breadth of his reading, it is useful to remind us that he read more books than he cited. But what are we to say when we find Vittoria's basic formulations in St. Thomas Aquinas? And what when most of the conclusions at which the Spanish school arrived are obviously implicit in twelfth-century canonists with explicit elaborations in the fourteenth and fifteenth centuries?

Even Vittoria's freshest contribution (necessarily fresh since the problem was a fresh one), the right of the American Indians to protection by the law of nations, was a fairly obvious deduction from Alfonso X's *Las Siete Partidas* on the rights of infidels. In the Spain of 1430 it would scarcely have needed the buttress from Aristotle which Vittoria provided. When we note further that about all the theorists did throughout the sixteenth and seventeenth centuries was to provide, tardily and hesitantly, rationalizations for what European governments were actually doing, and that this, in turn, was still guided, as far as possible, by the maxims of the post-glossators and the century-old habits of Western Christendom, we may be pardoned for wondering whether we ought to talk about the founding of international law at all.

Of course we should and must. The very bewilderment of the theorists shows that fundamental problems had arisen of which the disputes about diplomatic rights were only acute and obvious symptoms. A chasm was opening in the European tradition. The public law of Christendom was crumbling and sliding into the gap. The theorists were confronted with a task far more difficult and painful than just enlarging and modifying an existing structure to meet new demands. They had to discover a new foundation for whatever remained. They had to reshape the familiar concept of a law of nations, a *jus gentium*, governing the relations of individuals and public authorities within the commonwealth of Christendom, into the notion of a law for sovereign states, a law, that is, not *of* but *among* nations, a *jus inter gentes*. Although there was never a time when relations within Christendom had not been regarded as under the rule of law, it is literally true that 'international law' was something which the publicists of the later Renaissance were obliged to invent.

We can understand the difficulty of that task better if we look again at the foundation which was slipping away. '*Jus gentium*' had been variously defined between the beginning of the thirteenth and the end of the fifteenth century, but the different definitions were not in conflict: they were differences of emphasis, different ways of describing the same thing. The theologian or devout canonist might speak of the law of nations as the sum of those rules of morality which God had implanted in the hearts of mankind, and equate it, very nearly, to divine law. The philosopher, relying upon Aristotle, might prefer to speak of those standards imposed by reason, and thus base *jus gentium* on what he called natural law. The lawyer, meanwhile, whether civilian or feudalist, looking chiefly at what made *jus gentium* an operative part of the code of his society, would simply say that it was that body of customs observed by all or almost all mankind, and so valid by common consent.

But these are distinctions in terminology, not fundamental disagreements. Lawyers generally kept the term 'Natural Law' for instincts common to men and animals, but they would have agreed that the customs of different nations were alike and therefore assimilable in a common code because they were governed by natural reason. For Thomists the ethical norms recommended by reason constituted Natural Law. But though St. Thomas preferred to reserve the term 'Divine Law' for the imprescriptible decrees of Revelation, he would never have denied that the light of reason was divinely implanted, and therefore, in a real sense, divine, or that the observance of the law it prescribed was enforced and sanctioned by custom.[1] In making and sustaining the law of nations, reason, revelation and custom were held to be collaborators, not competitors. Therefore the Bartolists were able to assimilate the decrees of the Church and the practices of existing governments into what they regarded as Roman Law, and, reinforcing it by the only authority left to the Roman Republic, the authority of its law schools, make *jus gentium* a living common law for Western Europe.

In the sixteenth century the collaboration of reason, revelation and custom broke down, and the publicists were left without a foundation for their theories. The first prop to fall was not custom, itself, but the consciousness of and respect for Western tradition which gave custom its authority and coherence. The Renaissance in its narrower sense — the revival of classical scholarship and classicizing pedantry — was, on the whole, a more devastating attack on tradition than the religious revolution. The enthusiasm of the humanists for Greece and Rome, their attempt to restore a direct connection with antiquity by a backward leap across the 'dark centuries', meant, in the end, a rejection of the greater part of the usable European past.

Not at once, of course. Tall folios of the post-glossators continued to come from the presses throughout most of the sixteenth century, just as other medieval textbooks continued to be printed for use in university class-rooms. In the long run, too, the enrichment of European culture by a fresh infusion from classical sources may have been worth more than the humanists' contempt for medieval language and logic cost. Cujas and his fellows have been praised, perhaps justly, for liberating the law schools from bondage to the post-glossators and bringing back classical jurisprudence and the bare text of the *Corpus Juris*. Certainly they did leave the civil law, in France and ultimately in Europe, different from what they found it, better adapted, probably, to the needs of bureaucratic states and a pecuniary society. But the point here is that the return to the classics undermined the traditional method of interpreting the law of nations.

For instance, history and philology leave no doubt that the word *legatus* in the *Corpus Juris* usually meant not 'ambassador' but a delegate or representative of a municipality or province to the central government at Rome. In using these passages to rationalize the customs of late medieval states about ambassadors, the post-glossators were twisting (ignorantly or deliberately?) the word's original sense. More tolerant and historically minded scholars might have held that any body of law often grows in just this way. But the letter-worshipping humanists seem to have thought that a mistake about a word destroyed the argument. In the pride of their new scholarship they felt obliged to discard their predecessors' modes, not only of writing, but of reasoning. This drove them to try to derive the legal principles underlying contemporary practice without noticing the doctrines on which practice had been consciously based, or referring to the experience out of which the doctrines had arisen.

Having rejected their own tradition, all they had left to work with was the remote experience of the ancient world. It did not prove very fruitful. After about 1550, no writer on diplomacy who valued his reputation as a scholar could afford to omit a long disquisition on the sacred herbs, woollen fillets and flint knives which had been the insignia of those earliest Roman envoys, the priests of the fetial college. But no working diplomat can have felt much confidence that such details would be useful for checking his own or his opposite number's credentials. No writer on the laws of war, not even the hard-bitten soldier-lawyer Balthazar de Ayala, fails to describe how the Spartans or the Macedonians or Tibarenians declared war on their enemies.[3] But none of them gives so much as a sentence to the proper summoning of a town with drum and trumpet, according to contemporary custom, or to the forms normally observed at the outbreak of war by the states of their own time. Jean Hotman, practical diplomat and no great scholar, felt he had to stuff his little treatise with dozens of tales from Greek history cribbed out of other men's books for every bashful allusion to the recent past. Hugo Grotius, advocate-fiscal of Holland and pensionary of Rotterdam, intimately connected with the active diplomacy of the young Dutch republic for the better part of two decades, wrote six chapters on treaties and illustrated each point with profuse examples, none of them less than fifteen hundred years old.[4]

Grotius's avoidance of his own experience and of modern history has been commented on, and well-informed scholars, defending him, have protested that, in fact, Grotius drew oftener on the relatively recent past than did most publicists of his time. That would seem to be true. Every ten pages or so in *The Laws of War and Peace*, a little oftener in *Mare Librum*, if one keeps a sharp eye one can come upon a reference to some event that occurred after the fall of the Roman Empire. And though, characteristically, Grotius does say, 'to settle this we must ask what the custom of nations has actually been', and then cite Livy and Sallust,[5] one can often guess that some classical instance was selected to make a point about a current controversy.

But no one would claim that Grotius, a poet and a man of

humanistic letters, drew as often on the tradition of Latin Christendom as did Alberico Gentili. Gentili was no humanist. His Latin is rougher than Bernard du Rosier's. For the upstart school of Cujas he felt mainly hostility and scorn. He was a Bartolist. Probably no publicist of his century made more use of medieval and early modern authors and illustrations. But the citations of classical authorities in his two chief books outnumber references to writers and events since the sixth century by almost twenty to one.[6] The trend of literary taste, the general feeling that on practically any question only classical authority was respectable, swept along with it even so self-conscious a conservative as Gentili.

Since the prevailing climate of opinion obliged the Renaissance publicists to explain and justify the existing system of interstate relations without referring to its history or to the reasoning on which its habits had long been based, since even when they knew what the old foundation was (as they often did) they had to construct their theories on a base hastily put together from random fragments of an alien past, it is small wonder they made heavy work of it. But the harm resulting from the loss of the tradition of Latin Christendom went deeper than this. If the age of Greece and Rome seemed to the humanists the most glorious the world had known, it was, nevertheless, in many ways a far more savage and barbarous time than their own. Out of sheer pedantry some of the publicists were tempted to recommend harsher laws of war, less regard for the safety of ambassadors, the rights of neutrals, and the sanctity of treaties than even deteriorating contemporary practice warranted.

Moreover, probably because each state in its time was claiming more and more outspokenly to be a law unto itself and to regard nothing ahead of its own self-preservation and aggrandizement, the publicists turned oftenest to a period between the rise of Macedon and the final triumph of Rome, when the passionate local rivalries of the self-centred Mediterranean city states were embittered and distorted by the clash of contending empires. It was an ominous choice. In those centuries, though it was not hard to find a precedent for almost any treachery or aggression, one would look in vain for such ties of brotherhood and chivalry, for such a sense of common origin and common destiny as still bound together the Western world. European society in the late Renaissance had not yet fallen so far apart as the Hellenic world in its 'time of troubles', but it was moving in that direction. Whether the classicizing of the publicists did anything to encourage that disintegration, or whether the humanist break with tradition was merely a symptom of a movement beyond the power of literature to affect, is probably an idle question.

At the same time that the law of nations lost most of its support from customary law because the humanists had broken with the legal tradition of Latin Christendom, the support of divine law was gravely weakened. Revelation, the basis of divine law, instead of unifying Western culture, for the time being divided it. The same literal-mindedness, the same demand for a return to original sources, as interpreted by the new philology, which sapped the medieval structure of civil law, undermined also the authority of canon law.

After mid-century, large areas of Northern and Western Europe revolted from the Roman canon law altogether, or at least from all that part of it which had helped to underpin the public law of the Latin West. It became useless for publicists to appeal to sanctions of the Church to guarantee treaties or protect ambassadors, or to mitigate the horrors of war. Most Protestants indignantly rejected the suggestion of any earthly sanctions superior to the conscience of their rulers. At the same time Catholics began to contend that restraints once applied universally should not be invoked to protect heretics and rebels. Europe was losing its sense of moral unity. The levers which had moved Western public opinion no longer had a solid fulcrum.

In vain Trent reasserted the authority of tradition and of the canon law, and the supremacy of the Sovereign Pontiff. Protestant Europe mocked the Tridentine decrees, and Catholic monarchies received them only tardily and coldly. Meanwhile the religious ground of argument had shifted. Instead of referring to saints and popes and canonists, the publicists, Catholic and Protestant alike, were compelled, in deference to the temper of their time, to buttress their theories by quotation directly from the Bible. Joshua and David and Solomon, Judith and Jehu and Ehud the son of Gera became models of international conduct.

Again, the choice was not altogether fortunate. One can find a great many things in the Bible, including, perhaps, a valid system of international relations, but one would have to search rather differently from the way the Renaissance publicists did. They were looking for concrete examples of how states ought to behave towards one another, for the kind of historical precedents which fashion prevented them from seeking in the past of their own society. Therefore the whole of the New Testament was excluded. What human history it contains is about a withdrawn and outcast minority, not much interested in statecraft. That left the historical parts of the Old Testament, which Renaissance men accepted, naïvely and immediately, as they accepted Livy and Plutarch, as the record of states like their own and men like themselves, only more heroic and admirable, having, in the case of the ancient Jews, so direct a relation to God as to lift them altogether above criticism. The most potent precedents in international law were drawn, then, from the legends of a society more savage and barbarous than historic Greece and Rome.

These legends were dominated by the fierce tribal exclusiveness and self-righteous national egotism which had made the Jews unique, as far as we know, among the peoples of the ancient Near East, and made them unusually hard to live with. In the rise of national feeling which was beginning to divide European society, the imitation of classical patriotism was already supplying one element: the worship of a special fatherland which the humanists drew from their favourite reading was replacing the sense of belonging to an œcumenical community. But the imitation of ancient Judaism was more divisive still. As the Bible became the common property of the people of Europe, it was open to any group of them, national or religious, to imagine themselves, like the ancient Jews, divinely authorized to any lengths of guile or violence in the pursuit of their peculiar ends.

In the 1640s a New England assembly is said to have adopted the following resolutions: '1. The earth is the Lord's and the fullness thereof. Voted. 2. The Lord may give the earth or any part of it to His chosen people. Voted. 3. We are His chosen people. Voted.' With more sophistication, Papists and Covenanters, Spaniards and Dutchmen, Frenchmen and Englishmen, Austrians and Swedes all employed much the same argument.

Under the circumstances one must admire the discretion with which Renaissance publicists selected their biblical precedents.

Mainly, though with some unhappy exceptions, they chose examples of conduct which Latin Christendom had always admired and tried to imitate. Actually, they no more wanted their fellow-Europeans to become ancient Jews than they wanted them to become ancient Romans. They were simply seeking terms in which to explain and justify, and so to confirm and consolidate, the shaky structure of customary law within which, mostly by blind habit and conservative prejudice, the European community still continued to function.

Since classical and biblical precedents were at best poor substitutes for the living traditions of civil and canon law, serious Renaissance publicists were driven to rely chiefly on arguments based on Natural Law, unconscious of how incomprehensible much of their 'Natural Law' would have seemed to the people of India, or China, or the Americas, unsuspecting how much of that 'Law which natural reason has established among all men' was, in fact, the product of a single positive ethical and legal tradition. ' The assumption that natural reason induces universal agreement on basic principles of conduct, and the further assumption that the agreement of all (or most) peoples has legislative force enabled writers from Vittoria to Grotius to re-establish the existing rules of *jus gentium* on what they thought was a Natural Law basis. But the logic of their arguments depended, really, on the inner coherence of the Western tradition, just as their eloquence derived its force from the persistent sentiments of Christendom.

In the first, and perhaps greatest of the school, Francisco de Vittoria, the logic and sentiments of medieval Christendom, challenged by the egotism of the new power-seeking states, produced a ringing response. 'Since each state is a part of the whole world,' Vittoria said, 'if any war should be advantageous to some one state but disadvantageous to the world, for that very reason such a war is unjust.' (And therefore sinful, and not to be supported by the subjects of the guilty state, and to be punished by common action.) And further on: 'Just as the majority of members of a state may set up a king over the whole state, although not all consent, so the majority of Christians may lawfully establish a ruler whom all are bound to obey. For unanimous consent is rarely or never found in a multitude . . . therefore the will of the majority should prevail.' And again, 'The law of nations (*jus gentium*) has not only the force of an agreement among men, it has the force of law. For the world as a whole, being in a way a single republic, has the power to make laws just and fitting for all . . . And in grave matters it is not permissible for one country to refuse to be bound by laws which have been established by the authority of the whole world.'[8]

But Vittoria was speaking rather to the thirteenth century or the twentieth than to his own time. There was no one any more who could say to a king, 'It is not permissible', except professors who did not expect to be heard beyond their class-rooms. Even Vittoria was too much a Spaniard, too much a man of his century, to claim such a prerogative in temporal affairs even for the papacy. He could only appeal to accepted ethical principles as a check on the behaviour of the prince, and this at a time when the moral consensus of Europe was less secure than it had been for centuries, and was being weakened further by the passage of every decade. The dilemma gives the friar's flights of idealism a more than medieval unreality, and his returns to practicality an almost cynical air. Though he demolished the customary claims of Castile to its American empire with ruthless logic, and spoke up for the natural rights of the Indians as eloquently as Las Casas, in the end he conceded enough rights to the Spanish crown to enable it to do about what it was doing. Though he marshalled all the old pleas against aggressive war with unsurpassed cogency, he still saw war as part of the eternal scheme of things. He never pressed his argument about the moral duty of subjects to refuse to fight in an unjust war and of third party states to help repress it to the point of saying that since no war can be 'just' on both sides, then, if men would do their moral duty, there would be no wars at all. And though Vittoria restated the medieval rejection of an omnicompetent parochial state with a sharpness born of Europe's new experience, his remedies are less practical than Dante's. For the civil power which so much concerned him, his logic never devised a workable bridle.

That was the crux of the problem: how was the European community to escape anarchy if no check could be imposed on the absolute monarch and the absolute state? In the heat of the religious wars, the two religions which thought of themselves in œcumenical terms both offered solutions which were reformulations of the medieval answer. Both Rome and Geneva invoked against the claim of the State to the final and unquestioning allegiance of its subjects the claim of the Church to a higher allegiance. But the Calvinist solution could be applied only by internal rebellion, and the Catholic one only by the intervention of what many Europeans had come to think of as a foreign power. Each threatened civil war, and the rivalry between them widened the schism in Christendom.

Nor had the problem been correctly formulated. What Europe had to come to terms with was not just the absolute monarch, the tyrant-prince who put himself above the law in relation to his subjects, but the absolute state, the tyrant-nation which acknowledged no superior and no law more potent than that of its own interests. Not until mid-century were Puritan revolutionists to demonstrate how separable were royal divine right and absolute sovereignty, and an English observer of the Long Parliament and its sequel, one Thomas Hobbes, to find the word to describe the new monsters which men had created to rule over them. 'He is a great beast,' says Hobbes's title-page, 'no power on earth can bind him.' 'His heart is as firm as a stone,' said the Voice from the Whirlwind, 'yea, hard as a piece of the nether millstone.'

The two descriptions differ only at first glance. They both mean, 'A king over all the sons of pride.' And the quality of the extraordinary creature they allude to, its appearance of independent life, its stark power, its freedom from the trammels and scruples which complicate most human behaviour, would draw many generations of men after Thomas Hobbes into idolatry. The community of Europe, from the early seventeenth century for more than three hundred years, was to be composed not of individuals, not of estates and cities and provinces, but of these voracious, amoral, man-made monsters, the Leviathans. The real problem of the founders of international law was the one which mocked Job: by a slender line of logic to draw up Leviathan with a fish-hook.

Perhaps Hugo Grotius was the first to see the problem quite clearly, and therefore, if for no other reason, really does deserve his fame. He was mainly concerned, like publicists for more than half a century before him, with trying to save as much as possible of the old public law of medieval Christendom by providing new rationalizations for such of its rules as the governments of Europe still followed. He still spoke of the 'law of nations' (*jus gentium*), not of 'international law'.* He formulated no new rules. He seems to have invented no entirely new arguments. It is a temptation to guess that he did not, from one end to the other of his major work, *The Laws of War and Peace*, employ so much as a single fresh illustration. But he was notable for what he avoided doing.

Soto and Suarez had been unable to escape the influence of scholastic theology, and even if their medieval form had not closed their books to following generations, much of their argument would have proved unusable by Protestants or by the eighteenth century. But though Grotius had been reared a Calvinist, his mind had begun to outgrow the straight-jacket of dogma even before he had experienced its political dangers, and in his mature writings he left no trace of any doctrine not belonging to a vague, generalized Christianity. He threw none of the real burden of his proofs on revealed religion. From the arguments of his predecessors he selected those which would appeal to his successors down into the nineteenth century.

The success of his book owes much, of course, to its style, to a simplicity and lucidity which even today more than half overcome one's revulsion from the baroque classicizing which was once its literary passport. But it owes more to what Grotius was willing to cut away. From first to last his argument was arranged to appeal to rational men and men of goodwill, yes, but to such men living in a society which had accepted Leviathan. He seems to have been the first to adopt fully the basic axiom common to his successors: that the State is sovereign, subject to no exterior controls and amenable mainly to consideration of its own self-interest. He aimed to show that on these terms it is to the interest of the State to accept the rule of law, since to preserve its existence there must be some community of nations.

Sentiments of European unity and regard for the moral code of Christendom still survived in Grotius's day, as they have, in some fashion, ever since. They were strong in Grotius himself, and are obvious on many of his pages. So that, seeing so much still left and remembering how recently much more had been lost, at first one is tempted to condemn the prudence which discarded so many timbers of the stately medieval ship to make a simple liferaft. But Grotius cannot be blamed for the break-up of the old vessel. If it is a mistake to believe that in any dynamic society a dependable structure of law can be maintained for long without judges to administer it and police power to enforce it, the error does not begin with Grotius. After the failure of papacy and empire, the law schools had already embraced it. Grotius did no more than adapt and make explicit for his generation the reliance on persuasion which is clear enough in Bartolus. In a world in which the Leviathans were loose, clearly the terms of persuasion had to be altered.

Granting this, Grotius's system had two great merits. In the first place, by accepting absolute sovereignty, it implied the equality of all sovereign states. In the long run, to the extent that this doctrine triumphed, it probably limited the violence and frequency of wars. More important still, it helped guarantee that healthy variety which was the chief advantage of the direction European development was taking. In the second place, by abandoning theological argument and basing the plea for a law of nations purely on reason, Grotius extended the path marked by St. Thomas and Vittoria towards a more inclusive world community.

In the same century in which they lost their last chance to unify their society around the traditions of Latin Christendom, Europeans began their unique mission. Through traffics and discoveries, through conquest and colonization and the dissemination of their goods, their technologies and their ideas, they began to unite in one society the peoples of the globe. The next significant effort to achieve the rule of law among nations could not confine itself to the heirs of a single tradition. It would have to embrace mankind.

NOTES

A GENERAL NOTE ON BIBLIOGRAPHY

Most histories of diplomacy are devoted to foreign policies and diplomatic relations without much attention to diplomatic institutions. This is less true of the recent Russian history of diplomacy edited of V. P. Potemkin (Spanish translation, Buenos Aires, 1943; French, Paris, 1946), of David Jane Hill's *A History of Diplomacy in the International Development of Europe*, 3 vols. (London, 1921), still the best thing of its kind in English, and of *Histoire des relations internationales* (pub. sous la direction de Pierre Renouvin) T. I^e *Le Moyen Age*, by François-L. Ganshof (Paris, 1953). This last, while very brief (it covers the period 300-1500 in three hundred pages, devoting much space to economic and cultural relations), has several chapters on 'the techniques of international relations', and valuable bibliographies.

The trail was broken for the history of diplomatic institutions in the Renaissance by Alfred von Reumont's essay in his *Beiträge zur italienischen Geschichte* (Berlin, 1853), later expanded into a short book, *Della diplomazia italiana dal secolo XIII al XVII* (Florence, 1857). Three nineteenth-century treatments still dominate the field: a monograph by Otto Krauske, *Die Entwicklung der ständigen Diplomatie* (Leipzig, 1885); a review article about Krauske's book by Adolf Schaube, 'Zur Entstehungsgeschichte der ständigen Gesandtschaften' in *Mittheilungen des Instituts für Oesterreichische Geschichtsforschung X* (1889), 501-52; and a three-volume study by M. A. R. de Maulde-la-Clavière, *La diplomatie au temps de Machiavel* (Paris, 1892-93), intended as one panel of a monumental *Histoire de Louis XII*. For the continuing importance of Schaube and Krauske, see 'Italien und die Anfänge der neuzeitliche Diplomatie' in *Historische Zeitschrift* (1942-43) by Willy Andreas, and 'Über Gesandtschaftswesens und Diplomatie an der Wende vom Mittelalter zur Neuzeit' in *Archiv für Kulturgeschichte* (1950) by Fritz Ernst. Everything written since 1893 about Renaissance diplomacy, including the present study, is indebted to Maulde-la-Clavière's great monograph.

If recent books on international law no longer begin their historical introductions with Grotius, credit is due to the Belgian scholar, Ernest Nys. Nys's works, *Les origines de la diplomatie et le droit d'ambassade jusque à Grotius* (Brussels, 1884), *Les origines du droit international* (Brussels, 1894), the essays in *Études du droit international* (2 vols. Brussels, 1896) and later elaborations of the same themes, broke new ground, and in so far as they concern the fourteenth and fifteenth centuries have been very little amplified or corrected. E. R. Adair's *The Exterritoriality of Ambassadors in the Sixteenth and Seventeenth Centuries* (New York, 1929) is not only a thorough treatment of its subject, making conscientious use of concrete historical instances to illuminate the writings of the jurists, but a good general introduction to the later Renaissance literature about the international law of diplomacy.

For the theorists, the bibliographical study of Vladimir E. Hrabar, *De Legatis et legationibus tractatus varii* (Dorpat, 1906) is indispensable. It prints three important tractates in full, and describes forty-five others printed before 1625. Cf. B. Behrens in *The English Historical Review*, LI (1936), 616-27.

The full texts or extended summaries of a considerable mass of diplomatic documents for the period before 1620 are available. Texts of treaties in Rymer's *Foedera* and Dumont, *Corps universel diplomatique du droit des gens*, etc.; texts or summaries of ambassadors' dispatches and other state papers chiefly in the publications of governmental agencies and learned societies. A complete bibliography of these would double the size of the present volume and would, for the most part, simply duplicate listings in existing historical bibliographies.

Enormous masses of material for the diplomatic history of the period 1400-1620 remain in the archives, unpublished, uncalendared, and sometimes uncatalogued. I have been able to examine a few small segments of this material, but this study is, necessarily, mainly based on printed sources.

NOTES

[1] For the fifteenth-century proponents of the *res publica christiana* see J. N. Figgis, *From Gerson to Grotius* (Cambridge, 1923), pp. 31-54, and R. W. and A. J. Carlyle, *A History of Medieval Political Theory in the West*, VI (London 1936), 111-71 *passim*. For the prolongation of these sentiments, F. L. Baumer, 'The conception of Christendom in Renaissance England' in *Journal of the History of Ideas*, VI (1945), 131-56; 'The Church of England and the Common Corps of Christendom' in *Journal of Modern History*, XVI (1944), 1-21; and 'England, the Turk, and the Common Corps of Christendom' in *American Historical Review*, L (1944), 26-48. The last appearance I know of the term *res publica christiana* in an official public document is in the preamble of the Treaty of Utrecht (1714).

[2] For the problem of a 'common law' in Latin Christendom, and a survey of the literature since Savigny, see Francesco Calasso, *Storia e sistema delle fonti del diritto comune* (Milan, 1938), I, 13-97, supplemented by Carlo Calisse, 'Il diritto comune con riguardo speciale agli Stati della Chiesa' in *Studi di storia e diritto in onore di Enrico Besta* (4 vols. Milan, 1939), II, 417-33. Also, Enrico Besta, *Introduzione al diritto comune* (Milan, 1938).

[3] Articles in the *Catholic Encyclopedia* on 'Canon Law', 'The Peace and Truce of God', etc., provide an introduction. C. J. H. Hayes, 'Medieval diplomacy', in Walsh, *The History and Nature of International Relations*, pp. 69-92, a crisp general statement. Both Nys and Maulde-la-Clavière assume the predominance of the ecclesiastical element in medieval international law. See also A. C. Krey, 'The International State of the Middle Ages' in *American Historical Review*, XXVIII (1933), 1-12, and the symposium of citations from Isadore of Seville to the sixteenth century assembled in John Epstein, *The Catholic Tradition of the Law of Nations* (London, 1935).

[4] Cf. W. S. Holdsworth, *A History of English Law*, V (London, 1924), 60-129.

[5] On Honoré Bonet, earliest 'systematic' writer for the laity on the laws of war, the influence of the canonists is clear. It has been traced almost entirely to Bonet's dependence on one book, *De bello*, by John of Legnano. For this and for Bonet's influence on subsequent writers, see the introduction to *The Tree of Battles of Honoré Bonet*, translated and edited by G. W. Coopland (Liverpool, 1949), pp. 21-65.

[6] Francesco Ercole, *Dal Comune al Principato* (Florence, 1929), pp. 119ff; Francesco Calasso, 'Il problema storico del diritto comune' in *Studi . . . in onore di Enrico Besta*, II, 461-536; Enrico Besta, *Fonti del diritto italiano* (Padua, 1938), pp. 181ff; cf. F. W. Maitland, *English Law and the Renaissance* (Cambridge, 1901), pp. 7-8, 24-5.

[7] Bartolus is cited hereafter from his *Opera quae nunc extant omnia* (5 vols. Basel, 1588-89); for his career and an interpretation of his views, C. N. S. Woolf, *Bartolus of Sassaferato* (Cambridge, 1913); also Francesco Ercole, *Dal Bartolo al Althusio* (Florence, 1932), pp. 49-231.

[8] Maitland, op. cit., 50-1, summarizing Sir Thomas Smith's inaugural oration at Cambridge (1544), Camb. Univ. Lib. *Baker MSS.* XXXVII, 414; Holdsworth, op. cit., IV, 233-4, citing Somerset, Francis Bacon and James I; John Locke, *On Education*, para. 186. Continental instances are too numerous to mention. No writer of advice on a diplomatic career, from Dolet to de Callières, fails to commend the study of the civil law.

[9] A. J. Carlyle, 'Some aspects of the relation of Roman Law to Political Principles in the Middle Ages' in *Studi . . . in onore di E. Besta*, III, 185-98.

NOTES

[1] 'Legatus est seu dici potest, quicumque ab alio missus est; sive a principe vel a papa ad alios, sive ab aliqua civitate vel provincia ad principem vel ad aliam . . legatus dicitur vicarius muneris alieni.' Durandus in Hrabar, p. 32.

[2] F. Ercole, *Dal Bartolo al Althusio*, pp. 143ff.

[3] Bartolus, *Opera Omnia*, V, i, 34.

[4] The principal source for the life of Bernard du Rosier is Nicolas Bertrand, *Les gestes des Tolosains* [Toulouse?] (1555). Bertrand closes his account with a formidable list of Rosier's writings. Some of these are to be found in the manuscript collection of the Bibliothèque Nationale, including the *Ambaxiator brevilogus prosaico moralique dogmate pro felice et prospero ducato circa ambaxiatas insistencium excerptus.* (MSS. Lat. nᵒ. 6020, ff. 45-66.) I have been unable to locate another manuscript. The Paris MS. (*cir.* 1500) is published in full in Hrabar, leaving the slips of the pen uncorrected.

[5] Gondissalvus de Villadiego, *De legato*, III, i, 25 (Several sixteenth-century eds.), cited from *Tractatus Universi Juris* (Venice, 1584) (hereafter *TUJ*), XIII, ii.

[6] There is no good account of the diplomatic functions of heralds in the later Middle Ages. A brief discussion in A. R. Wagner, *Heralds and Heraldry in the Middle Ages* (London, 1939), pp. 31-45; cf. Maulde-la-Clavière, I, 428-38.

[7] Nicolaus Uptonus, *De studio militari* (London, 1654), I, 12.

[8] For Arundel's mission, J. H. Wylie, *The Reign of Henry V* (Cambridge, 1914), I, 98 and references there cited. For Machado's first mission (to Italy, 1494-95), Calendar of State Papers, Venetian, ed. R. Brown (London, 1864-) (hereafter *Cal. Ven.*), I, 260; for his second (to Spain), James Gairdner, *Memorials of King Henry VII* (2 vols. London, 1858). For Toison d'Or in England (1506), J. Chmel, *Urkunden, Briefe und Actenstücke zur Geschichte Maximilians I* (Stuttgart, 1845), pp. 238, 268, 276.

CHAPTER III

[1] Hrabar, pp. 4ff.

[2] G. Vedovato, *Note sul diritto diplomatico della repubblica fiorentina* (Florence, 1946), pp. 29-30; A. Larsen, 'The Payment of fourteenth century English Ambassadors' in *Eng. Hist. Rev.* LIV (1939), 406ff; G. de Villadiego in *TUJ*, XIII, ii, 2, iv; Martin of Lodi in *TUJ*, XVI, Quaes. XV, XXVI, XXXVI; J. Bertachinus in Hrabar, pp. 71-6.

[3] Maulde-la-Clavière, II, 176-201.

[4] H. Finke, *Acta Aragonensis* (Berlin and Leipzig, 1908), *Intro.* cxxvii-clvi publishes part of the formulary of the crown of Aragon, *cir.* 1340; for England, G. P. Cuttino, *English Diplomatic Administration, 1259-1339* (Oxford, 1940), pp. 108-15; Bib. Nat. *MS. du fonds français: Ancien fonds*, 6022 contains a formulary from the reign of Charles VII containing credentials (or powers) addressed to the pope, the emperor, the king of Castile, the marquis of Montferrat, etc. (ff. 85-7ᵛᵒ). G. de Villadiego, op. cit., II, i, gives a general formula for the content of credentials, citing Bartolus, a formula which was used by Spanish and Italian chanceries, often practically verbatim. Cf. Bartolus, *Op. Omn.*, IV, iii, 13, 39.

[5] Hrabar, pp. 14-16. For eloquence in Italian diplomacy see Emilio Santini, *Firenze e i suoi 'oratori' nel quatrocento* (Milan, 1922).

[6] Cf. Maulde-la-Clavière, II, 119-54 and D. Marzi, *La cancelleria della repubblica fiorentina* (Rocca S. Casciano, 1910), pp. 353ff.

[7] Bartolus, *Op. Omn.*, IV, iii, 39; Martin of Lodi, op. cit., Quaes. XXV; G. de Villadiego, op. cit., II, v, 2; III, i, 3-18. Actual discussions about powers in sixteenth-century negotiations often invoked these jurists.

NOTES

[1] Rosier in Hrabar, pp. 22-7. In the *Corpus Juris Civilis*, the section most frequently cited by medieval jurists was *Digest*, L, vii, 17; cf. *Las siete partidas*, VII, xxv, 9. Leading places in Bartolus, *Op. Omn.*, I, i, 269, 500; II, ii, 666-7; III, ii, 666, 683; IV, ii, 458. For fifteenth-century opinion, see G. de Villadiego, op. cit., and Martin of Lodi, *De Legato* (both in *TUJ*, for other editions see Hrabar), especially, Villadiego, III, iii-v, and Martin of Lodi, Quaes. V, VI, XII, XVIII, XXXI, XXXVIII. Also Johannes Bertachinus's popular *Repertorium* (see Hrabar) which collects the answers to some fifty-odd questions concerning diplomacy, ranging from the security of the ambassador's person to how he can collect indemnity for a horse that dies on his journey. All the later writers show a wide range of reference to other jurists, and a remarkable harmony of opinion.

[2] L. Mirot, 'L'arrestation des ambassadeurs florentins en France' in *Bibliothèque de l'Ecole de Chartres*, XCV (1934), 74-116.

[1] Jacob Burkhardt's famous phrase. For an analysis of Burkhardt's influence on historiography see Wallace K. Ferguson, *The Renaissance in Historical Thought* (Cambridge, Mass., 1948).

[2] A. Gherardi, 'La guerra degli Otto Santi' in *Archivio Storico Italiano*, Ser. 3, vol. V (1867), pt. ii, 35, 131 for the war of the Florentines against Gregory XI. Nino Valeri, *Signorie e principati, 1343-1516* (Verona, 1949), provides the best general guide to the history of Italy during the whole period. Good critical bibliography.

[3] There is no even partially adequate study of the logistic factor in European history before the sixteenth century. Some idea of courier speeds *cir.* 1500 may be gathered from Pierre Sardella, *Nouvelles et speculations à Venise au début du XVIe siècle* (Paris, n.d. 1947?), and of their progressive decrease in H. Robinson, *The British Post Office* (Princeton, 1948) and E. Vaillé, *Histoire générale des postes françaises* (Paris, 1947, 1949). Both Robinson and Vaillé tend, however, to distort the problem by following the general custom of citing minimum times, records for the period over the course. Such records are of far less importance for the political and economic history of Europe than the normal speeds, and the volume and regularity of the traffic. Sardella's statistical approach to this question would seem to be capable of wide and fruitful application. For the consequences of the logistic factor from the tenth to the thirteenth centuries, see Marc Bloch, *La société feudale: La formation des liens de dépendance* (Paris, 1949), pp. 99-115; and for some suggestive remarks on the 'greater size' of the Mediterranean world in the sixteenth century, Fernand Braudel, *La Méditerranée et le monde méditerranéan à l'époque de Philippe II* (Paris, 1949), pp. 309-24.

[4] Piero Pieri, *La crisi militare italiana nel Rinascimento nelle sue relazioni con la crisi politica ed economica* (Naples, 1934). W. Block, *Die Condottieri* (Berlin, 1913); E. Ricotti, *Storia delle compagnie di ventura* (Turin, 2nd ed. 1893).

[5] E. Santi, *Firenze e i suoi 'oratori' nel quattrocento*; C. Curcio, *La politica italiana del' 400* (Florence, 1932).

[1] A. Pieper, *Zur Enstehungsgeschichte der ständigen Nuntiaturen* (Freiburg, 1894), p. 2; O. Krauske, *Entwicklung der ständigen Diplomatie*, pp. 7-8 and references cited.

[2] H. Finke, *Acta Aragonensis*, I, cxxvi ff.

[3] G. P. Cuttino, *English Diplomatic Administration*, esp. pp. 96-9; cf. G. B. Guarini, *Legazione stabili prima del' 400* (Rome, 1909); R. von Heckel, 'Das aufkommen der ständigen Prokuratoren' in *Studi e Testi*, XXIX, 290.

NOTES

[4] A similar development took place at the same time in the chancery of the French monarchy. Philippe le Bel's diplomatic activity led to the establishment of no permanent embassies unless we count his proctors at Avignon, but it did lead to a fanciful suggestion for them in a Utopian book, *Le songe du vieil pèlerin*, by one of his counsellors.

[5] L. Ferraris, *Prompta Bibliotheca Canonica* (Bologna, 1746), article 'Procurator'; A. Pieper, op. cit., pp. 28-9; Maulde-la-Clavière, I, 298-9, 312.

[6] B. Behrens, 'Origins of the office of English Resident Ambassador in Rome' in *The English Historical Review*, XLIX (1934), 640ff. A. de la Torre (ed.) *Documentos sobre relaciones internacionales de los Reyes Catolicos* (Barcelona, 1949), I, 441.

[7] *Cal. Ven.*, III, 334.

[8] R. de Roover, *The Medici Bank* (New York, 1948), pp. 5-18; B. Buser, *Die Beziehungen der Mediceer zu Frankreich* (Leipzig, 1879), pp. 78-188 *passim*; C. S. Gutkind, *Cosimo de' Medici* (Oxford, 1938), pp. 176-93.

[9] First so signalized by Adolphe Schaube in *Oesterreichisches Geschichtsforschung*, X (1888). Cf. W. Andreas, 'Italien und die Anfange der Neuzeitlichen Diplomatie' in *Historiche Zeitschrift*, CLXVII (1942), 279 for an emphatic, uncritical acceptance of Schaube's dictum.

CHAPTER VII

[1] Maulde-la-Clavière, I, 306, mistakes Gonzaga's agent in Germany for one from the court of Naples on the basis of Winkelmann, *Acta imperii*, No. 1152. Relevant documents listed in A. Luzio, *L'Archivio Gonzaga di Mantova* (Verona, 1922), II, 94ff.

[2] L. Osio, *Documenti diplomatici tratti dagli archivi milanesi* (Milan, 1864), I, 177-202. Another, more marginal, instance is furnished by the Venetian ambassador who resided in Milan from November 1379 to March 1381. See Vittorio Lazzarini (ed.) *Dispacci di Pietro Cornaro* (Venice, 1939).

[3] D. M. Bueno de Mesquita, *Giangaleazzo Visconti* (Cambridge, 1941).

[4] G. Mattingly, 'The first Resident Embassies' in *Speculum*, XII (1937), pp. 428ff.

[5] Archivio di Stato di Venezia *Sen. Sec.*, IX, f° 13, 27, 42. Cf. P. M. Perret, *Relations de la France avec Venise* (Paris, 1896), I, 133.

[6] Perret, op. cit., I, 150-8, and II, 316ff (documents).

[7] G. Canestrini and A. Desjardins, *Négociations diplomatiques de la France avec la Toscane* (Paris, 1859), I, 59; B. Buser, *Die Beziehungen der Mediceer zu Frankreich*, pp. 39, 364; cf. C. S. Gutkind, *Cosimo de' Medici* and Perret, op. cit., I, 408ff *passim*.

CHAPTER VIII

[1] L. Osio, *Documenti diplomatici . . . milanese*, III, 268-78; J. Simonetae *Rerum Gestarum Francisci Sfortiae*, G. Soranzo (ed.) in *Raccolta degli storici Italiani*, the revised edition of L. A. Muratori, *Rerum Italicarum Scriptores*, Vol. XXI, pt. 2 (Bologna, 1932-34).

[2] Osio, III, 369 and ff *passim*.

[3] Ibid., III, 420, 458.

[4] Nicodemo Tranchedini's letters to Sforza (Bib. Nat. *fonds italien*, 1585-91) were published in part by B. Buser, *Beziehungen der Mediceer* and his career summarized by Schaube, op. cit. See also R. Parodi, 'Nicodemo da Pontremoli' in *Archivio Storico Lombardo*, 5th ser., XLVII (1920), 334ff.

[5] Francesco Antonini, 'La pace di Lodi ed i segreti maneggi che la prepararono' in *Archivio Storico Lombardo*, LVII (1930), 233-96.

[6] Ibid., III, 300; Simonetae *. . . F. Sfortiae* in rev. Muratori, pp. 350, 357, 399; Buser, op. cit., 36-42, 362, 367.

NOTES

[7] Antonini, op. cit., 236-62 *passim*; Perret, op. cit., I, 210ff; G. Soranzo, *La lega italica* (Milan, 1924), pp. 8, 14-36 *passim*, 73. Simoneta, op. cit.

[8] Text in Dumont, III, i, 202. Antonini, op. cit.; Soranzo, op. cit.; G. Nebbia, 'La lega italica del 1455' in *Archivio Storico Lombardo* (1939), pp. 115-36.

CHAPTER IX

[1] For this war see, besides Soranzo, op. cit. and references there cited, N. F. Faraglia, *Storia della lotta fra Alfonso V d'Aragona e Renato d'Angiò* (Lanciano, 1908); Albano Sorbelli, *Francesco Sforza a Genova* (Bologna, 1901); and J. Ametller y Vinyas, *Alfonso V de Aragon en Italia*, Vol. II (Gerona, 1903). Agostino Giustiniani, *Annali della repubblica di Genova* (Genoa, 1835) prints the correspondence between the Genoese and Neapolitan chanceries, II, 385-404.

[2] Cf. E. W. Nelson, 'The Origins of modern balance-of-power Diplomacy' in *Medievalia et Humanistica*, I (1942), 124-42. For further discussion see bibliography in N. Valeri, *Signorie e principati*, p. 830, especially C. Cognasso, *I problemi politici del Rinascimento* (Turin, 1930); Keinast in *Historische Zeitschrift*, LIII (1936); and Carlo Morandi, 'Il concetto della politica d'equilibrio nell' Europa moderna' in *Archivio Storico Italiano*, XCVIII (1940).

[3] For the Milanese embassy in France, see B. de Mandrot (ed.), *Dépêches des ambassadeurs milanais (1461-1466)* (Paris, 1916-23), 4 vols.; *Lettres de Louis XI* (Paris, 1883-1909), 11 vols. and Gingins la Sarra, *Dépêches . . . sur les campagnes de Charles-le-Hardi* (Paris, 1858), Vol. I. The dispatches of Galeazzo Maria's ambassadors in France, 1466-75, a considerable number of which are preserved in the Archivio di Stato di Milano (*Visc.— Sforz., Potenze Estere, Francia*) have been published only in brief excerpts in *Lettres de Louis XI* and elsewhere.

Recently Fritz Ernst in *Archiv für Kulturgeschichte*, X (1950), 77-81 has voiced a doubt that the Milanese ambassadors in France should be regarded as residents. The argument turns on Louis XI's reluctance, which he expressed to one of the Milanese diplomats in 1464, to receive resident ambassadors at all, and concludes that therefore none of the Italian ambassadors in France before 1483 may properly be called residents. But even from the published documents it is clear that for twelve years, with only two short breaks, there was a continuous series of Milanese envoys at the French court, that they behaved as residents behaved in Italy, regarded themselves as residents, and were so regarded in Milan. It is also clear that Louis XI recognized and dealt with all of them as properly accredited ambassadors, whatever he called them. That Louis did not reciprocate by sending a resident ambassador to Milan scarcely matters since many resident embassies at the time and much later were unilateral, but it makes it possible to argue that though Louis recognized the ambassadors, he did not recognize the existence of a resident embassy. Perhaps he did not.

[4] Mandrot, op. cit., II, 125.

[5] Bernardo Bembo, res. 1470-74. Perret, op. cit., I, 555ff, *passim*; G. M. Malipiero, 'Annali veneti' in *Arch. stor. ital.* (1843), p. 230; Chmel, *Monumenta Habsburgica*, I, 101.

[6] For Galeazzo Maria's motives and his preliminary negotiations with Burgundy, see Fabio Cusin, 'Impero, Borgogna e Politica Italiana' in *Nuova Rivista Storica*, XIX (1935), 137-72; for his residents, F. de Gingins la Sarra, op. cit.; for his attempt to make up with Louis XI, Commynes, *Mémoires*, ed. Mandrot, 2 vols. (Paris, 1902-03), I, 352-3. A more recent edition of Commynes, ed. J. Calmette, 3 vols. (Paris, 1924-25).

[7] Perret, op. cit., II, 98-114.

[8] Ibid., II, 131-214; G. Mattingly in *Speculum*, XII (1937) and references there cited.

[9] B. Buser, *Beziehungen der Mediceer*; Kervyn de Lettenhove, *Lettres et négociations de Philippe de Commines* (Brussels, 1867), II, 39-40, 60, 78; G. Canestrini and A. Desjardins, *Négociations*, Vol. I.

NOTES

[1] L. Bittner and L. Gross, *Répertoire des représentants diplomatiques de tous les pays depuis la paix de Westphalie*, Vol. I (Oldenburg and Berlin, 1936).

[2] Maulde-la-Clavière, I, 369-74.

[3] 'Traité du gouvernement de Venise' in App. to Perret, op. cit., II, 292ff; E. D. Theseider, *Niccolò Machiavelli, Diplomatico* (Como, 1945), p. 102.

[4] Vedovato, *Note sul diritto diplomatico della repubblica fiorentina* analyses at length the Florentine regulations for junior aides, and prints in full the regulations for ambassadors (1421-1525), pp. 47-82; also in Maulde-la-Clavière, III, App.

[5] As the later *quatrocento* popes, particularly Sixtus IV and Innocent VIII, got more deeply involved in Italian politics, their nuncios tended to remain for longer periods at major Italian capitals. One, Giacomo Gherardi, stayed in Milan for more than two years (1488-90). But his papers show that he was not considered by the papal chancery or by his hosts as a resident. See *Dispacci e Lettere di Giacomo Gherardi*, ed. E. Carusi (Rome, 1909).

[6] A. Pieper, *Zur Enstehungsgeschichte der ständigen Nuntiaturen*, pp. 28-9.

[7] Maulde-la-Clavière, II, 155-260; Theseider, pp. 154-78; *Commentaries of Pius II*; the *Diarium* of Johannes Burchard (ed. Thouasne, 3 vols., Paris, 1883-85); *Diarium* of Paris de Grassis (Vat. MS); see Pio Paschini in R. Paribeni, *Ambasciate e ambasciatori a Roma* (Milan, 1927), pp. 47-74.

[1] For E. Barbaro see: Ermolao Barbaro, *Epistolae, Orationes et Carmina*, ed. V. Branca (2 vols. Florence, 1943); T. Stickney, *De Hermolai Barbari vita . . .* (Paris, 1903); A Ferriguto, *Almorò Barbaro* (*Miscellanea di Storia Veneta*, Ser. III, Vol. XV, No. 2, Venice, 1922); V. Branca, 'Ermolao Barbaro Junior' in *Repertorio degli Umanisti Italiani* (Florence, 1943); P. O. Kristeller, 'Un codice Padovano di Aristotle postillato da Francesco e Ermolao Barbaro' in *La Bibliofilia*, L (1950), 162-78.

[2] V. Branca in *Repertorio degli Umanisti Italiani*, p. 3 lists six MSS of *De officio legati*. Of these, Hrabar prints the full text of Vatican, *Lat.* 5392. Another MS, Correr, *cod.* PD 397, No. 41 was printed in part in *Thiara et purpura Veneta* (Rome, 1750) and is summarized by Ferriguto, pp. 430-1.

[3] Hrabar, p. 65.

[4] 'Ut ea faciant, dicant, consulent et cogitent quae ad optimum suae civitatis statum et retinendum et amplificandum pertinere posse judicent', ibid., p. 66.

[5] Between May 1st, 1503, and April 30th, 1504. *Dispacci di Antonio Giustinian*, ed. P. Villari, 3 vols. (Florence, 1876).

[6] D. Marzi, *La cancelleria . . . fiorentina*, p. 356; E. D. Theseider, *N. Machiavelli, Diplomatico*, pp. 94-5, 186-92.

[7] Maulde-la-Clavière, III, 141-3, 382-8; A. Degert, 'Louis XI et ses ambassadeurs' in *Rev. Hist.*, CLIV (1927), 18; for Florence, Theseider, pp. 96-198; Marzi; and Machiavelli, 'Memoriale a Raffaello Girolami' in *Scritti Politici Minori*; for Venice, A. Baschet, *La diplomatie vénitienne* (Paris, 1862), more eloquent than reliable, should be supplemented by W. Andreas, *Staatskunst und Diplomatie der Venezianer* (Leipzig, 1943); Perret, op. cit., II, 292 on the recording of *relazioni*, *cir.* 1500. For the texts of these, E. Alberi (ed.), *Relazioni degli ambasciatori veneti al senato* (15 vols. Florence, 1839-63).

[8] Hrabar, p. 67.

[1] E. Fueter, *Geschichte des Europäischen Staatensystems von 1494 bis 1559* (Munich and Berlin, 1915) is still valuable for the political and diplomatic history of the Italian

wars and has the best short critical bibliography for publications up to 1914. For more recent scholarship see Corrado Barbagallo, *Storia Universale IV* (Turin, 1950); or J. Calmette, *L'Élaboration du Monde Moderne* (Coll. Clio, Paris, 1949). A valuable discussion of the considerable literature concerning the crisis of 1494 in Nino Valeri, *Signorie e principati*, pp. 830-1. See, especially, F. Ercole, *Da Carlo VIII a Carlo V* (Florence, 1932).

<h3 style="text-align:center">CHAPTER XIII</h3>

1 *Mémoires*, II, 97-100; see chap. XII, note 1.

<h3 style="text-align:center">CHAPTER XIV</h3>

1 R. B. Merriman, *The rise of the Spanish Empire* (New York, 1918), II, 28-40, 46-53, 271-3, and references there cited.

2 J. Zurita, *Anales de la Corona de Aragòn* (Saragossa, 1669), IV, 280-1; Merriman, op. cit., II, 60-1.

3 Antonio de la Torre's magnificent publication of the documents from the Barcelona Archivo de la Corona de Aragòn, *Documentos sobre relaciones internacionales de los Reyes Catolicòs*, 4 vols. (Barcelona, 1949-52), is now the chief printed source for Ferdinand's Italian affairs. The Archivo General de Simancas also contains relevant material in *Estado, Negs. de Venezia, Estados pequenos de Italia*, and *Patronato Real*. (For the last see *Catalogo V*, 1946.) So does the library of the Academia de Historia at Madrid (see *Bol. de la R. Accad. de Hist.* XCVII, 363-416). See also A. Rodriguez Villa, *Don Francisco de Rojas* (Madrid, 1896), and the articles and monographs of Joseph Calmette, especially 'La politique espagnole dans la guerre de Ferrare' in *Revue historique*, XCII (1906), 225-53; 'La politique espagnole dans l'affaire des barons napolitains' in *Rev. Hist.*, CX (1910), 225-46; and *La question des Pyréneés et la Marche d'Espagne au Moyen Age* (Paris, 1947).

4 The standard monograph on the diplomacy of the Breton crisis (from French sources) is still A. Dupuys, *Histoire de la réunion de la Bretagne avec la France*, 2 vols. (Paris, 1880), to be supplemented by J. Calmette, 'La politique espagnole dans la crise de l'indépendance bretonne' in *Revue historique*, CXVII (1914), 168-82.

5 For Juan de Fonseca and Francisco de Rojas, see, besides *Calendar of State Papers, Spanish* (hereafter *Cal. Span.*), I, *passim*, and sources cited above, A. Rodriguez Villa, *La reina dona Juana la Loca* (Madrid, 1892) and *Don Francisco de Rojas* (Madrid, 1896). Scattered letters from both Fonseca and Rojas are to be found at Simancas, *Estado, Negs. de Flandes*. For what may have been an earlier approach to Maximilian, see A. de la Torre, op. cit., II, 39-40.

6 De Puebla's surviving correspondence is calendared in *Cal. Span.*, I (London, 1862) ed. Gustave Bergenroth; G. Mattingly, 'The Reputation of Dr. De Puebla' in *The English Historical Review*, LV (1940), 27-48.

7 'ut mos est francorum', M. Sanudo, *La spedizione de Carlo VIII in Italia* (Venice, 1873), p. 48. For de Silva see also G. Zurita, *Anales de la Corona de Aragón*, V, 37-9, and Merriman, *Spanish Empire*, II, 285.

8 M. Sanudo, *Diarii* (Venice, 1879), I, 377, 441ff *passim*; Pieper, op. cit., 30; *Cal. Span.*, I, 62.

9 Commynes, *Mémoires*, II, 222ff.

<h3 style="text-align:center">CHAPTER XV</h3>

1 *Cal. Span.*, I and II, and *Cal. Span., Further Supplement* (1513-43), ed. G. Mattingly (London, 1947). R. B. Merriman, *Rise of the Spanish Empire*, II (New York, 1918) remains the best account of Ferdinand's foreign policy in English. (Good critical

NOTES

bibliography.)   See also the works of J. M. Doussinague, especially *La politica internacional de Fernando el Católico* (Madrid, 1944).

[2] Maulde-la-Clavière, I, 308; A. Rodriguez Villa, *Juana La Loca*, pp. 155, 483; J. Gairdner (ed.), *Memorials of King Henry VII* (London, 1858), p. 433.

[3] For instance his treatment of Caroz in 1513-14, *Cal. Span.*, II, 162-248, *passim*.

[4] *Cal. Span.*, I, 413; II, 32 and *passim*.

[5] *Cal. Span.*, I, 161-7; Duque de Alba (ed.), *Correspondencia de Gutierre Gomez de Fuensalida* (Madrid, 1907), pp. 131-5.

[6] Ibid., p. 483.

CHAPTER XVI

[1] *Cal. Ven.*, I, 189, 211, 221; Marino Sanudo, *Diarii* (Venice, 1903), I, 116, 145; F. Calvi, *Bianca Maria Sforza* (Milan, 1888); G. Canestrini and A. Desjardins, *Négociations . . . avec la Toscane*, I, 230, 235; Commynes, *Mémoires*, II, 118-19; H. F. Delaborde, *L'expédition de Charles VIII en Italie* (Paris, 1888), pp. 220ff.

[2] Sanudo, I, 865; *Cal. Ven.*, I, 227, 865.

[3] Malipiero, pp. 336, 505, 507; Sanudo, I, 51, 199, 618; *Cal. Ven.*, I, 233, 236, 251ff *passim*.

[4] Desjardins, *Négociations . . . avec la Toscane*, I, 221ff.

[5] The banker, Neri Caponi, accompanied Charles VIII to Naples and followed him back to France. Whether he was officially accredited or recognized as resident ambassador is uncertain, but he was certainly in communication with the Florentine Signory, represented its views and held an official cipher. He was associated with the special embassy of G. Guasconi and F. Soderini in December 1495 just as if he were a resident, and was still there on the arrival of Ridolfi, whom Desjardins calls 'the first resident' in 1497 (Desjardins, I, 496, 584, 638-9). The series of residents only becomes completely clear from Tosinghi's embassy in 1500 (ibid., II, 24, 42).

[6] A. Pieper, *Zur Entstehungsgeschichte der ständigen Nuntiaturen*, remains the best study.

[7] I. Bernays, 'Die Diplomatie um 1500' in *Historische Zeitschrift*, CXXXVIII (1928), emphasizes this point (p. 23); W. Andreas, 'Italien und die Anfänge der neuzeitlichen Diplomatie', in *Hist. Zeit.*, CLXVII (1942), 34 repeats it.

[8] A. J. G. Le Glay, ed., *Négociations diplomatiques entre la France et l'Autriche* (Paris, 1845), I; J. Chmel, ed., *Urkunden . . . Maximilians I*, in *Bib. Lit. V. Stut.*, X, 126, 149, 166; *Cal. Ven.*, I, 260; *Cal. Span.*, I, 80, 93, 98.

[9] Le Glay, *Négociations*, I, xxviii-xxix, 122-5, 131-91 *passim*, 370-455; Maulde-la-Clavière, II, 20ff.

[10] F. Vindry, *Les ambassadeurs français permanents au XVI siècle* (Paris, 1903). Cf. Jean des Pins, 'Autour des guerres d'Italie' in *Revue d'Histoire Diplomatique*, 1947, pp. 215-46.

[11] *Cal. Ven.*, I, 260; B. Behrens, 'Origins of the Office of English Resident Ambassador in Rome', in *Eng. Hist. Rev.*, XLIX (1934), 640-56.

[12] For Thomas Spinelly, with some remarks on John Stile, B. Behrens in *Trans. R. Hist. Soc.*, XVI (1933), 161-96.

[13] The surviving diplomatic correspondence of Henry VIII's ambassadors is fully calendared in *Letters and Papers of Henry VIII*, 21 vols. in 33 parts (London, 1862-   ) (hereafter *L. & P.*).   The addenda (London, 1929-   ) add many documents valuable for foreign affairs.   The best accounts of Henry's diplomacy are A. F. Pollard, *Henry VIII* (London, 1905) and *Wolsey* (London, 1929); to be supplemented by W. Busch, *Drei Jahre englischer Vermittlungspolitik* (Bonn, 1884) and *Cardinal Wolsey und die kaiserlich-englische Allianz* (Bonn, 1886).

NOTES

CHAPTER XVII

[1] *History of Diplomacy*, II, 294.

[2] *Lettres de Louis XII* (Brussels, 1712), I, 48; *L. & P.*, III, 1248; *Cortes de los antiguos reinos de León y de Castilla* (Madrid, 1861-1903), Vols. IV and V, *passim*.

[3] Villari, *Dispacci di A. Giustiniani*, I, 243.

[4] Text in Rymer, *Foedera*, XIII, 624ff.

[5] A. F. Pollard, *Wolsey*, p. 117; H. A. L. Fisher, *The Political History of England*, V, 203-5; Pastor, *History of the Popes*, VII, 242-3; Sir Charles Petrie, *Earlier Diplomatic History* (New York, 1949), p. 23.

[6] G. Mattingly, 'An early Non-aggression Pact' in *Journal of Modern History*, X (1938), 1-30.

[7] F. Nitti, *Leone X e la sua politica* (Florence, 1892), pp. 250ff.

[8] *Cal. Span.*, II, 434.

[9] Fisher, op. cit., p. 240.

[1] Eduard Rott, *Histoire de la représentation diplomatique de la France auprès des Cantons Suisses*, etc. (Berne and Paris, 1900), Vol. I.

[2] For Passano's mission, G. Jacqueton, *La politique extérieure de Louise de Savoy* (Paris, 1892), and for the first news of the divorce, *La première ambassade en Angleterre de Jean du Bellay*, V. L. Bourilly and P. de Vaissière (eds.) (Paris, 1905).

[3] In *Reports of the Deputy Keeper of the Public Records*, XXXVII (1876), app. i, 180-94, Armand Baschet published a list of French ambassadors in England which does not distinguish adequately between residents and special envoys. Conyers Read, *A Bibliography of British History, Tudor period* (Oxford, 1933), lists the principal publications of dispatches from French residents in England.

[4] Hasenclever, *Die Politik der Schmalkaldener* (Berlin, 1901).

[5] Documents in E. Charrière, *Négociations de la France dans le Levant*, Vol. I (Paris, 1848). Narrative, J. Ursu, *La politique orientale de François Ier* (Paris, 1908); R. B. Merriman, *Suleiman the Magnificent* (Cambridge, Mass., 1944), pp. 126-44.

[6] H. F. Rördam, 'Résidents français près de la cour de Danemark' in *Bulletin de l'Académie royale des Sciences et des Lettres de Danemark* (1898). For Danzay, see A. Richard, 'Un diplomate Poitevin du XVIe siècle: Charles de Danzay' in *Mémoires de la Société des Antiquaires de l'ouest*, 3e s., III, 1909 (Poitiers, 1910), 1-241; 'Correspondance de Charles Dantzai, ministre de France à la Cour de Danemark; Dépêches de l'année 1575' in *Handlinger rörande Skandinaviens Historia*, XI (Stockholm, 1824), covering actually the period 1575-86; and C. F. Bricka, *Intheretninger fra Charles de Dançay til det Franske hof am forholdene i Norden, 1567-1573* (Copenhagen, 1901).

[7] Charrière, I, 285-94.

[1] For Florence, G. Canestrini and A. Desjardins, *Négociations diplomatiques de la France avec la Toscane*, 6 vols. (Paris, 1859-96) and cf. L. Romier, *Les origines politiques des guerres de religion*, 2 vols. (Paris, 1913-14); for Genoa, Vito Vitale, *La diplomazia Genovese* (Milan, 1941) and ibid., *Diplomatici e consoli della republica di Genova* (Genoa: Società Ligure di Storia Patria, 1934), a list of the ambassadors and consuls of the republic from 1494 to 1796.

[2] Visconde de Santarem, *Cuadro Elementar das Relaciones . . . Diplomaticas de Portugal* (Paris, 1842), 15 vols. is still to be consulted. Honoré de Caix, the first French resident

NOTES

at Lisbon was at his post in the summer of 1522; he remained until 1535. Dr. Barroso, the Spanish ambassador, reached Lisbon, December 30th, 1521; he was replaced after about a year by Juan de Zuñiga. Archivo General de Simancas, *Estado, Negs. de Portugal*, legajo 367, nos. 32-86 *passim*. Archivo do Torre do Tombo, Lisbon, *Gavetas Antigas*, IV, 37.

[3] Archivo do Torre do Tombo, Lisbon, *Corpo Cronologico*, Maço 27, Docs. 103, 106, 109; Maço 39, Doc. 60. Because of the diplomatic dust-up over Magellan's voyage to the Moluccas, Luis da Silveira was only in Spain a short time and though diplomatic contacts between Spain and Portugal (the Badajoz conference and the marriage negotiations) were continuous during the next three years, the first Portuguese who really acted as resident ambassador in Spain was Antonio de Azevedo Coutinho (April 1525-May 1529), Arch. Gen. de Simancas, *Estado, Negs. de P.*, 368 and 369; Torre do Tombo, *Corpo Cronologico, Index* (numerous scattered letters). For Portuguese residents in France, see E. Gomez de Carvalho, *D. João III e os Franceses* (Lisbon, 1909).

[4] Christopher Mont (Mount, Mundt) served England in Germany over a period of forty years, with an interruption during the reign of Mary. He died at his post in Strasbourg in 1572. Reports from him in *Letters and Papers of Henry VIII* and in *Calendar of State Papers, Foreign, Edward VI, and Elizabeth*, though the latter collections, limited to documents in the Public Record Office, do not notice all his surviving correspondence. For Henry VIII's diplomacy in Germany, 1535-40, see F. Pruesser, *England und die Schmalkaldener* (Leipzig, 1929); for Somerset's, A. O. Meyer, *Die englische Diplomatie in Deutschland zur Zeit Eduards VI und Mariens* (Breslau, 1900).

[5] For Charles V's policies and administration, A. Ballesteros Beretta, *Historia de España*, IV (Madrid, 1927); R. B. Merriman, *Rise of the Spanish Empire*, III; K. Brandi, *The Emperor Charles V*. Dip. correspondence with England at Simancas and elsewhere, mostly calendared in *Cal. Span.* With Italy, mostly unpublished and in Arch. Gen. de Simancas, *Estado, Patronato Real* (Cat. V), *Negs. de Venezia* and *Estados Pequeños de Italia* (no printed cats.), some in Haus- hof- und staatsarchiv, Vienna. With France, now mostly in Simancas, see J. Paz, *Capitulaciones con Francia y negociaciones diplomaticas, Cat. IV* (Madrid, 1914) and ibid., *Documentos relativos a España existentes en los archivos nacionales de Paris* (Madrid, 1934). (These documents have now been restored to Simancas.) See also C. Weiss, *Papiers d'État du Cardinal de Granvelle*, 9 vols. (Paris, 1841-52.)

[6] *Cal. Span.*, III, 50ff and *Further Supplement*, xx-xxxvii.

[7] For Catherine's diplomatic rôle and Spanish and imperial ambassadors in England to 1536, see G. Mattingly, *Catherine of Aragon* (Boston, 1941).

[8] *L. & P.*, XVI and XVII (esp. XVI, No. 1109 and XVII, Nos. 319-20, 329, 360-1, 397, 435; XIX i, Nos. 799, 866, 987, 989, 1004; ii, 5, 12, 45, 53, 105, 181, 236. Marillac's account in J. Kaulek, *Correspondance Politique de MM de Castillon et de Marillac* (Paris, 1885) contrasted with the actual record above shows how thoroughly Chapuys outwitted his French rival.

[9] For Renard and the clash of French and imperialist diplomacy in England, see E. Harris Harbison, *Rival Ambassadors at the Court of Queen Mary* (Princeton, 1940).

CHAPTER XX

[1] J. B. Casale was withdrawn from Venice, March 17th, 1535 and not replaced (*Cal. Ven.*, V, 18) until Edmund (alias Sigismund) Harvel, Casale's former secretary, returned there in March 1541. Harvel died at his post. The official account of his funeral (January 7th, 1550) states that the Signory regarded him as merely 'nuntius' or vice-ambassador. In August 1550, Peter Vannes presented his credentials from Edward VI as English resident ambassador to the republic. He was recalled by Mary in 1556 without replacement. For an account of papal pressures to prevent a resumption of diplomatic relations with England under Elizabeth see G. C. Bentinck's preface to *Cal. Ven.*, VII (London, 1890), pp. xi-xxii.

NOTES

[2] A. O. Meyer, *Die englische Diplomatie . . . Eduards VI*, pp. 16-17.

[3] Philip II was inclined to discourage any permanent exchange of ambassadors between the English and Austrian courts. So, and most emphatically after 1570, were the papal nuncios in Germany. A. G. de Simancas, *Estado, legs.* 683, 687, *passim*.

[4] For the Spanish embassy in England, *Calendar of State Papers, Spanish, Elizabeth*, M. A. S. Hume (ed.), 4 vols. (London, 1892-99) (hereafter *Cal. Span., Eliz.*), should be supplemented by the full texts in *Colección de Documentos Inéditos para la historia de España* (Madrid, 1842-1931) (hereafter *CDIE*), vols. 87, 89, 90, 91, 92 and J. B. C. Kervyn de Lettenhove and L. G. van Severen, *Relations politiques des Pays-Bas et de l'Angleterre*, 11 vols. (Brussels, 1882-1900). The history of the embassy 1558-68 has been re-studied by Manuel Fernandez Alvarez, *Tres Embajadores de Felipe II en Inglaterra* (Madrid, 1951) from the Simancas archives.

[5] Some of the correspondence of Elizabeth's ambassadors, mostly what is preserved in the Public Record Office, is summarized in *Calendar of State Papers, Foreign, Elizabeth* (hereafter *CSPF, Eliz.*) through the year 1588. F. J. Weaver, 'Anglo-French Diplomatic Relations, 1558-1603' in *Bulletin of the Institute of Historical Research*, Vol. IV (1926) to Vol. VII (1930) *passim*, serially, gives a complete list of Elizabeth's envoys to France, resident and special, with a copious bibliography of the sources, printed and MS., for each mission. C. Read, *Mr. Secretary Walsingham*, 3 vols. (Cambridge, Mass., 1925), is an excellent guide to the main lines of English diplomatic activity, 1570-90. For a general picture of the Queen's foreign policy, J. E. Neale, *Queen Elizabeth* (London, 1934).

CHAPTER XXI

[1] *CDIE*, LXXXVII, 91-2.

[2] *CSPF, Eliz.*, I, 426-8, 438, 558.

[3] *CSPF, Eliz.*, I, 379.

[4] For the impression made by Throckmorton's dispatches, compare Cecil's memorandum on French relations, *CSPF, Eliz.*, I, 523-4 with Throckmorton's reports in the preceding two hundred pages, *passim* and cf. J. B. Black, *The Reign of Elizabeth* (Oxford, 1945), pp. 39-50 *passim*.

[5] *CSPF, Eliz.*, IV, 521.

[6] In 1559 Feria, probably the best-informed of all Philip's ambassadors, estimated that 'most of the nobles are tainted with heresy' (he meant not just peers but, as his inclusion of Cecil, Peter Carewe and Nicholas Throckmorton in his list shows, also the gentry around the court), and in addition most of the people in London, Kent and the seaport towns. The rest of England, he repeated, was solidly Catholic. *CDIE*, LXXXVII, 132. In other words, Protestant sentiments predominated in the circles and areas he had been able to observe himself, and he took the word of his Catholic informants for the solid Catholicism of the rest of the country. Statistical estimates covering large areas are not the most reliable part of diplomatic reporting in the sixteenth century.

[7] *CDIE*, LXXXVII and XC; *Mémoires de Michel de Castelnau, seigneur de Mauvissière*, ed. J. Le Laboureur, 3 vols. (Paris, 1731) and G. Hubault, *Ambassade de Michel de Castelnau en Angleterre* (Saint-Cloud, n.d. [1857?]).

[8] *CDIE*, CXI, 181-92; CXII, 528-33.

[9] Excerpts from Mendoza's dispatches from France in *Cal. Span. Eliz.*, IV. The greater part, still unpublished, are now in Simancas. Except for a short notice by Col. Guillaume, prefixed to Loumier's translation, *Commentaires de Bernardino de Mendoza (1567-1577)* (Brussels, 1860), there is no biography of Mendoza, but see G. Baguenault de Puchesse, 'La politique de Philippe II dans les affaires de France' in *Revue des Questions historiques*, XXXV (1879), 31-42 and refs. there cited.

[10] Sir William Harborne presented his credentials at the Sublime Porte in 1583 and remained five years. The embassy was normally continuous thereafter. By that time

NOTES

not only France and Venice, but the emperor and the king of Spain had residents at Constantinople. A. L. Rowland, *England and Turkey* (Philadelphia, 1925); H. G. Rawlinson, 'Embassy of William Harborne to Constantinople', *Transactions of the Royal Historical Society*, V (1922); *CSPF, Eliz.*, 1-27.

¹¹ A regular exchange of resident ambassadors between the two Habsburg courts did not begin for some years after the abdication of Charles V. The Spanish series up to the Thirty Years War runs: the count of Luna (1559-62), who remained in touch with the Austrian court as Philip's ambassador to the Council of Trent until December 1563; Thomas Perrenot de Chantonnay (Granvelle's brother), 1562-70; Francisco Hurtado de Mendoza, count of Monteagudo, 1570-77; Juan de Borja, 1577-81; Guillén de San Clemente, 1581-1608; and Balthazar de Zuñiga, 1608-17. The Austrians were served during this time by Adam Dietrichstein, 1564-73, and Johan Khevenhueller (1571)-1573-1606. The documents at Simancas, mostly in *Estado, Negs. de Alemania* have been catalogued, but published only in small part, a haphazard selection of the dispatches 1559-74 in *CDIE*, vols. 98, 101, 110, 111 and a better edited collection by the marquis of Azerbe, *Correspondencia Inédita de Guillén de San Clemente (1581-1608)* (Saragossa, 1892). See also Bohdan Chudoba, *Spain and the Empire* (Chicago, 1952). Bratli and other historians ever since Ranke have made much use of the reports of Venetian ambassadors at the court of Philip II, but those of the Spanish residents at Venice, A. G. de Simancas, *Estado, Negs. de Venecia* have been little used.

Correspondence with the papacy at Simancas mostly under *Patronato Real* has been used for numerous special studies. See also R. de Hinojosa, *Los despachos de la diplomacia pontifica en España* (Madrid, 1896), Vol. I to 1605.

Genoa and Florence both normally maintained diplomatic representation with Philip II and occasional resident Spanish agents in both cities can be traced in Simancas, *Estado, Estados pequeños de Italia*, and *Patronato Real, Diversos de Italia*, but in neither city had Spain anything like continuous official representation.

¹² There is no adequate monograph on the French diplomatic service in the sixteenth century, and nothing for its later half to replace Edouard Frémy, *Essai sur les Diplomates du temps de la Ligue* (Paris, 1873). Gaston Zeller's announced Vol. II in P. Renouvin's *Histoire des relations internationales* should shortly supply a guide to the abundant special literature.

CHAPTER XXII

¹ Sir Thomas Elyot, *The Governour*, I, xi.

² Dolet, Etienne, *De officio legati* . . . [etc.] (Lyon, 1541); see also *Am. Jour. Int. Law*, 1933.

³ Braun, Conrad, *De legationibus libri quinque*. The only text of this work I have ever seen, and the only one listed by Hrabar, occupies the first 244 pp. of the folio, D. Conradi Bruni, *Opera tria* (Mainz, 1548). See B. Behrens in *Eng. Hist. Rev.*, LI (1936), 616-27, for a critical summary.

⁴ In his *De origine et auctoritate rerum judicatarum*, Tit. XVI (Paris, 1573). For subsequent editions and redactions see Hrabar, 104-12.

⁵ *Legatus seu de legatione legatorumque privilegiis officio ac munere libellus* (Paris, 1579). The second edition (Hanover, 1596) bound with Maggi and A. Gentili's *De legationibus* is much commoner. There are no differences except a few misprints.

⁶ Tasso Torquato, *Il Messagiero*, Venice, 1582. I have used the text in *Opere di* . . . *Tasso*, ed. Rosini (Pisa, 1822), VII, 48-117.

⁷ *De legationibus, libri tres* (London, 1585), see Hrabar, 123-30. The best modern edition is that published in 'The Classics of International Law' by the Carnegie Endowment for International Peace (New York, 1924). Vol. I has an introduction by Ernest Nys and a photographic reproduction of the edition of 1594; Vol. II, a translation and index.

NOTES

[8] Hrabar, pp. 131-9.

[9] *Legatus* (Rouen, 1598) (see Hrabar, 140-7). I have used the handy and fairly common Elzevir 12° (Amsterdam, 1645), 543 pp.

[10] *The ambassador*, London, 1603. (With a dedication to the earl of Pembroke.) *De la charge et dignité de l'ambassadeur* (Paris, 1604). An enlarged and corrected edition of the MS. from which the English translation was printed, cited hereafter. For subsequent editions see Hrabar, pp. 154-62.

[11] Hrabar, pp. 163-204, gives a full summary.

[12] *KHPYKEION sive Legationum Insigne* (Antwerp, 1618). (For other editions see Hrabar, pp. 224-6.) I have used the Weimar edition of 1663, the text of which does not differ from Marselaer's revision, *Legatus libri duo* (Antwerp, 1626).

[13] See the two examples of model general instructions in *Revue d'histoire diplomatique* (1914-15): Pierre Danès, 'Conseils à un ambassadeur', MS. of *cir.* 1561, ed. L. Delauvaud, p. 607ff, and Anon., 'Instructions générales des Ambassadeurs', from a MS. *cir.* 1600, ed. Griselle, p. 772ff. Both models were almost certainly known to Hotman.

[14] Hotman (1604), f. 5. Hotman, in fact, borrowed most from his immediate contemporary, Paschalius (Carlo Pasquale), including, apparently, Pasquale's borrowings, but this debt he omitted to mention. The omission earned him a furious attack by the slighted author under the pseudonym of Colazon. *Notes sur un petit livre premièrement, intitulé L'ambassadeur.* Par la Sieur de Colazon (Paris, 1604).

[15] Dolet in *Am. Jour. Int. Law* (1933), p. 85; cf. Marselaer (Weimar, 1663), pp. 63-4.

[16] *El Embajador*, I, 126ᵛᵒ; cf. Gentili's emphatic praise of Henry Stanley's magnificent special embassy to France, mounted at his own expense. *De legationibus* (N.Y., 1924), I, 152.

[17] Gentili, I, 153; De Vera, I, 134ᵛᵒ-6ᵛᵒ.

[18] Maggi, *De legato* (Hanover, 1596), ff. 55-7ᵛᵒ, Marselaer also urged the importance of Turkish, p. 143.

[19] Gentili, I, 148-9.

[20] '. . . y tambien porque es grandeza de un Principe que su lengua corra en toda parte', II, 9.

[21] Maggi, op. cit., ff. 18-21ᵛᵒ; Tasso, 'Il Messagiero' in *Opere*, VII, 108-9; Gasparo Bragaccia, *L'Ambasciatore* (Padua, 1627), p. 36.

[22] Op. cit., I, 197. See, however, Gentili's *De abusu mendaci* (Hanover, 1599), in which he makes out quite a case for those *missi ad mentiendum reipublicae causa*.

[23] *De la charge et dignité*, f. 27ᵛᵒ.

[24] *El Embajador*, I, ff. 74-112ᵛᵒ.

[25] 'Il Messagiero' in *Opere*, VII, 111.

CHAPTER XXIII

[1] There is no comparative study of the development of this office. For England, an excellent monograph, F. M. G. Evans, *The Principal Secretary of State* (Manchester, 1923), to be supplemented by C. Read, *Mr. Secretary Walsingham*, 3 vols. (Oxford, 1925). For France, a summary discussion in R. Doucet, *Les institutions de la France au XVIᵉ siècle* (Paris, 1948), I, 159ff with bibliography and valuable material in J. Nouaillac, *Villeroy* (Paris, 1908); see also C.-G. Picavet, *La diplomatie française au temps de Louis XIV* (Paris, 1930). For Spain, A. Ballesteros Beretta, *Historia de España* (Madrid, 1927), IV², 10ff which still leans heavily on J. Gounon-Loubens, *Essai sur l'administration de la Castille au XVIᵉ siècle* (Paris, 1860). G. Maranon, *Antonio Perez* (Buenos Aires, 1947), a brilliant biography, is disappointingly meagre about the *Secretario's* official duties, but its bibliography provides the best guide for the study of the office.

313

NOTES

[2] Evans, op. cit., p. 9.

[3] Cf. Hotman, *De la charge et dignité* (1604), 21vo.

[4] Read, *Walsingham*, I, 431.

CHAPTER XXIV

[1] In all the diplomatic correspondence of the sixteenth century there is a superabundance of information about the pay which ambassadors received (or expected). For some general statements see Frémy, *La diplomatie au temps du Ligue*, pp. 77ff; A. Richard, *Un diplomate poitevin*, p. 172; J. Paz, *Arch. Gen. de Simancas, Cat. IV*, p. 664; A. O. Meyers, *Englische Diplomatie* . . . (Breslau, 1900), pp. 10-11. By taking as a base line John Stile's pitiful 4s. 2d. a day (1505-09) Meyer is able to say that the pay of English ambassadors had increased seven-fold by 1550, but Wingfield's 13s. 4d. (1510), a little over three ducats (of Venice or of Aragon) is a juster comparison. Edward VI's ambassadors drew about twice that or little more. For France, in 1560, Throckmorton drew £3 6s. 8d, but that was unusually high, partly because of adverse exchange. For E. Chapuys's fortune, G. Mattingly, 'A Humanist Ambassador', in *Jour. Mod. Hist.* IV (1932), pp. 175-85.

[2] A. O. Meyer, op. cit., pp. 6-8.

[3] A. Richard, op. cit., pp. 18-20; J. Hotman, *De la charge et dignité*, p. 14.

[4] A. Gentili, *De Legationibus* (Hanau, 1594), p. 14.

[5] Ibid., pp. 103, 191.

[6] *Legatus*, p. 462.

[7] According to Isaak Walton, Wotton inscribed in the album of an Augsburg merchant, in 1604, 'Legatus est vir bonus peregre missus ad mentiendum Reipublicae causa'.

CHAPTER XXV

[1] The *Calendar of State Papers, Spanish* (London, 1862-1947), 11 vols. and two supplements, and the *Calendar of State Papers, Spanish, Elizabeth*, 4 vols. (London, 1892-99), are the basic guide to the correspondence of the Spanish ambassadors in England, though incomplete. (See Conyers Read, *Bibliography of British History, Tudor Period, 1485-1603*, Nos. 620, 621 and *Further Supplement* to *Cal. Span. (1513-1543)* (London, 1947), pp. v-ix.) No publication for 1553-58 and much material either at Brussels or Simancas (most of it formerly at Paris) omitted especially from *Cal. Span. Eliz.*, cf. chap. XX, Note 4.

[2] Longlée to Villeroy in Bib. Nat. *Fonds français*, MS. 16110 ff. 208-87 *passim*; Letters of Sir Edward Stafford in *CSPF, Eliz.*, 1586-87 *passim*.

[3] For the theory of ciphers in the Renaissance, see Maulde-la-Clavière, III, 133ff; De Vera, *El Embajador*, II, 19ff; Fletcher Pratt, *Secret and Urgent* (Indianapolis [1939]); and Mariano Alcocer, 'Criptographia Español' in *Boletin de la Academia de Historia*, CV (1934), 331ff; CVII (1935), 603ff.

[4] De Puebla held two ciphers of his own, and one in common with the Netherlands embassy between 1496 and 1507. They were as complicated as any in the next hundred years and more complicated than most. Bergenroth said he had counted more than four hundred symbols in one. I have been unable to find so many in all three, even adding in as separate symbols some which are certainly just variants. But one key does run to about one hundred and twenty signs. Cf. *Cal. Span.*, I, XIII. For the Duke of Feria's absurdly simple cipher (1558) see M. Fernandez Alvarez, *Tres Embajadores de Felipe II*, p. 263.

[5] *L. & P.*, III, 1090.

[6] Up to the middle of the sixteenth century, the Empire, France and England were,

NOTES

most heralds agreed, in that order the three ranking crowns in Europe. Then followed the other crowned heads in an order increasingly uncertain; then independent republics (Venice first); then vassal states. This was the practice at Rome, Venice and the French court. Towards mid-century the Portuguese made occasional trouble by their claim to precede the English. For the dispute between Sir Edward Carne and the Portuguese ambassador at Rome, in 1555, *CSPF*, p. 180.

[7] *CDIE*, XCVIII, 280 (re Venice). See also Frémy, *Diplomates du temps de la Ligue* for Franco-Spanish disputes about precedence. Luna's correspondence from Trent is in *CDIE*, XCVIII.

[8] In the first part of the seventeenth century those theorists with the most experience as working diplomats placed the most emphasis on precedence. Hotman, for instance, *De la charge et dignité*, ff. 58-62vo and De Vera, *El Embajador*, I, 41-53 and special remarks for each court in Part IV. Cf. Wicquefort, *Mémoire touchant les ambassadeurs* (Cologne, 1679), II, 48ff.

CHAPTER XXVI

[1] Bohdan Chudoba, *Spain and the Empire, 1519-1643*; G. Ritter, *Deutsche Geschichte im Zeitalter der Gegenreformation und dreissigjährigen Krieges*, Vol. III (Stuttgart, 1908).

[2] See E. Rodriguez Maris, *El gran duque de Osuna* (Madrid, 1920) and A. Ballesteros Berretta, *Historia de Espana*, IV, for the considerable literature about Bedmar.

[3] Don Diego Sarmiento de Acuna, conde de Gondomar, Spanish resident ambassador in England, 1613-18 and again 1620-22 is referred to throughout this chapter by the title by which he is most familiar in history, though he was not created count of Gondomar until 1617. There is a sketch of him by Martin Hume (Madrid, 1903) and another by F. H. Lyon (Oxford, 1910) in English, to be supplemented by Francisco Javier Sánchez-Canton, *Don Diego Sarmiento de Acuna, conde de Gondomar, 1567-1626* (Madrid, 1935), but the best and freshest source is *Correspondencia oficial de . . . Gondomar*, 4 vols. in *Documentos inéditos para la historia de Espana* (new series). Vol. I (Madrid, 1936) contains mainly dispatches for the year 1617, Vol. II covers 1618-20 and has a preface and valuable notes by Don Antonio Ballesteros Beretta. Vols. III (1944) and IV (1945), also with preface by Ballesteros Beretta, cover the first two years of the embassy (hereafter cited as *DIE*). J. S. Gardiner's *History of England* made use of Gondomar's dispatches, especially for 1618.

[4] E. C. Bald (ed.), *A game at chess*, by Thomas Middleton (Cambridge, 1929).

[5] T. Scott, *The second part of Vox Populi* (London, 1624), pp. 11-17.

[6] *DIE*, II, 183-9; III, 269-79.

[7] Ibid., IV, 7-22, 99-100, 125-6.

[8] Ibid., *passim*. The index of persons, IV, 269-84 lists most of the numerous references to all these personages, usually under their actual, but sometimes under their code names. See especially III, 86ff, 123, 131, 271-4; IV, 32ff; I, 129; II, 189.

[9] Miguel Gomez de Campillo, 'El Espía Mayor y el Conductor de Embajadores' in *Boletin de la Real Academia de Historia*, CIX (1946), 317-39.

[10] *DIE*, III, 135 (October 5th, 1613); I, 131 (November 15th, 1617).

[11] Ibid., I, 35-41, 53-64 *passim*, 66-78; cf. J. S. Gardiner.

[12] Ibid., III, 71-8. Sir William Monson, *Naval Tracts* (Navy Records Soc., 1913), III, 33-6, and Oppenheim's notes, pp. 45-55 on 'the Honour of the Flag'; Monson's 'The Ceremony of Wearing the Flag', op. cit., IV, 120-1 contains his account of the Portsmouth incident.

[13] *DIE*, I, 221ff, 231-4, 237-8, 341-2.

[14] Ibid., II, 131-47. Gondomar's own summary of the internal and international situation of Spain, end of March 1619, a striking document.

NOTES

[1] For this subject, E. A. Adair, *The Exterritoriality of Ambassadors in the Sixteenth and Seventeenth Centuries* (New York, 1929) remains indispensable.

[2] See chap. IV above.

[3] B. Ayala, *De iure et officiis bellicis* (Washington, 1912), I, 88-9; Zeller, *La diplomatie française*, pp. 260-1; Lanz, *Correspondenz*, II, 316-17; F. Lopez de Gomara, *Annals of Charles V*, ed. R. B. Merriman (Oxford, 1912), pp. 110-11 and references there cited.

[4] *Cal. Span.*, III, i, 677-81, 763-4, 1015-17; III, ii, 16-84; *L. & P.*, IV, 1163-88 *passim*.

[5] Adair, pp. 110-11, takes a different point of view. Cf. A. Gentili, *De legationibus*, II, iii; Hotman, *De la charge et dignité*, ff. 76-7vo, Grotius, *De iure belli ac pacis*, II, xviii, 5, for shift in views of theorists.

[6] For de Puebla, Bernard André, *De vita . . . Henrici VII*, in J. Gairdner, *Memorials of King Henry VII*, pp. 104-5; for Frauenberg, *Cal. Span.*, I, 552. Other examples in Maulde-la-Clavière, II, 36ff.

[7] *De iure belli ac pacis*, II, xviii, 9.

[8] B. Ayala, op. cit., I, lx, 3; the consensus of the post-glossators may be traced in J. Bertachinus, *Repertorium*, cf. Adair, p. 47.

[9] Polydore Vergil, *Anglicae Historiae* (Basil, 1570), p. 624; Edward Hall, *Chronicles* (London, 1809), p. 527; Sanudo, XII, 269; Desjardins, II, 454; *Cal. Span.*, II, 50; *L. & P.*, I, 56, 58, 426-8, 462.

[10] For de Praet's case, the calendared accounts, *L. & P.*, IV, 508, 542 and *Cal. Span.*, III, 50-6, 62-5, 74-5 and 79 *passim* should be supplemented by the original documents at Brussels, Simancas and Vienna, and the transcripts (P.R.O.) since editors were inclined to omit or abbreviate legalistic arguments. Hall's account (op. cit., 691-2) is over-simplified.

[11] For Wyatt, *L. & P.*, XIV, 217 and *passim*; for Noailles, E. H. Harbison, *Rival Ambassadors*, pp. 271-96; for the Ridolfi and Throckmorton plots, C. Read, *Walsingham*, I, 159-61, 271-2; II, 381-7.

In Mendoza's case both Alberico Gentili and Jean Hotman were consulted. Both recommended sending Mendoza back to Spain 'to be punished', but as an act of clemency, not of justice. Hotman felt that severe punishment would have been warranted (*De la charge et dignité*, f. 66). Gentili based his argument on the fact that no overt act had been committed, adding, 'I hold that an ambassador should be put to death if he has inflicted even the slightest injury upon the prince.' (*De legationibus*, II, xviii.)

[12] *De iure belli ac pacis*, II, xviii, 4.

[13] Sir Matthew Hale, *History of the Pleas of the Crown* (London, 1736), cited by Adair, p. 32.

[1] Besides books previously listed, see, for an introduction to the vast and growing literature about the Spanish jurists, James Brown Scott, *The Spanish Origin of International Law* (Oxford, 1934); ibid., *The Catholic Conception of International Law* (Washington, 1934); both chiefly valuable for F. de Vittoria and summing up Scott's earlier books and papers; also J. B. Scott, *Suárez and the International Community* (Washington, 1933). For Domingo de Soto, V. D. Carro, *D. de Soto y el derecho de gentes*, Covarrubias, 'the Spanish Bartolus', has had little recent recognition as a member of this group, perhaps because he was no theologian. W. Knight, *Life of H. Grotius*, remains the standard biography in English. H. Grotius, *De jure belli ac pacis* is cited by book, chapter and section, which correspond in all editions.

NOTES

[2] A. Bonilla y San Martin, *Francisco Suárez, El escolasticismo tomista y el derecho internacional* (Madrid, 1918).

[3] Ayala, *De iure et officiis bellicis* (Douai, 1582), ff. 1-4vo.

[4] *De iure belli*, II, xi-xvi. Following the custom of the post-glossators, Grotius discussed treaties as governed by the civil law about contracts.

[5] Ibid., II, xviii, 4.

[6] In *De legationibus*, for instance, Gentili cites Cicero seventy times, Plato sixty-three, Livy forty-nine, and a dozen or more other classical authors more often than the modern he cites oftenest, Francesco Guicciardini. His *Storia di Italia* is cited nineteen times and Paolo Giovio's various writings three times, Commynes and Machiavelli once each, no other historian or memoirist later than Procopius, at all. Among the jurists, Alciatus, Alesssandro Alessandri, Baldus and Jason Mainus get occasional mention, but none of the four chief older authorities on Gentili's special subject, Bartolus, Martin of Lodi, Gondissalvus de Villadiego and Bertachinus, though Gentili must have read them all. Gratian, the Roman emperor, gets referred to, but not Gratian, the decretalist. And so forth.

[7] An exception should be made here of Juan Ginés de Sepúlveda. His proposition was that the law of nations was only to be found among 'gentes humanitiores', more civilized peoples. In his view, of course, Western Europeans. See J. H. Parry, *The Spanish Theory of Empire in the Sixteenth Century* (Cambridge, Mass., 1940), pp. 31ff.

[8] Francisco de Vittoria, *De Potestate Civile*, paragraphs 13-22, *passim*. Parry's view (op. cit.) is that Vittoria's 'majority' equals Sepulveda's 'gentes humanitiores' and means Europeans. In view of the over-estimate in sixteenth-century Spain and Portugal of Asiatic populations, and the tendency to exaggerate the indigenous population of the New World, this seems doubtful. Vittoria insisted on the equality of the Indian communities, and except in theological matters was not prone to invidious comparisons between societies. Cf. his remark that the Indians are stupid only because they are uneducated, and that if they live like beasts, so, for the same reason, do many Spanish peasants (*De Indiis*, I, xxiii); and his assertion that discovery gave the Spaniards no more rights in America than a canoe-load of Indians would have acquired had they 'discovered' Spain (ibid., II, iii).

[9] This term, in its Latin form, first used by Richard Zouch, *Juris et Judicii Fecialis, sive Juris inter Gentes* (Oxford, 1650). Of course Vittoria had spoken more than a hundred years before of 'ius quod naturalis ratio inter omnes gentes constituit' and there were other places where Zouch might have caught the phrase. Jeremy Bentham introduced the term 'international law' into English while the French were still using their more exact equivalent of *jus gentium*, 'droit des gens'.

INDEX

INDEX

INDEX

INDEX

Montoya, 244
More, St. Thomas, 166, 281
Morison, 257
Most Holy League (1455), 87-92, 137, 143, 204

NAPLES, 31, 78, 84, 86-7, 91-4, 96-8, 101, 105, 108, 116, 134-6, 139, 143, 145, 155, 162, 165, 175, 181
Naturelli, Philibert, 157
Navarre, Queen of, 199
Neale, Profr. J. E., 11
Neroni, Dietisalvi, 81, 86
Netherlands, 126, 130, 139, 141-2, 145, 148, 182, 187, 205
Nicholas of Cusa, 18, 20
Nicholas of Upton, 32
Nicholas V, 55, 87-8, 105
Nicodemus of Pontremoli, 69, 85-6, 110
de Noailles, Antoine, 190, 277
Northampton, Earl of, 259
Northumberland, Duke of, 189-90
Nuncios, Papal, 29, 30; resident, 154-5
Nuncios (Nuntii) Secular, 30-1

OLIVARES, 211, 214
Orleans, House of, 97, 130, 134

PADUA, 58, 75, 77, 108
Pasquale, Carlo, 213ff, 239
Passano, Gian Giacomo, 175-6
Pazzi Conspiracy, 95
Perez, Antonio, 226, 228, 230, 247
Perez, Gonzalo, 228, 230
Petrarch, 10, 62
Philip the Good, 23, 60, 74
Philip II, 189, 191-4, 198, 200-4, 227-8, 230, 237, 246, 252, 263, 277, 279
Philip III, 223, 228, 255-6
Philip IV, 43, 223
Pisa, 58, 68, 72, 75, 77
Pius II, 93, 106
Pole, Cardinal, 277
Portugal, 34, 123, 128, 131, 145, 182-3, 186, 189
Powers, 36, 42, 107
de Praet, Louis, 186-7, 240, 274
Precedence, 37-8, 251-3, 261-4
Prince, The, 116, 166
Princes, 26, 47; interviews between, 102, 172, 252-3
Procurators, 29, 31, 65-7
de Puebla, Dr. Rodrigo Gonzales, 141-3, 145, 147-51, 156, 159, 215, 233, 235

QUADRA, Bp., 199-203
de Quintana, Pedro, 146

RALEIGH, Sir Walter, 262
Relations, 112
Renard, Simon, 186, 189
Reports, 112
Richelieu, 177, 180, 231
Richer, Christophe, 178
Ridolfi Plot, 277
de Rienzi, Cola, 62
Rincon, Antonio, 177, 270-1
de Rojas, Francisco, 141-2, 150-1
Rome, 65, 67, 75, 78, 80, 86-7, 89, 101, 105-8, 110, 139, 143, 145, 159, 175, 178
du Rosier, Bernard, 28-30, 34-46, 107, 115, 218-19, 240, 288
Rudolph of Austria, 233

ST. MAURIS, 186
Salutati, Coluccio, 62-3, 75
Sardinia, 139, 144
Sarpi, Fra Paolo, 213-14
Savonnières, Seigneur, 173
Savoy, 102, 105, 180-1
Savoy, Duke of, 80
Savoy, House of, 97
Schepper, Cornelis, 186
Scheyve, 246
Schmalkaldic League, 183
Scotland, 78, 131, 145, 184
Secretaries of Embassies, 103, 241
Secretaries of State, 224-31
Selden, John, 216
Sforza, Bianca Maria, 84, 153
Sforza, Francesco, 55, 83-7, 89, 92, 96-7, 153
Sforza, Galeazzo Maria, 97-8
Sforza, Ludovico (il Moro), 121, 135, 137, 143, 153-5, 157, 159
Sicily, 139, 144, 181
Siena, 58, 72, 75, 77, 87, 102, 105
Sigismund, Emperor, 34, 76-7
de Silva, Alfonso, 143, 146
de Silva, Diego Guzmán, 203-4
Simancas (archives), 230
Simonetta, Cecco, 248
Sixtus IV, 94
Solemn Entries and Receptions, 37-9, 107, 240
Somerset, Protector, 184, 224
Soncino, 159
Soto, 284, 294
Spain, 67, 100, 122, 129, 131, 138-54, 182, 191, 221
Spies and counterspies, 114, 226, 243-5, 259-61
Spinelly, Thomas, 160, 249
Spinola, 267-8
Stile, John, 159-60, 233
Suarez, 214, 284, 294

INDEX